T0340309

Giving Wings to Her Team

Denise dreamed of being the kind of leader who empowered and engaged her people, but was becoming frustrated and disillusioned.

Denise – a fast-rising, young consultant at a large advisory firm – lands a job as a manager in industry. Crisis strikes as low-cost competitors take market share and general chaos generates late shipments. Denise goes into Lean consulting mode but quickly learns her supervisors are not buying it. They're not engaged, and they find the Lean tools confusing and a distraction from their goals of getting product out. It's going to take some magic – magic that's available to you, the reader, too!

Come with Denise on a journey of discovery and skill development, as she moves beyond the tools and concepts of Lean and focuses on daily practice that helps her supervisors achieve their goals. It's about an approach called Toyota Kata that helps anyone develop and apply scientific thinking – an exploratory mindset of curiosity and experimentation. A mentor from an unlikely place appears and shares with Denise how to coach her team. Once her supervisors dig into real problems they face every day, they begin to engage. Step by step, with insightful inputs from her mentor, Denise starts developing the skills to become a coaching manager. She watches her team meet their current challenges and be ready for more.

When you teach and practice scientific thinking and coaching skills you give wings to your team, and new worlds of opportunity open up. If you're a manager you'll identify with how the team in this story goes beyond general preaching about best practices, to practicing how to get to where they want to be. If you're a Lean practitioner frustrated with applying tools with a limited half-life, you'll learn how to develop people so they can achieve their most important goals and keep going. And if you're already a Toyota Kata practitioner, well … you will love this book!

Giving Wings to Her Team

A Novel About Learning to
Coach the Toyota Kata Way

Tilo Schwarz & Jeffrey K. Liker

Routledge
Taylor & Francis Group

A PRODUCTIVITY PRESS BOOK

First published 2023
by Routledge
605 Third Avenue, New York, NY 10158

and by Routledge
4 Park Square, Milton Park, Abingdon, Oxon, OX14 4RN
Routledge is an imprint of the Taylor & Francis Group, an informa business

ISBN: 978-0-367-36553-0 (hbk)
ISBN: 978-0-367-36228-7 (pbk)
ISBN: 978-0-429-34702-3 (ebk)

DOI: 10.4324/9780429347023

Typeset in Minion
by Deanta Global Publishing Services, Chennai, India

Contents

PART IV   Upping the Pace: It's a
Sprint and a Marathon to the Finish

Foreword

A Manager Learning to Coach Her Team … in Scientific Thinking

DENISE, FORMER LEAN consultant, has taken on her first managerial job, as the manager of a small assembly team. She is under pressure to produce … big time! Instead of going along with management edicts to throw labor at the problem, she decides to develop her people to improve their way to reach their targets. As we follow the feats and follies of Denise in this novel, she learns how to coach her team members in a way of thinking, acting, and *reacting* scientifically. You should be able to identify with Denise easily, her ups and downs, and angst and elation (yes, there is even a romance), no matter what business you are in.

The story is based on Tilo Schwarz's experiences as a plant manager in Germany. You'll see how Denise struggles to learn to coach rather than command, encountering problem after problem and reflecting on and learning from each. Over time, Denise develops a coaching approach, based on deliberate practice, learning micro-skills for different situations. As her coaching practice evolves, she is able to mobilize surprising capabilities among her team members. Those team members achieve tough goals while also developing greater confidence in themselves.

To achieve this, Denise must move beyond reading books and watching videos that teach management strategies. Her growth as a leader and ultimate success comes from facing real problems in her management work that require her to learn on the job. But this itself is not enough. As every manager knows, facing problems alone does not lead a person to successfully practice and acquire new habits – we can easily use failing strategies again and again when up against difficult challenges at work. A key ingredient in Denise's skill development as a manager is receiving coaching from her friend, Maggie, also a former Lean consultant, who now owns a gym and who has practiced the coaching skills that provide a model and structure to learn scientific thinking. So Denise gets challenging workouts and works out her management coaching dilemmas with Maggie as they occur. Get on your treadmill and get ready to sweat and learn with Denise and Maggie.

When I put Toyota Kata out into the world, my goal was to help people get started in developing scientific thinking skills for themselves and in learning how to coach others in the process. I deliberately called them Starter Kata not finishing kata. Kata are like drills in sports or scales in music, tools to build up basic competencies. My hope was that others would add to, deepen, and elaborate on these Starter Kata. Tilo's work on Toyota Kata coaching exceeded my expectations – he has developed outstanding methods by which coaches can advance themselves and their ability to teach others. In this novel, you will see those methods at work. You will see Denise experiment, learn, and grow as she discovers further nuances of coaching that make her better every day. She is continually running experiments in coaching sessions and learns most when something she tries fails. Why didn't my approach work as I expected? What can I learn from this? What can I test next? Denise is the ultimate learner in order to become a better coach.

By picking up this book, you already have demonstrated an interest in improving how you and your team strive to achieve even the most difficult goals. If so, you've got the right book. Likewise, if you're tasked with developing managers into better coaches and scaling deliberate coaching throughout your organization, reading Denise's story will give you real life tips on how to do so.

This book is about you becoming a better coaching leader by practicing specific routines in your work. If you're not coaching yet, this book will help you get started and will show you how to keep getting better at it. If your organization already has committed to a particular method of coaching, the story can help strengthen what you already do and take it to the next level. Our story expands your toolkit as a manager by illustrating a specific kind of management that builds powerful scientific thinking skills in any team, which can be directed toward any goal.

With that, let's get going and meet Denise and her colleagues!

Mike Rother

Cast of Characters

Denise Shelsky, Department Manager, Large Pump Assembly
Maggie Petrikova, Fitness Studio Owner
David Meyers, Plant Manager, Goldberg Power Pumps
Joe McIntyre, Team Leader, Large Pump Assembly
Mark Fowler, Team Leader, Large Pump Assembly
Jason Wilson, Head of Sales Administration

SUPPORTING CAST

Fred Goldberg, former Director of the Board, Goldberg Power Pumps
Roger Deng, Director of the Board, Goldberg Power Pumps
Harold Rosen, CEO
Roland Palmer, CFO
Sam Watson, VP Sales
Dick Murdoch, VP Operations
Pete Cheng, Head of Purchasing and Scheduling
Rob Cedrec, Department Manager, Plant Logistics
Joshua (Josh) Olson, Team Member, Large Pump Assembly

Part I

Learning to Think Scientifically while Producing Results

1

This is not what I've signed up for

MONDAY, JANUARY 17, 7:05 AM, A CHANGE OF COURSE

"DENISE, ARE YOU in the office yet?" asked the voice on the other end of the line.

It was a cold, but sunny Monday morning, and Denise was driving to work along her usual route. Denise's parents got her hooked on classic rock at a young age and she had been listening to Fleetwood Mac on the radio and rocking her head to Stevie Nicks' soft tones when the phone rang. *Well, I've been afraid of changin'*, Stevie crooned in the background, as David, Denise's boss, the plant manager, spoke tersely into her ear. David sounded tense. He hadn't even said good morning.

Denise felt anxiety rising within her, but she tried to sound positive. "Hope you're having a good morning David," she said as brightly as she could. "I'm on my way, just ten minutes to go!"

"Good morning is not how I would describe it," David replied, without an ounce of humor. "Please meet me in my office as soon as you get here."

Now, Denise was seriously worried. *What could be wrong?*, she wondered. *Did something happen on my team this morning? Is the sales team going ballistic again about some delayed delivery? Am I in trouble?*

The truth was her department's delivery performance wasn't exactly great. It had already been bad when she first joined Goldberg Power Pumps and took over the small assembly department three months ago, and it hadn't improved as much as she would have liked. *It is not our fault, though*, she thought to herself. *Sales changes priority on customer orders nearly every day. The supply chain is a mess. It seems like we have thousands of suppliers, and they are either very small or super large. Neither performs well. The small ones have quality issues and delivery delays every single day. The global players build and ship in large quantities whether we need it or*

DOI: 10.4324/9780429347023-2

not and fill our warehouse with large containers that are almost impossible for my people to handle and pick from. And my gosh, engineering changes designs on a whim and half the time they don't even warn us about it.

Denise tried to calm her racing mind.

"Of course, David," she said, as evenly as possible. "I'll be there shortly. It sounds like there's a problem. Is there an issue on my team or with my management that I should be aware of?"

"No, no, nothing like that. Frankly, this is much bigger than that, Denise. Haven't you read your emails this morning? I need an all-hands with the whole management team to coordinate. We're going to meet at 7:30. Come to my office as soon as you're here."

Denise struggled to remain calm.

"No, I haven't read my email yet," she said apologetically. "What's going on?"

But as soon as Denise spoke, she realized there was no one else on the other end of the line. David had already ended the call. She felt her pulse racing; her heart was in her throat. *What is this about?* She felt an urge to check her email on her phone while driving but stopped herself – she had to pay attention to the road. It was rush hour; everybody was in a hurry; getting into an accident wouldn't solve anything. She checked the time. It was 7:10, and she still had another 8 minutes to drive. She shifted to the left lane and sped as quickly as she could toward her office.

As soon as she found a spot in Goldberg's parking lot, she checked her email on her phone. Here it was, an email from Fred Goldberg, the owner and chairman of the board of Goldberg Power Pumps:

Date: January 17, 6:08 am
To: Managers-All
From: Fred Goldberg
Subject: Strictly Confidential – Change of Personnel
Priority: Highest

Managers,

This is for your eyes only, as I wanted you to have this information before it became public. The official announcement will go out to all employees at noon today. Until then please keep this information strictly confidential.

Harold Rosen will retire as CEO of Goldberg Power Pumps for personal reasons effective immediately. We thank him for his effort and accomplishments over the past three years and wish him all the best for the future.

We are happy to announce that Alexander Aspen, who has been a highly successful executive in the technology and automotive sector and a member of our board over the last 12 months, will take over the role as CEO starting May 1st. He brings a fresh perspective and will lead us into our next stage of competition in this rapidly changing world. In the interim, our CFO Roland Palmer will act as CEO. Please address all urgent matters to him.

Also effective immediately, I will step back from my role as chairman of the board. Having turned 73 in December, I feel now is the right time for me to stand aside so that Goldberg Power Pumps can be set up for a successful future.

After an exhaustive external search we selected Roger Deng as chairman of our board. He has a successful track record as CFO of several global companies and is an expert in international finance. I have benefited greatly from his advice many times.

I will stay on as a member of the board representing the owners and ensuring Goldberg Power Pumps maintains the family spirit with which my grandfather founded the company all those decades ago.

It is no secret that recently we have been attacked by fierce competitors, especially companies abroad with lower labor costs. The technological edge our great pumps once enjoyed has stagnated. While we work on future technologies, we need to focus on tightening up manufacturing by cutting costs and becoming the best in the business at on-time delivery for our customers.

I fully believe that we have all we need inhouse to strengthen our position as the market leader when it comes to pumps. I'm counting on all of you to successfully lead the necessary efforts with your teams.

With gratitude and hope for the future,
Fred Goldberg

Denise gasped. *Goldberg Power Pumps is still owned by the founder's family, in its third generation. Now Fred, the last of the Goldberg's to run the company, is stepping down as chairman of the board, and they are bringing in an outsider. And who is this Alexander Aspen? I do not think there has ever been a CEO from the outside. Who knows where this new guy will try to take the company?*

Denise felt clueless. She was aware that, as the memo stated with total frankness, Goldberg was losing its edge when it came to innovative technology. So the goal seemed to be to push engineering for new products and then lean on manufacturing in two ways, and two ways only, to get products out the door and radically cut costs. He didn't give any indication of how he wanted it done. *Command and control at its worst*, thought Denise. *Give marching orders and demand results without a clue about what is actually happening at the front line.*

When she joined Goldberg three months ago, it had seemed like the usual mid-size family-owned business. It was an old story, started by a superb engineer with a brilliant product idea whose passion was to design the next big thing to lead the industry. Pumps were his life. It had all started here in this small, but charming, isolated town in upstate New York. Over time, the business had grown to nearly 3,500 employees with sales subsidiaries around the world, three manufacturing plants, and three logistical hubs, one in the United States, one in the Eastern part of Germany, and one in Vietnam.

Denise enjoyed working at the original headquarters and manufacturing plant in Guilderville, New York, a town founded by the Dutch in the colonial period and full of small, beautiful homes and historic touches. Sales, engineering, and manufacturing were all here, along with the senior executives, and everyone who worked here seemed to like Guilderville too.

Denise especially loved the small town charm, nestled in the scenic beauty of upstate's rolling hills. She loved hiking and running in the nature surrounding Guilderville, though every now and then she ached for city living. At least there was a coffee shop with decent lattes and a few excellent restaurants. There were even rumors that a Japanese place was opening soon. And she had found a great loft apartment on the fourth floor of a downtown building—her little slice of city living. Guilderville was about an hour west of the state capital, Albany, and just an hour north was the Royal Mountain Ski Area. *Thank goodness for the skiing*, she thought. *At least I can exercise my frustrations there.*

Denise had joined the company in part because it was a family-run business with a commitment to customers and employees. She had been aware at the time that it was struggling a bit. Overwhelming growth and a strong focus on meeting current demand over the past years had led management to neglect the development of cutting-edge products. New competitors had emerged in developing countries that made bread and butter pumps, with lower labor rates and therefore could be sold at a lower cost. Goldberg Power Pumps was still the market share leader but was slowly losing share month by month.

But she needed to stay positive. She was hired because of her lean manufacturing skills, and in her former career as a consultant she had more than once attacked costs and helped turn around a failing business. She could certainly do it again in assembly. *Are things really that bad?* she wondered, sitting in her parked car, still staring at Fred's email. To Denise, the company seemed like an old car with a great engine, sitting underutilized in someone's garage. Sure, it had gathered a little dust. It needed updates and improvements, but it was a hidden champion. It could still win the race; it just required some tender loving care.

What Goldberg needed was to straighten out its strategy, focus on execution, and develop a continuous improvement process at all levels, then start knocking off problems one by one. At least, that had been her assessment when she had applied for the job months ago.

Denise looked at the dashboard. 7:25 am. *I better get out of this car and run to that meeting,* she thought. *What a start to the week … and then there is that very first workshop I was planning to hold for my team today.* She sighed, locked the car, and walked briskly to the building where David's office was located. En route, she called Joe, her team leader for today's morning shift, to tell him the workshop had to be postponed by at least an hour.

Three months ago, she had taken over the small assembly department from Bill, who retired after being with the company for many years. Assembly put together all the components into a finished pump. Most of it was manual work, but there were a few robots and some other equipment to sort parts, do inspection, and several other things. She managed thirty-four production members across two shifts and one team leader for each shift, the title Goldberg used for the first-line supervisor. At 29, this was her first management position, and, after three months in the role, she was still both excited and nervous.

She knew she had an opportunity here to help her team improve by drawing on the lean-conversion expertise she had gained during her time with Francis & Drake (F&D), a large and prestigious consulting company. After earning her master's degree in manufacturing engineering and a year of volunteer work in Malawi, she had gone to work at F&D as a consultant for five years. She knew nothing about what they called "lean manufacturing" when she started. She vaguely knew it was associated with the Toyota Production System and was supposed to eliminate waste. She found the focus on improving and standardizing processes appealing and it fit her obsession with orderliness. It was not long before she got good at it.

Admittedly, she had enjoyed her consulting job more than her time as a student. And she had probably learned more, too. She was assigned to many different and challenging projects across all industries. Mostly, her work involved streamlining processes using the company's standard lean toolkit. The most unpleasant part was when she had to oversee downsizing, better known as firing people. Of course, the job involved lots of travel, but Denise had enjoyed the cosmopolitan lifestyle and especially loved working in a team of smart and driven people. Francis & Drake had really invested in her development, even encouraging her to go part-time for a PhD, which she started but then got hung up on actually writing her dissertation. She gave up, satisfied with her master's degree. Writing was just not her thing. She preferred hands-on work.

Denise had allowed her mind to wander, but now she realized that Joe still hadn't answered her call. What was taking him so long? *It must be a very busy morning shift*, Denise thought, feeling even more tense. *Maybe he is dealing with the mess created by sales re-prioritizing orders again. That never seems to go well.*

The truth was Denise did not anticipate things would be this difficult at Goldberg when she jumped ship from Francis & Drake to join the company. In her short time at F&D, she had become their youngest and most accomplished junior project manager. She had been surprised but also excited when a senior partner at Francis & Drake, a mentor who had taken a special interest in her career, suggested she'd gain more credibility with her clients if she stepped away from consulting for a few years and took a management role in a company of the kind she spent her days restructuring from the outside. Her clients would respect her more if she could reassure them she wasn't just a person who came in and told them what to do, that she had experience working on the inside, too, he argued. Then, they would believe that she knew what she was talking about. In some ways, the move would be a kind of demotion – she would no longer be the big-deal consultant coming in to save the day but instead would be living the daily grind of managing a department. And she took a sizeable pay cut. She had been concerned about stepping away from what she saw as the fast track to becoming a partner in the firm, but her senior colleagues assured her that time on the front lines of manufacturing would more than pay for itself. And a break from constant travel was an upside – the glamor of that aspect of the job was wearing.

One day, she had received an email from her mentor forwarding a job posting from Goldberg Power Pumps; the note said they were hiring an assembly manager. She had never heard of Goldberg but soon learned that it was a well-established company with a strong brand and high margin products. Her research indicated that it was about ready to start the next transformation cycle, taking them beyond the one-billion-dollar revenue line – or at least that is what she would have advised them if she'd been hired to come in and consult.

She had landed the job at Goldberg relatively quickly. The managers who hired her had been impressed by her credentials, a bit concerned she was young and overqualified, but willing to take a chance. To Denise, the role had seemed like the perfect starting point for a management career: a technology-driven, family-owned, slightly old-fashioned, business. They had asked her to start in the trenches running one department with the promise of rapid promotion if she succeeded there.

"Hi Denise, what's up?" Joe finally answered

"I'm really sorry," Denise replied, "but we have to delay our workshop by at least an hour. David just called me and told me I need to attend an urgent meeting. I'm already on my way to his office. I know this is last minute, and I'm so sorry, but it's out of my control."

"Ha, watch out, Denise, the missiles are flying. Keep your head down." Joe laughed dryly. "I'll be rooting for you," he added.

Denise winced. "What do you mean, Joe?" It seemed like everyone knew more than she did this morning.

"Well, there are rumors that musical chairs are happening at the executive level. I heard Harold Rosen got axed and now old Ronald McDonald Palmer, the bean counter is temporarily acting as CEO. I wonder who the next CEO will be?"

Denise was caught off guard. News traveled fast at Goldberg. "Thanks for the warning, Joe," she said. "I have to go. David and the team are waiting."

Joe was one of her two team leaders, along with Mark, and they had both been with the company for over 15 years. They knew Goldberg's processes inside and out. It seemed like there was nothing they hadn't seen before. They also had a wide network within the company. They were opinion leaders – good people to have on her side.

When Denise had first begun working with them, she had quickly understood the challenge of leading people who had far more experience and knowledge about their processes and products than she ever would. From her consulting days, she knew that getting them on board was a top priority. She had tried to teach them about some of the lean management approaches she used in consulting, but Mark and Joe had easily countered each of her suggestions for improvement with a plausible explanation of why "that won't work here." Denise had also understood that trying to give them technical advice or offering solutions to problems would be a waste of time. These were humbling lessons, ones she had never had to learn as a consultant helicoptering in and out.

That was last month, and now she was left asking herself what management approach she should take and how she could best contribute to the team's success. Clearly, it was not through technical expertise, micromanaging, and telling everyone what to do.

She also was surprised to learn how much the team had relied on her predecessor's expertise. Bill had 30 years of experience in the business, and he knew every process and product in the field. If a serious problem arose, everyone on the team was happy to stay on the sidelines and let Bill come up with a solution and decide what to do.

Denise was already running late for the all-hands meeting and stepped up her pace. It was ironic she was rushing to get to a meeting that she thought was probably a waste of time. *Why is it so important to have a meeting right now when we just learned there will be a new CEO?* Denise wondered. *What is there to learn until the CEO is in place and actually does some planning? There must be something else going on behind the scenes.* The meeting was in the plush administration building, separate from the dim, noisy manufacturing building that Denise actually preferred. Outside David's office, she straightened her company-issued gray jacket, let out a deep breath, and entered the room to find that the rest of the team had already convened.

David gave Denise a polite nod and started the meeting.

"OK, you've all read the email," David said. "So, here's the situation. That news came as a total surprise to all of us. Even Dick was caught unaware. He still seemed shocked when he informed senior staff in a last-minute call late last night. But Dick also said that he believes some of the problems came from family members running the company, and he reassured us that overall he was pleased with the changes."

Dick Murdoch was the VP of Global Operations at Goldberg Power Pumps and David's boss. Denise had only seen him once in an all-employees town hall last month. He looked to be in his mid-fifties, was gray haired and sturdy, and seemed like one of those "get things done or get out of the way" executives she had met so many times during her consulting days. *Strange that someone like him would get caught unaware by such a major change*, thought Denise.

"On the operations side, as you know, we've been under pressure for most of the last two years," continued David. "Our delivery performance is totally unacceptable, but I realize you are all working hard and a lot of the delays come from other departments, part shortages, late engineering changes, the list goes on. When push comes to shove, manufacturing is always in the cross hairs. But pointing the finger at others will not solve the problem.

"Now, I am going to share with you something that I probably shouldn't. Dick also told us that Harold, our now former CEO, had been discussing a major strategic shift with the board. It was a concept he and CFO Roland Palmer had carved out to dramatically cut costs. Since our past competitiveness has come from new pump technology, they believe we are simply not competitive when it comes to basic manufacturing and never will be. They are now talking about outsourcing some of our fabrication of components, mainly for the motor, and we would simply bolt together the purchased parts in assembly. Now, nothing has been decided and you did not hear this from me. I just want to warn you that there is a lot at stake here and we need to do our best to restore our competitiveness."

Are they serious? Denise thought to herself. *Goldberg is a technology company in its DNA, but we also have some proprietary production technologies and a core competence is manufacturing. How can you trust outside companies to learn to make motor components, the core of our product, as the technology is developed, and deliver the quality our customers expect? If they do this, our plant would almost certainly be demolished, leaving the plants in Eastern Germany and Vietnam, which have much lower labor costs. Maybe it's a good thing Harold left, so he didn't have a chance to pursue this lose-lose proposition for all of us.*

As if he could hear Denise's thoughts, David continued, "Dick doesn't see this plan as having ended with Harold, though. Roland will now be acting CEO, and he and his financial team are seriously investigating this strategic proposal."

Denise felt her stomach churn. This was not what she had signed up for. She fought to bring herself back to what David was saying as he continued on.

"Okay, so, what do we do now? The immediate problem Dick wants us to tackle is our backlog of deliveries to our customers. They are waiting for pumps and getting impatient, and we need the cash flow. Dick has ordered us to ensure all lines run at full capacity and do whatever is needed, including hiring more temporary workers and allowing for max overtime. Purchasing has already increased numbers on all orders and raised forecasts for our suppliers."

"That sounds kind of dangerous to me," said Rob, a department manager from plant logistics. He was standing in the back of the room, and it was hard for Denise to tell if he had raised his voice so he could be heard or because he was angry – probably both. "Our productivity will plunge," he continued, "costs will multiply, and who knows how long it will take until we really get more parts from our suppliers. Why can't we start working on the problems that are biting us in the butt like sorting out the issues with the damn electronics supplier, and seriously working on our bottlenecks in the production lines? That's what…"

But David interrupted Rob mid sentence. "These are not suggestions up for debate. The leadership team has thought through the issues carefully, and we have decided on our course of action. Go through the backlog and production plans with your team and get your best estimates for additional resources needed and the necessary overtime by tomorrow morning. Dick wants to see a significant reduction in backlog within the next four weeks. The sooner the better. Let's get going."

With that, it was clear the meeting was over. The team filed out of David's office in groups of two and three, murmuring to each other. Most were shaking their heads in disbelief. Denise saw many angry grimaces, but some of the older department managers seemed calm, an almost expressionless look on their faces. During their careers, they had probably experienced these kinds of upheavals many times. *Surely that can harden people and make them skeptics.* She tried to think positive thoughts, but she couldn't help but wonder what she had gotten herself into.

So, the answer is to throw people and money at the problem and just start pushing pumps out. And this order follows the clear message that cost reduction is meant to be the strategy. These leaders don't know whether they're coming or going, Denise thought as she caught herself gritting her teeth.

She knew from experience that the best way to clear her head and calm any racing thoughts was to pause and reflect. She was a consummate notetaker, going back to grade school. When she started working, she formed the habit of writing what she learned each day in a small notebook she called her *Personal Learning Handbook*. She used it to highlight key points, and she always carried it with her. She pulled out some of the notes she had scrawled during the day and wrote a succinct summary in her notebook (see Figure 1.1).

January, 17th

Team meeting with plant management team

☐ The founding family is out and a new outside CEO will be coming in.

☐ Interim CFO, Roland Palmer will act as CEO: bean counter.

☐ Goldberg is good at fire fighting and big projects, but not at continuous improvement.

☐ David blames the old regime on the current crisis--out with the old.

☐ David seems stressed and feels pressure to act now.

☐ "Rightsizing for growth"--outsourcing manufacturing like a commodity, it is someone else's problem, scary.

☐ Short-term focus on clearing backlog, next 4 weeks, will fail.

FIGURE 1.1
Denise's notes from January 17th.

2

Getting to Work

MONDAY, JANUARY 17, 8:30 AM, KNOWN WATERS AND A GOOD START?

DENISE WAS IN shock after the memo and meeting with David. But the deal was done, and she had no influence over the machinations of the executives up top. She was determined to move ahead with her plans to transform assembly rather than waste time stewing over the suits' poor decisions. She went back to her notebook to review some points she had recorded early in her time at Goldberg about how she would approach managing assembly (see Figure 2.1).

First: **Make direction clear**. She wanted to ensure her team had a clear direction for improving their processes – in both the short and long term.

Denise had observed that her team leaders jumped from one daily problem to the next. She also noticed that most improvement efforts at Goldberg began as big projects that came from the top. These projects looked good on paper but usually had very limited effect across the plant. They were mostly aimed at introducing computer-aided information systems and buying new automated equipment to replace workers. They rarely focused on how to improve what they had, and development of current personnel seemed to be out of scope for senior managers.

For that reason, she had planned a workshop with her team today, which of course was delayed by the meeting and general chaos. She wanted them to get a bigger picture view of how materials flowed through assembly and all the waste along the way. Then together they would create a future state map of how products should flow through their part of the value stream: smoothly, stably, without interruptions. Finally, they would break down the biggest problems and begin to attack them. The best part of this process was that it was a team effort – everyone involved would see that she cared about their opinions and thus have some ownership over the results.

DOI: 10.4324/9780429347023-3

January, 18th

<u>Key-points for Change:</u>

☐ Make direction clear.

☐ Give priority to continuous and sustainable improvement.

<u>Purpose statement:</u>

Make continuous improvement part of everybody's daily work. Everybody - every process - every day.

FIGURE 2.1
Denise's notes from when she started at Goldberg.

Second: **Give priority to continuous and sustainable improvement**. Right now, the whirlwind of daily business diminished most of these efforts. To address this issue, Denise established daily meetings with her team leaders to discuss their key performance indicators (KPIs) and the targets they had set on cost, quality, and on-time delivery. They created a big board with graphs showing trends on the KPIs for all to see. For Denise this was the starting point for continuous improvement.

She had also crafted a purpose statement: **Make continuous improvement part of everybody's daily work – everybody, every process, every day**, which Denise continually mentioned when talking with her team.

Denise walked back from the administration building across the parking lot to Building 3, where her assembly team was located. She checked the time on her cell phone. She hated wearing a watch. It was already 8:30 am. The email about the senior management changes would go out at noon to all employees. So three and a half hours to go. Joe and Mark were probably already waiting for her to return, hoping to hear some more about the rumors.

Denise looked up and took a deep breath. It was a sunny day, the January air still crisp. *Oh well, I'll just tell them what I learned,* she decided. *Let's get that off the table, and then we can at least get a start on our value-stream analysis workshop. We've lost an hour and a half, but we'll make up for it. If we can identify our biggest bottlenecks and develop solid ideas on how to remove them, maybe I can convince David to give it a shot. We need to improve our processes and not cover up our inefficiencies by throwing temporary hires and overtime at the problem.*

Over the next hours, Denise, Joe, and Mark walked the shop floor following the value stream of three products backward. Starting with complete pumps, they could see how the pumps were built. As they walked, they drew what they saw, making boxes for each process and drawing triangles to reflect inventory, like a map of the flow of the product through the plant. For each process, they gathered and made a note of key data like the percent of defective product coming out of the process, how much time was lost because a machine was down, and how long the process took. One by one, they identified where the bottlenecks were and where they were coming from. *We could increase the output by 50% just by addressing the bottlenecks*, Denise reckoned.

Then, Denise led them to develop the future state map. She asked Joe and Mark to think about what *should* be happening rather than what was happening. What would a lean value stream look like? This turned out to be much tougher than she expected for her team leaders who knew nothing about lean. They were so mired in all their daily struggles; her ideas for the future state just seemed like science fiction to them, and they let her know it.

Still, Denise pushed on, dominating the discussion. *This part is just like being a consultant*, she thought. Helping them move past minutia and toward the big picture was something she felt comfortable with and even enjoyed. But, at the end of the day, Denise was a little disappointed with the results. She had compromised on some of her key ideas. The plan they had come up with was not, in her estimation, a particularly ambitious future state map. *It's honestly more like the current state without the problems, and we just put in a bunch of specific problems that have to be fixed*, she thought to herself. Still, she reasoned that maybe now was not the time to push Joe and Mark too hard. She couldn't really expect them to develop a breakthrough new vision using tools and concepts they had never experienced before. *It's enough to get started*, she tried to convince herself.

TUESDAY, JANUARY 18, 8:00 AM, MAKE SURE I DON'T REGRET THIS

In the wake of the all-manager meeting, Denise had decided it was a good idea to meet with David one-on-one. Before leaving work on Monday, she had arranged a meeting with David for early the following morning.

She wanted to show him the results from her value-stream workshop and convince him that they could improve the output and chisel down their backlog, without increasing cost to a level they'd soon regret.

David was in his late thirties and had become the plant manager at Guilderville two years earlier. He was just a little taller than Denise, had short, brown hair, and was dressed in casual business attire most of the time.

He must have been an athlete in college, Denise thought. He always stood completely straight and carried himself with that kind of discipline. Today, he was wearing a blue button-down shirt and a pair of khaki-colored chinos. He had clearly changed into his safety shoes just before Denise entered his office, and she could see a pair of brown, narrow-tipped business shoes, probably Italian made, sitting underneath the bookshelf behind him.

Denise had carefully prepared for the meeting, and, in her mind, she expected to wow David with her convincing arguments and the incontrovertible data of the value-stream map. After 20 minutes of presenting data, analysis, and just plain pleading, the conversation devolved into a tense debate that was going nowhere. David seemed more disinterested than anything else.

"But listen, David, we only have one line running on the late shift this week because we ran out of parts for the three others. What do we win if we fully staff them?"

David shook his head. He looked out the window and spoke sternly. "Denise, this is not some game we are playing," he said. "We need positive numbers, and we need them soon. As much as I appreciate lean methods and agree there are lots of opportunities, I'm not willing to risk my job for this. They just walked Harold out of the door and Dick will not accept any setbacks just because we might do better in the long run."

Denise followed David's gaze out of the window. It was snowing again, just like the night before.

After a pause, she said more gently, "David," then waited for him to turn his attention back to her. When he finally looked at her, she continued, "you know just as well as I do that covering up waste is a lure. It may appeal in the short term to big-picture thinkers, but it only creates more waste overall.

"To eliminate waste, we need to solve problems at the root cause, which does not always have to take an enormous amount of time. I have done this as a consultant many times with great results. That's why you hired me." Denise could see him shift uneasily in his chair. Their eyes met. She smiled. "Just give me a chance, David, please."

David took a deep breath. At last, he seemed to be engaging with her. He took one last look out the window, and then the magic happened.

"OK, but make sure I don't regret this. I want an update on your backlog numbers every evening, and I'll meet you on site every Friday so you can show me your progress. And keep in mind, if things don't change quickly I'll pull the plug sooner than later."

"Deal," Denise replied. "I'll call you every day at 5 pm, ok?"

David nodded and smiled unconvincingly.

"Talk to you later then," she said, grabbing her value-stream maps as quickly as she could and scooting out the door before David could change his mind.

As Denise enjoyed the walk back to her office through the cover of fresh snow, she considered her conversation with David. *He is one of the good ones*, she thought. *He's trying to do the right thing for the plant and his team, and he does want to solve the actual problems. He's clearly torn between challenging his boss and just doing what the higher ups are demanding, but, deep down, I think he knows their plan will get quick results, but won't work in the long term. I do appreciate that he is working to protect us department managers from nonsense politics.*

But Denise could also see all this was taking its toll on David. He looked tired and had put on a little extra weight even in the few months since she knew him. He was married, with two kids, cute little boys who were six and eight, and he regularly clocked close to 80 hours a week. Denise knew about long hours. They considered 80 hours to be a usual week when she was working as a consultant. But she was younger and single. It was no way to live if you had a family.

Arriving at her desk, she glanced up at the trophies she kept displayed in her office. They were for high school track and field and a state competition for college skiing. Next to them were photos of her parents and brother, her foundation. Hanging beside the photos of her family was a picture of the day she graduated from high school, her with her closest friends jumping in the air while flipping their caps. *Those were the good old days*, she thought wistfully. Denise was not the prettiest girl or the most popular. She'd been a bit of a nerd, really. She was a straight A student, in the chess club, and had been valedictorian, too. But she had prided herself most on being an athlete. Her time on the field made life seem so simple: work hard, compete, win, get rewarded. Not so much anymore. Still, while her days of competitive sports were over, she stayed in shape by eating healthy and exercising daily, preferably outdoors. Working out helped manage her stress, and if she were being honest, Goldberg was a pretty stressful place to work.

I appreciate David giving me a shot at doing things differently, she thought, trying to stay positive. *He is risking his career. If that ain't trust…*

She wandered out of her office and saw Joe poring over their current state map. He was focused on the problem areas that needed work to get to the future state.

Not looking up, Joe said, "I think we should focus on reducing equipment downtime on the bottleneck processes on each of the two assembly lines. The more the machine runs, the more pumps we can make, without spending a dime."

Denise felt so pleased that Joe was trying. It seemed like the workshop *had* lit a spark after all.

"You know Joe," she said, "this is my job on the line, and I need you and Mark in my corner. I obviously cannot do this on my own. Thank you so much for jumping in and taking responsibility. You are a lifesaver."

Joe smiled, a twinkle in his eye. "You better believe I am bailing you out," he said, "and do not forget it when it comes time for my raise."

Denise smiled back at him. "Thank you again," she said.

Joe was short, stocky, and balding. With a wife and four children, he was a traditional family man all the way. He provided for his family by working hard to get from a line worker to a team leader, and he was constantly doing home improvement projects, busily updating his home and yard. He was no nonsense and preferred action to talk. *If he can do it at home, why not here?* Denise wondered.

As Denise had done so many times during her consultant years, she suggested to Joe that they use what in the lean world was called an A3 form to describe what needed to be achieved for each of the most urgent bottlenecks, and then later they could continue filling them out as they worked on the problems. She explained that the A3 was simply the size of the paper, bigger than standard letter size to fit the different boxes needed to capture the problem solving process – the story – from problem definition to the current condition to the root cause to solutions and follow-up. With only one side of the paper to write and sketch on, it created a succinct summary of major points. Graphics were even better than bullet points.

By the end of the shift, Joe and Denise had filled out parts of A3 forms for each of the three most urgent equipment bottlenecks in the lines Joe would work on. They then agreed on a milestone schedule for the next four weeks and a list of the major tasks Joe needed to complete.

"I'd like to meet with you and Mark on a daily basis," Denise said at the end of the meeting. "It is probably best that we meet just after the shift handover, while you are both still here. Then we can check our progress and see where you need help."

Joe nodded. "All this paperwork has got me kind of tired," he said. "You know I'm an action guy, not a paper tiger. I'm glad we're at the action part now. You wait, I'm going to dazzle you now with what we can do. Keep thinking about my raise."

Denise nodded and smiled – she believed him. Then, she stayed through the first half of the second shift to work with Mark in the same way. They developed three more A3s describing what needed to happen at his bottlenecks. Mark also agreed to work on these areas over the next four weeks.

Driving home, Denise felt a sense of satisfaction with what they had achieved. They were starting to work like a team, instead of antagonists. She even allowed herself to daydream a little. *If this works out the way it has with some of my clients, it could serve as a best practice example for others at Goldberg on how improvement could become part of every team's daily work*, she thought to herself, with renewed excitement about what was to come.

FRIDAY, JANUARY 21, 5:45 PM, WHO SHOULD I BE MAD AT?

Denise had been excited to meet with Joe and Mark after the shift handovers on Wednesday and Thursday to check in on their work on the A3s. To her frustration, they hadn't made any progress.

After the value-stream workshop, Denise had been glad to have such a clear direction. The improvements they planned were modest but still significant. But for some reason, as soon as they had started working on implementing the plan, Joe and Mark seemed to throw up their hands. They said that they did not have the time to spend on fixing the bottlenecks that they themselves had identified. What happened to the idea of feeling ownership and taking responsibility?

"We understand this is important to you Denise, but we just don't have the time for this improvement work along with our real work," Mark explained during a tense check-in on Thursday.

Denise had finally realized that Mark and Joe not only struggled to make room in their daily schedule of mostly fire fighting for working on their improvement targets, but were simply overwhelmed by the number and magnitude of topics to work on. Besides, they both believed that the processes they had written about in the A3s could not actually be improved. They had lived with the problems for so long that they seemed unfixable. They argued that there were too many constraints, that what she was asking for was technically impossible.

Denise was dreading her first weekly update with David at 4 pm. She knew she had no progress to report. All she could do was share the A3 papers and then complain about how difficult it was to get her two team leaders involved.

David did not seem impressed by her struggles or explanations.

"Denise," he said, "I can see that you are doing great foundational work, which will bring us closer to lean value streams. We'll benefit greatly from that in the long run, so keep working on it in the background. But right now we need results. Dick is giving us hell to reduce our backlog. He even lost his temper and started yelling in the operations team meeting on Wednesday. So, I need you to go to full overtime every day.

"We have the green light for working Saturdays until July with the labor council. I want to see your lines running every Saturday. If you run out of parts, switch to another product or pre-assemble products so we can quickly finish them once the missing parts arrive. Fill up the finished goods warehouse, even if it is with products customers have not ordered. I know that won't solve anything, but at least we can show the guys upstairs that this damn backlog isn't a production problem."

Denise left her meeting with David feeling completely discouraged. She had been right to dread it – it had been just as bad as she'd imagined. Then, she met with Mark, which only made things worse.

"Mark, I just had an awful meeting with David and he is pissed," she said at the start of their check-in. "He feels I let him down. He gave me the green light to work on improvement in the background, but wants quick results even if it means filling the warehouse with stuff that can't be shipped.

"Mark seemed surprised. "I didn't think you would cave in so fast, boss. We would have gotten the hang of the A3s and the action lists. But orders are orders, and we are aces at ramping up and wasting the company's money. So let's do it."

Something about this really aggravated Denise and she got defensive, even though she told herself not to.

"I am not nearly ready to give up," she said, hoping she didn't sound as angry as she felt. "I am hoping this stopgap plan will only last until Tuesday. I hate this game we're playing, but I can't disobey David."

When the day was over and the weekend had finally begun, Denise could not stop ruminating on each of these meetings, on her and her team leaders' collective and individual failures. Driving away from Goldberg, she was becoming more and more frustrated, angry even. *What a stupid plan this is. But who should I be mad at? Blame the guys upstairs, blame David, or blame myself. Maybe I did cave, just like Mark said.*

Denise realized she was beating on the steering wheel absent-mindedly, her rage getting the better of her. She told herself to calm down. She couldn't do anything about it now. She decided she would speak with all teams at the beginning of both shifts on Monday to explain the situation. It was important to not only tell people what to do but also give some context on the why. Now if she could only figure out what the why was.

The traffic in front of her had come to a halt. Denise noticed that her knuckles had turned white from gripping the steering wheel. Her face muscles were tense. She shook her shoulders, rotated her neck left and then right to try and relax a bit. *Today I am going to kill it at the gym*, she thought. She had packed her workout clothes so she could go directly from work to the gym, anticipating she would need to burn off the stress.

3

What's our Challenge?

DENISE WAS IN the middle of a vigorous workout, doing squats with a barbell, when she heard a familiar voice.

"Hey, Denise, make sure your knees don't move to the outside when you push up. You can easily control that by placing your feet absolutely parallel and having your toes pointing straight forward."

It was Maggie, one of the fitness coaches. She actually owned the studio but still worked as a coach because she loved it so much. She could also be seen on the gym floor, working out herself in her down time. Denise often wondered how Maggie had the freedom to do whatever she liked, even though she was in charge of the studio. *She must have a very engaged and self-reliant team*, Denise thought to herself.

"Hi Maggie, thanks for the tip," Denise replied. Maggie was now standing next to her to check that Denise was keeping her back straight. Maggie looked like she was in her early forties, with beautiful silver, braided hair. It was hard to know if the silver was real. From her hands, Denise could tell that she was probably actually in her early fifties – she just looked fabulous for her age. She was a little taller than Denise and in remarkable shape in a way that made Denise feel inadequate. After all, Denise still thought of herself as an athlete.

"How was your day?" Maggie asked with a smile after Denise finished the exercise.

Denise wiped her face with the towel she had flung around her neck, then glanced up with a false cheeriness. "Just great, Maggie," she said. But as she looked into Maggie's kind eyes, she felt she could be honest with her. "Actually," Denise said, taking a deep breath, "the whole week has been a disaster."

DOI: 10.4324/9780429347023-4

"Oh no, what happened?" Maggie asked sympathetically, then motioned to Denise to move to the next station. "Don't interrupt your workout. We can talk while you exercise."

Denise moved on, and Maggie followed her. Denise generally avoided mixing shoptalk with her personal life, but she could hardly stop herself from venting about her problems at work. Maggie just had a way about her that made Denise want to spill her guts. True, Maggie barely knew her, but she just seemed so nice and empathetic.

Denise started dumping her frustrations on Maggie, explaining what happened this week, leaving out the names and focusing mostly on what she wanted to achieve with her team. She realized she was probably going into too much detail, but it sure felt good to get it out.

"I want to give my team leaders control over their processes, and I want them to take initiative in improving them, too," Denise said, as her rant came to a close. "There is so much we can improve. Maybe I am overly optimistic, but I think Goldberg production really could be a gold mine.

Our future value-stream map clearly indicates what is possible. It certainly made sense to me, and the guys seemed into it. But when it came to actually doing the work, Mark and Joe just told me why things can't be changed. I thought the value-stream map, focusing on the major problem areas we identified, and having detailed A3s would help them to get started. But it absolutely did not. Shoot, sorry, I'm falling into lean jargon. All this probably means nothing to you."

Maggie had been listening intently without speaking, but now finally broke her thoughtful silence.

"Your story reminds me a lot of my situation when I started the gym several years ago," she said. "I haven't told you this before, but I was also in lean transformation for many years."

"Wow," said Denise, "I didn't know that."

Denise wondered which company Maggie had worked for. She realized how little she knew about her, not even her full name. Everyone here just called her Maggie. *I have to ask her*, Denise thought. *We have a lot more in common than I realized.* But she also didn't want to interrupt. Maggie had listened to her for so long, and Denise was excited and surprised by where the conversation was going.

"Yeah," Maggie responded, smiling. "And so when I started the gym I was excited to use everything I'd learned as a consultant to make my gym the best it could be. I went through all the usual lean tools, just like you're trying, and I learned a lot. At first, it seemed all the tools were making a big difference. Over time, though, I got more and more frustrated with the uphill battle to maintain and improve what we had implemented.

"Even back when I was a consultant, I was convinced there had to be a better way than piling all these tools and concepts onto overwhelmed supervisors and team members. The managers I was working with simply could not absorb it all. At the end of the day, they were just complying, instead of thinking for themselves. That's when I decided I wanted to open the gym, to create the type of environment I wanted to work in. Here, I can still use lean concepts, but on my own terms."

Denise was dying to drill Maggie with questions about her background and experience, but at the moment, she was doing another round of sit-ups with some extra weight on her chest and trying to catch her breath. Denise managed to press out a "wow, interesting" between her teeth. Maggie continued.

"Starting my own business was quite the eye-opener for me," Maggie said. "I realized that lean tools can be helpful, but they come second. The most important thing, in any business, is the way people work together to achieve the goals we set for ourselves, again and again. It is a dynamic business, and every customer is different. We can always do more and better for our customers.

Maggie went on, "building a business, just like improving and innovating in an existing business, is about discovery, not just planning and executing. We test our ideas, experiment, learn from what happens, and adjust. It's a team sport. It isn't something we'll achieve by me being the lone wolf at the top. For my new business I decided to focus on developing a team of voyagers who think and act scientifically instead of jumping to conclusions."

"That's exactly what I want for my team," Denise exclaimed, finally having finished her round of sit-ups. I remember in consulting we were always trying to teach our clients problem solving. We brought them through our six-step process, did some exercises, but they never really got it. They continued to jump to conclusions and rarely changed their thinking. I like your idea of 'scientific thinking.' I would love to develop my team leaders to think that way.

"I kind of got that impression," Maggie replied. "Just like you, I had an inspiring vision in the beginning but didn't really know how to get there. By accident, I went to an annual conference called KataCon where I met an author named Mike Rother. He talked about developing a model of practical, everyday scientific thinking and a way to develop it in our team through practice, which he called Toyota Kata."

Denise was getting excited, but also feeling information overload – after all, she was still exercising.

"I like the idea, but to be honest I'm not sure exactly what you mean by scientific thinking", she said panting.

"It's pretty difficult to describe a way of thinking", Maggie replied. "Here's one way I like to look at it: scientific thinking means realizing our knowledge is limited, that we have to experiment to learn more, and, this is the hard part, appreciating that when things go differently than we expect it helps us learn.

"Hmm, the very basics I would like to get to", Denise said getting up from the ground and grabbing for her water bottle, "but I've never heard of that kata stuff. What's Toyota Kata?"

"Toyota Kata is a way to develop that kind of thinking in teams through practice", Maggie replied. Then she continued:

"The word *kata* means practice routine or 'way of doing something'. It comes from the martial arts in Japan, like karate. The black belt, the teacher, knows what each movement should look like to effectively defend yourself. But there are way too many, and they are too complex to learn all at once. So the teacher breaks down all these motions into kata, small movements like kick and evade, for his students. He knows an effective way to do each of these small skills. The students have to learn each of these kata through practice, just like the black belt did when starting out. The student keeps doing each kata over and over until they can do them correctly, and they begin to feel natural – like a habit. As the student learns more kata, they can begin to put them together situationally, in defense against an attacker. I know I am dating myself, but have you ever watched *Karate Kid*?"

Denise murmured, "Yes, it's been a while."

Maggie continued, "remember the wax on, wax off, waxing the car? That is a kata. The kid thinks it is a waste of time and the teacher is just using him to get a free wax, but later learns the motion is a useful element in defending himself.

"The skills Mike wanted to teach were more mental. He calls them a mindset. He wanted to help people learn how to approach reaching big goals scientifically, based on experimenting and learning. But that's actually a complex and somewhat unnatural skill set to learn – like learning how to defend yourself in karate. It needs to be broken down into smaller skill elements that can be practiced: kata.

He started with a simple four-step model for how to use scientific thinking to improve that he called the Improvement Kata. You can easily look it up. It's pretty simple. First, you define a big challenge over a longer period of time, like six to twelve months. Second, you study your current condition. At this point, you know where you want to go and where you are, but the gap is huge, so you have to break it down into bite-sized pieces. So, third, you set a short-term target condition, say 1–2 weeks out. And then, fourth, you learn your way to the target condition by testing your ideas, one at a time, running experiments. Then, you keep setting new short-term target conditions and experimenting toward them until you finally meet the challenge. It is the same sort of thing you would do if you were climbing a new mountain, facing the unexpected. You might have an overall plan, but you have to break it down into smaller plans, like what is my goal by the end of the day, and then adapt to reality as it hits.

What Mike wants the learner to do with these four steps is practice them, repeatedly, with feedback from a coach, to get good at them, just like kata in karate. To do that Mike developed a set of practice routines for each step of the model. Mike calls them Starter Kata because they are to practice the basics, not necessarily to get you to a high level of mastery of scientific thinking.

"Rother also developed what he calls the Coaching Kata. In karate, the black belt is a coach, right? The job of the coach is to know the right way of doing each kata, observe the student, and give corrective feedback. You need the coach because people are not great at giving accurate self feedback. Well, the same is true in business. The goal is for every leader to be coached by their boss and then coach their team members – a chain of coaching, instead of a chain of command and control."

Denise felt overwhelmed by all this new information, but she was also deeply excited, energized even.

"Maggie," she said, breathless from the latest round of sit-ups, "what you're describing sounds amazing. It seems just like what I need to engage my team leaders. Why's it called *Toyota Kata*, though?"

"Oh, that's because Mike spent decades learning about the Toyota Production System, you know, TPS, the model for lean. When he observed TPS experts at work, he realized that they were not simply mapping and then implementing what they put on the map. They saw the future-state map as a vision to work toward, scientifically, step by step, learning from each step. It was not a recipe or road map to follow. Scientific thinking is ingrained in everybody by their supervisor, who is really a coach. That's the Toyota part. Thus, Toyota Kata."

"Fascinating. Well, this sounds just great. I would like for my team leaders to learn to think more scientifically, and be open to change. And of course be creative about it. So, how can I learn to be a coach?"

Maggie laughed. "Slow down, slow down," she said. "I probably already said too much. We can get more into Kata and coaching at another time, but step one in the model, understanding the direction is something you have to do for yourself and I would suggest that you might want to work on that first."

"I think the direction from above is clear," Denise blurted out, pausing between sit-ups, "by now everyone knows that reducing our back-log as fast as possible is our number one challenge. Our Vice President of Operations, Dick, has been completely up front about that and the heat is on, and the threat."

"Nope," Maggie said, waving her hand, "that's not a challenge that gives your team direction, that's a desired outcome."

"What do you mean?" asked Denise, as they moved over to the treadmills, and Maggie stepped on the one next to Denise, choosing to accompany her on a short run.

"While measuring outcomes is important, setting result targets alone doesn't give direction to improvement efforts," said Maggie. "Usually there are several, even opposing options to pursue on the process level for achieving the desired outcome. As a result, everybody has a different opinion on what to do. Then you end up in debate mode about who is right and who is to blame.

"Worst of all, chasing outcome targets invites work-arounds rather than sustainable improvement. You are experiencing that first hand at the moment with your VP forcing all of you to install superficial and expensive measures to reduce the backlog. The antidote is to define a broader challenge over a longer period that we can work hard to achieve through experimentation and learning."

"I think of it as three steps. **One, create pull, two, ensure focus, and three, establish pace.** The last one is not so important for you right now but creating pull and keeping your team leaders focused are super important, especially given their reluctance.

"So, let's start with 'create pull.' Your approach of value-stream mapping and A3s misses a key element – you've identified problems to solve without establishing a long-term vision your team leaders can work towards. You're missing the why, the motivation, the overall goal."

"Like our company vision you mean," said Denise. "Goldberg: number one in pumps."

"Not really," Maggie replied. "A company's vision is very long term and lofty by nature – too long term, too lofty. Also, 'number one in pumps' is not a very good vision. A vision should be about better serving the customer in ways you cannot yet today. In your company's case, you have a backlog of orders, a great deal of the wrong inventory, and you're just not building what the customers want. So, what I'm talking about is maybe developing a future-state vision that's like 'we're going to build the right products at the right time for our customers'.

"It's the mental perspective that's important here. Working toward a desired state makes people look forward, up to the mountaintop. Having a clear picture of that mountaintop, a desired state that would be a big step forward for the process and is inspiring for people is what helps you create pull – a common desire in your team to get there. This needs to be a direction your team can identify with.

Working on waste, bottlenecks, and seemingly individual problems makes people look down, or even back. Fixing broken things, like say the backlog, is not as motivating as aspiring to something. Working toward something raises the question, how can we get closer?

You jumped into value-stream mapping and A3s, and your team leaders were overwhelmed. On their level they don't have a clear overarching direction, just like you didn't have before developing the value-stream map. After your meeting with David, you only had a short-term outcome target.

"That's the second point I mentioned. You need one focus for your team, not a bunch of problem areas and three A3s for each of your team leaders. Establishing direction drives focus on every level. That's what you need to ensure first.

"What will your team focus on achieving for the next three months? Think of it like this: What is the wildly important thing you and your team need to achieve?"

Denise was getting frustrated. "I don't really know," she said, upping the speed on her treadmill to work out her anxiety, "but David insists we pull out the stops and use wasteful actions to reduce back orders, right now. We definitely need to work on multiple things to make that happen, and we don't have three months. I need to show progress in the next few weeks."

Maggie hit the pause button on her treadmill and then Denise's and suddenly looked very serious.

"No," Maggie said, "you're responsible for helping your team to achieve their goals. Having them work on many different things at the same time won't get you anywhere. That's what they already do, hopping from one issue to the next. You might see some short-term results, but they won't last."

Maggie restarted her treadmill and resumed running, even faster than before. Denise followed.

"Let me suggest some homework for you," Maggie continued, her voice rising above her footfalls, "at least as a thought experiment. What is the wildly important thing that you and your team can try to achieve in the next three months? I'm pretty sure that will also have a great impact on reducing your backlog."

Denise couldn't believe how Maggie could so easily talk while running. Denise's face was already red hot and covered in sweat. Denise gasped, "So, then what?"

Maggie switched off her treadmill again. She looked at Denise with empathy, as Denise stopped, totally winded.

"I know it's a lot," said Maggie, "but you can absolutely handle it. In fact, once you start, I bet you'll feel so much better. On Monday, have a look at your future-state value-stream map and figure out what your team needs to work on first. Then state it as a 3-month challenge. Then, let's talk again. I'm here for you, seriously. I have an appointment coming up so I need to hurry and shower, but let's connect next week, I mean it."

Denise had also stepped off her treadmill and was catching her breath.

"Maggie, how can I thank you? You are a lifesaver," Denise said.

"I'll do my best to keep you alive," Maggie chuckled, as she made her way to the changing room. "Let's talk Monday, ok?"

Denise smiled and nodded, then walked over to the water dispenser to refill her drinking bottle. Her brain was in overdrive trying to process everything Maggie had said, while her body was exhausted. *I have the weekend to digest it all, at least,* she thought. *What I need now is a nice hot shower.*

When Denise finally arrived home, she ordered carryout Chinese food and collapsed on the sofa, but before turning on Netflix™, she decided to write some key points from her talk with Maggie in her *Personal Learning Handbook.* Before she forgot everything Maggie had said, she wanted to be able to reflect on it all over the weekend. She knew recording not just what she remembered from their conversation, but her current thoughts, was an essential part of the process. She ended up boiling it down to five bullet points ending with a question. She was very curious about Maggie's last point on "pace" even though Maggie said to ignore it for now. Ignoring was not in Denise's DNA (see Figure 3.1).

January, 21st

Improvement Kata: A practical, everyday form of scientific thinking.

Helping my team to understand direction

☐ Understand Direction = Create Pull + Ensure Focus + Establish Pace.

☐ Create Pull: Picture of the mountain top: Long term vision for improving our processes.

☐ Ensure Focus: What is our wildly important goal on the value stream level? Next three months?

☐ Establish Pace: *Need to find out what that is???*

FIGURE 3.1
Denise's notes from January 21.

4

More Pressure and a Breakthrough in Thinking

MONDAY, JANUARY 24, BACK TO THE GRIND

Date: January 24, 5:30 am
To: All Managers, Guilderville Plant
From: Dick Murdoch, VP Operations
Subject: SENSE OF URGENCY
Priority: Highest
Cc: Pete Cheng, Head of Purchasing, Fernando Ruiz, Head of Global Logistics, Rolf Muller, Head of Controlling

To my great astonishment some of us seem to lack the necessary sense of urgency given our current situation.

Looking at last week's reports I can see that finished goods have risen in stock level. While availability of our finished goods is important, these are products for which we don't have pending customer orders. It's beyond my comprehension why some of you dare to produce these while we have a huge backlog of real orders on our more popular products.

Let me be 100% clear: We need every minute of production and every resource to be focused on producing the products our customers have ordered! Nothing else!! Any exceptions have to be approved by David Meyers.

I can also see that overall productivity has dropped on several teams. Let me be clear on that as well. This is a very bad time for taking a break

DOI: 10.4324/9780429347023-5

and letting things slip. Rolf Muller and his controlling team will make individual appointments with you to support you in analyzing your productivity and ensuring all lines get back on track over the course of this week.

—Dick

ANOTHER MORNING, ANOTHER wacko message from the top. So, Dick had finally discovered the problems that he himself had created thanks to the directives he had issued … last week. Denise saw the email first thing Monday morning when she sat at her desk and opened her laptop. Now Dick was bypassing David and directly interfering with plant operations. Things were getting worse. For the next 30 minutes, Denise checked on what pumps were ordered, but yet to be built, and what pumps were built and stored in inventory.

Indeed, productivity had gone down for all of her lines as well as for the plant overall. But to her, it was totally clear why. This was what she had anticipated when the orders came down to work more hours with temporary labor and overtime and continually push out products.

Yep, make more products without orders and you have more inventory. Kind of true by definition, Denise thought cynically. *Mark got it right, a waste of the company's money.*

They kept running out of parts for the pumps that were ordered by customers, but she had been told to keep making any pumps just to keep production going. Producing pumps that were not ordered with the parts they did have required making smaller quantities of each type of pump, which meant changing over the line more frequently. Different pumps required different fixtures to hold the parts in place and different tools which had to be changed out while production stopped. For every hour of changeover time that was an hour of labor with no pumps produced. Productivity dropped. Simple math.

But then Denise had an aha moment, like a detective, when suddenly the puzzle pieces started to fall into place. Maybe the next big step for productivity was to reduce changeover time. Denise recalled Maggie's advice from Friday. *Is reducing changeover time our wildly important thing to focus on?* She got up from her desk with determination and walked over to the current-state maps that she had drawn with Joe and Mark during their value-stream workshop and which were now hanging on the walls of her small glass office.

It was clear, right there in black and white, that line 3 had the highest changeover time. That was also the line where they assembled three of their top volume products and they had to keep switching to lower-volume items based on the parts they had on hand. More changeovers, more time lost.

Maybe there is an opportunity to get somewhere after all, Denise thought to herself. *The management team challenged us to reduce the backlog on our high-runners to zero within the next four weeks. Therefore we need to increase the output of line 3, which should be building what is ordered. Purchasing has been working to get the parts so we should have what we need to build more pumps.*

To do so we could work on many different things. We could reduce the cycle time needed to build each pump, reduce quality losses, reduce machine down time, or improve changeover time. And yes, we could cover up and improve nothing by just adding more operators and running overtime, but no, not on my watch. I've had enough with obeying orders.

She began to think like a scientist, engaging in hypotheticals, thought experiments. *Let's say we focus on reducing changeover time first, and everything else stays the same. Each minute of reduced changeover time gets us one more minute of production, for free. In our future-state map, we also wanted to use reduced changeover time so we could changeover more often and make smaller batches closer to what customers actually order, but that can wait for now.*

We can figure out how much we need to reduce our changeover time by calculating how many minutes of extra production we need to meet our target. Hmmm, rough guesstimate, and it looks like we can actually get there with reduced changeover time. Maybe that's what Maggie was talking about. It's not a 3-month goal, but it is a clear focus, and it's wildly important and short term. I can't wait to talk this over with Maggie at the gym tonight.

Denise returned to her desk and started writing in her notebook (see Figure 4.1).

Denise spent the rest of the morning meeting with the scheduling team to discuss expected deliveries from their suppliers and figure out how they could best match the production schedule with availability of parts.

January, 24th

What is our wildly important goal?

☐ Don't succumb to pressure to throw labor at the problem

☐ 3 months is too much

☐ Need short term focus on what's wildly important, for next 4 weeks

☐ Focus on changeover time increases production and gets us closer to desired value stream

☐ Must tell Maggie about this breakthrough

FIGURE 4.1
Denise's notes – what is our wildly important goal?

During her check-ins with Joe and Mark, she told them about her intention to focus on reducing changeover time.

"Let's have a look at our A3s and see which ones address changeover time," she said. "Look," Denise pointed to the wall, "out of the six we already have two addressing changeover time. One focuses on line 3, the other on line one." She took down the other four A3s. "Let's set these aside for now and focus only on changeovers. What do you think?"

Mark and Joe just stood there and said nothing, glancing at one another. Finally, Joe shrugged his shoulders.

"I don't know…you know it doesn't really matter how many issues you want us to work on. We haven't been able to work on any of these, and we won't be able to in the next few weeks either, given the current chaos."

Denise felt her frustration build. "But now it's just one issue for each of you," she said, "and reducing changeover time on these two lines is wildly important – especially because of the situation we're in. We need to get the backlog for our high runners down and improve productivity. That is a marching order to me and therefore I am passing it on to you," she added, with a little bit of a smile. "Seriously, who knows what bad things might happen if we, as a team, don't achieve it? Plus, we'll benefit in the longer term and get closer to our desired state for the value stream."

"We understand your idea," Mark said, jumping in, "but reducing changeover time on a line is not something you can just do as a side job. Believe me, changeover is a complicated process. I don't even know if it is possible. Most things need to be done the way we do them and if it were easy to simplify we would have done it already."

"I am not saying it will be easy," Denise agreed. "But trust me, it's in my wheelhouse to help. I've personally been involved in dozens of changeover time reductions, and we cut them all down at least by half, usually within a few days. We can use the SMED approach. I'll show you."

"SMED?" Joe fired back. "Is that a person or a thing?"

"It means Single Minute Exchange of Dies. It was developed at Toyota many decades ago to reduce the time to change dies on huge machines that stamped out car body parts," Denise said, launching into a speech she had given dozens of times, then stopped, catching herself. *Oh no, I'm back in consultant mode. I am racing out front doing a lot of telling and leaving them in the dust.* She realized that Mark and Joe were looking tense and confused.

Denise took a breath. "I'm sorry," she said. "After being a consultant for years, I got used to issuing orders when things were going south. And then I fall into lean jargon. I really don't want to do that with you guys. Let's have a fresh look at one of the changeovers tomorrow and see what we can do together. Maybe with what I know in general about changeovers and all you know about these lines, we can come up with something that is not too time consuming or disruptive."

Denise smiled at them, a little uncertain.

Joe and Mark nodded solemnly.

"Alright," said Joe, tentatively.

"Sounds good," echoed Mark, though he also sounded unconvinced.

MONDAY, JANUARY 24, 7:00 PM, RETREAT TO THE GYM

When Denise arrived at the gym that evening, Maggie joined her for a warm-up on the treadmill.

"So, what did you learn?" Maggie asked, upping the speed on her machine.

"That walking on the treadmill is a lot easier than my job!" Denise said, with a smile. "Do you have any openings for walking the treadmill for minimum wage?"

Maggie laughed. "I'll look into it. Maybe you can generate some energy to power the gym," she quipped. "But really. What did you learn?"

Denise launched into a detailed explanation of her revelation about changeover time and how it could be an easy first step to reduce their backlog and support their future-state value stream. Changeover time could be that wildly important goal that would get them focused, at least as a first step, she argued.

"Sounds good," said Maggie, somehow still completely relaxed, even as she increased her speed. "What else did you learn?"

Denise explained how she had reviewed the six A3s with Joe and Mark and kept only the two focused on changeover. So far so good. But then, just as she felt she was on a roll, Joe and Mark made clear they did not have the time to implement anything and that it probably wasn't possible to reduce changeover anyway. Denise confessed sheepishly that at that point she had lost it and started barking orders and throwing out terms like SMED.

Maggie smiled sympathetically. "Sounds like you're jumping ahead again," she said. "Remember the Improvement Kata we discussed. It is a scientific step-by-step process. Remember the four steps: 1. Challenge, 2. Current Condition, 3. Next Target Condition, and 4. Experiment.

You are still on step 1, where the purpose is to understand the direction. And Mark and Joe have to also understand it and identify with it. That is the problem with telling them a bunch of stuff, which quickly sounds like noise. Just because the direction is clear to you now doesn't mean it is so clear to your team leaders. Discuss it with them first, explain why you think this is the challenge to focus on. Then write it down with them. Best would be if you could make it a full sentence starting with 'Wouldn't it be great if'…"

"Do you honestly believe that will get them going?" Denise asked, clearly doubtful.

"No," Maggie replied, "but it might inspire them a bit. I think you may get them hooked in by doing step 2. Get them engaged in analyzing the current way of doing changeovers. They're likely to see opportunities for improvement. Then, they'll be active instead of just listening to you and coming up with counter arguments in their heads. This is how you shift from telling to coaching. Tellers try to get compliance, coaches try to get people to think for themselves.

Plus, analyzing the current condition sets you up for step 3, establishing the shorter-term target condition. I suggest you start with setting a target condition for one-week out. This will be more concrete, and I expect more real for your team leaders. Then you will have three consecutive target conditions to get to a one-month challenge. What do you think?"

Denise seemed to agree but was also clearly frustrated.

"At this point, Maggie, I'll try anything. I mean, what you're saying makes total sense. For me, personally, just looking at the future-state map is enough, and I can see what I need to do. But Joe and Mark don't have any experience with this stuff, and they seem to be naturally more focused on the here and now than abstract visions and concepts. It needs to be clear and concrete in their heads. I agree that looking at the way we do changeovers now, hopefully seeing a lot of waste, and then coming up with a short-term clear target for the week may be just what we need to get them unstuck. I'll certainly try it. I can see shifting from my past consulting role of being the person with all the answers, and telling people what to think, to coaching them to do the thinking will be a challenge for me. Patience has never been my strong suit. But I will try."

Maggie nodded, obviously relating to the frustration Denise was feeling. "A weekly target condition will give them something clear and manageable to focus on," she said. "Even the shorter target condition should be beyond what Rother calls their 'threshold of knowledge', what they currently know. So it is a bit scary. I learned that a good way to get clearly focused target conditions is to shorten the time frame. That's why I'm suggesting one week. Ask them, *where do we want to be one week from now on the way to our one-month challenge?* That will give your team leaders small chunks they can focus on. And it will allow you to check in with a coaching session daily, so problems do not go unresolved for many days."

Maggie stepped off the treadmill. Denise quickly followed. Unlike Maggie who seemed calm and refreshed, she was panting and covered in sweat. A towel draped over her head, Denise leaned forward and put her hands on her knees. From that position, she heard Maggie saying, "now don't jump ahead again. Remember that to establish a next target condition you need to grasp the current condition first."

Denise was finally able to speak. "That is what I've been doing every day this week," she said, "going on site and observing."

"Well, you need to do it again with your team leaders. Now, you have a clear focus on the changeover and can grasp and map the current condition of that one process in detail. Mike has a Starter Kata for that. Check it out." With that, Maggie was gone and Denise continued her workout. When Denise finally headed for the showers she was exhausted, from her workout and Maggie's advice.

After returning home from the gym, Denise checked the internet to find out more about Mike Rother's work. She knew about *Learning to See*, Rother's book introducing value-stream mapping. What was new to her was his research that led to his book *Toyota Kata*. He had also published another book called the *Toyota Kata Practice Guide*, which went into detail about how to practice Toyota Kata. Denise wasted no time in ordering both books. There also was a Toyota Kata website, where she found the Improvement Kata four-step model or "platform" for scientific thinking, as Mike described it. It also contained information about a Starter Kata for coaching.

Denise could see why Maggie was so into Toyota Kata. Rother's project was in many ways not so different from what Maggie did at the gym every day, trying to get clients to develop healthier habits when it came to exercise and eating. Rother wanted people to practice thinking more scientifically until it became a habit.

Denise then sketched the Improvement Kata into her notebook. She liked the four-step model. It was simple, intuitive, and easy to understand. The visual was more like a comic book than a master's thesis (see Figure 4.2). Perhaps her group leaders would take to it better than the A3s. One, figure out where you need to go, two, figure out where you are, three figure out where you need to go *next*, and four, experiment to get you there. It was more like taking a hike than sitting through a business lecture.

QR CODE 4.1
Visit the Toyota Kata website.

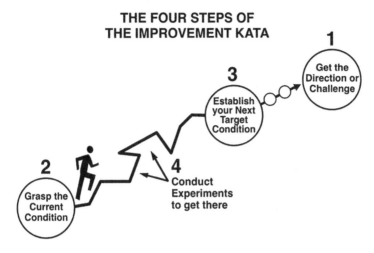

FIGURE 4.2
The Improvement Kata Model, Mike Rother, *The Toyota Kata Practice Guide*, McGraw-Hill (New York), 2018.

Before calling it a night, as usual Denise wrote in her notebook to try to synthesize all she had learned from Maggie. She still felt herself resisting some of it. Maybe Maggie was pushing her beyond her threshold of knowledge, she thought, smiling to herself (see Figure 4.3).

January, 24th

<u>Ensuring focus for my team</u>

☐ Individual A3s from value stream map still too big.

☐ Seem overwhelming to team leaders.

☐ Team leaders need a more concrete focus in actionable terms
  they understand.

☐ Must clarify a short term (1 week)
  Target Condition = Target + Condition.

☐ Next, go to the process with the team to understand the
  current condition of the changeover process.

FIGURE 4.3
Denise's notes – ensuring focus for my team.

5

Getting Down to Kata Planning

DENISE WAS SITTING at her office desk, and it was surprisingly peaceful. She wasn't sure why. Maybe it was the calm before another storm, but for now she could enjoy it. She opened her *Personal Learning Handbook* and took another look at the Improvement Kata diagram. She liked the combination of a longer-term challenge and a short-term, next target condition. Together, they gave direction and focus, just as Maggie had said. And they created pull, a positive way of thinking, striving toward something by experimenting forward.

The vision Maggie had laid out for her team was growing on her. *I need to develop a team of explorers, just like Maggie said she's done at the gym, people who are working together in a scientific way to reach challenging goals.* Denise flipped to a fresh page in her notebook and wrote: "Establish direction to create pull and focus." *The mysterious third thing was pace. I guess the weekly target conditions and daily meetings are one way to create a steady pace*, Denise thought.

A knock at the door brought Denise out of her thoughts. Mark was the team leader on shift, and he was stretching his head through the door.

"We are out of parts on line 3," Mark said. "Should we switch to building what we can with the parts we have, even if there are no orders for them?"

Denise covered her face with her hands, closed her eyes for a second, and swallowed. Then she replied, as calmly as she could, "no, just send the team home."

"But last week you asked us to keep up production by any means. Isn't that what David wants us to do?"

"Not this week," Denise replied, laughing darkly. "Dick wrote us an email saying so yesterday. The genius figured out that his previous strategy

DOI: 10.4324/9780429347023-6

did not help customers with back orders. He wants us to only build to real orders. Another week, another set of contradictory orders. At least these make more sense."

"Ah, well, direct order from the big boss. I guess he has the right to change his mind from week to week. At least it seems he still has some active gray cells," Mark replied, closing Denise's office door.

"Wait a second," said Denise, stopping him. "Once the team is gone, I'd like to talk with you about the A3s."

"I haven't had any time to work on them. I've been too busy fighting our daily fires," said Mark, his voice sharp and his tone defensive. "Nothing has changed since yesterday."

"No, no," Denise waved her hand, "I don't want to check up on you. It's more that I feel that the way we have filled the A3 isn't working. I'd like to discuss a different idea with you, something more manageable."

Mark looked doubtful, but nodded dutifully. "OK, you're the boss," he said.

"Oh, is Josh on the shift this morning?" Denise asked, before Mark could escape.

"Yes, he's with the line-three team today."

"Please ask him to stay. He can help us to run some test changeovers with line 3 now that we've halted production there anyway. Let me know once you're ready to start."

I might as well get Josh involved in this Kata process, Denise thought. *He still works on the line, but he is one of our brightest and most enthusiastic young team members, and he has leadership potential. Let's start developing him.*

"Will do boss," Mark replied, looking a little confused, and gingerly closed the door to Denise's office.

They had a basic challenge: shorter changeovers. This would in turn increase production time on the lines and thus increase output, which would help their customers by reducing the backlog of orders. And a bit later, it would allow them to run smaller batches to bring them closer to actually building what the customers wanted when they wanted it.

Wouldn't it be great if … Maggie had told Denise to think about understanding the direction with a sentence that began with those words. Now, Denise found she was doing it almost naturally. *Wouldn't it be great*, she thought, *if we weren't hamstrung by the changeover time anymore and could make smaller batches? That would be awesome for us and our customers. Team members can relate to serving our customers better than profit margins and budget variances.*

To get closer to that challenge we'll start with reducing changeover time for line 3. With that direction I think we move to step 2. Maggie was insistent our next step is to more deeply understand the way we currently do changeover. On the Toyota Kata website, Denise had also found instructions for grasping the current condition. Mike Rother called it a Starter Kata. Denise had been a bit confused by the difference between Improvement Kata and Starter Kata. *Oh well. Maybe it's like a recipe for beginners. I'll give it a try. When it comes to this Kata stuff I am definitely a starter.*

Mark peeked in. "Josh and I are ready to go, are you coming?" he said.

Denise grabbed her clipboard, got up, and followed Mark to line 3. She took along a printout of the Starter Kata for grasping the current condition on her clipboard but decided not to show it to Mark. It would just confuse him at this point. At the line, Denise began by explaining her thoughts about the challenge of reducing changeover time and why she thought they should focus on that.

"Reducing changeover time in the short term will increase our output and get the big bosses off our backs. In the long term it will allow us to run much smaller batches and make it easier to fulfill any customer requirements," she said.

Mark and Josh were nodding, but Denise was unsure if they understood and bought in or were just trying to appease her. Then, she explained what she would like to do to grasp the current condition. Getting to actually do something made more sense to them and they said they were ready to get started. "As a first step, we will look at data on multiple changeovers over time and graph the time it takes for each."

"You mean the time to change over the whole line?" Mark asked.

"Yes, exactly," Denise replied, "we're looking at how long it takes us each time we do a changeover. Let's have a look at the last two weeks."

Mark walked over to his computer to check. A few minutes later, he came back with the printout of a run chart. From what they could see, most changeovers took between 20 and 30 minutes with about four changeovers happening on each shift.

"Damn, that's three hours or more of production time per day gone just like that." Mark shook his head in disbelief. "We really need to do something about that."

"Look," Josh said, as he traced the run chart with his finger, "there seem to be three classes of changeovers. Some are as short as 15 minutes, a few are nearly 60 minutes, and the majority are around 30 minutes."

"That's because of the different types of products we have on the line," Mark replied. "The majority, the ones that are around the 30 minutes, are our high-runners, which we assemble most often. Usually, we run much larger batches of them, so changeover time doesn't really matter. But, with all the backlog chaos at the moment, we have to switch to the low runners a bunch of times. That's totally crazy."

"Perhaps we can start with the group of changes to low runners, which are done more frequently?" Denise suggested. She was thinking about Maggie's advice that a clear focus is motivating.

"OK," said Denise, "we are currently doing about four changeovers per shift. Now let's imagine we could do six. Then we could produce four of the eight high-runners we have on this line and two other products every shift. Given that we produce a total of eight high-runners on this line, we could do all of them every other day."

"The key word there is *imagine*," Mark said. "But I'll bite. It would be great if we could do it."

Was Denise imagining it or, hidden in his mocking her was some enthusiasm? Encouraged, she pressed on.

"Now, *imagine* we can do these changeovers in 10 minutes, resulting in 60 minutes of total saved time per shift," Denise said. "That would be an hour less than we usually waste, a found hour that we could use each shift to produce more pumps and reduce our backlog."

"Yeah, would be," said Mark., "But, come on, 10 minutes? That just doesn't seem possible."

"I agree it's not possible right now. It's a challenge, for sure, but isn't it one worth working toward? Besides, you guys are manufacturing Olympians. If anyone can do it, we can, right?"

"Well, yes," Mark replied, a bit hesitant.

"We don't have to get there right away," Denise said, reminding herself not to be too ambitious when it came to setting target conditions. "This just gives us a direction to work toward in small steps. Also, just to be clear, I am not suggesting that we stop the line and then do everything in 10 minutes. I suspect there is a lot we can do while the line is still running to prepare for the changeover. What matters for production is how many minutes the line is shut down." She pulled them over to a flip chart and began writing at the top.

Wouldn't it be great if we could run 6 changeovers a day at 10 minutes each, enabling us to run through all 12 high-runners every two days and giving us an extra hour per shift of assembly time and so reduce our backlog to 0?

"I like that," Josh said, speaking up confidently, even in the presence of his boss Mark. "I like that a lot actually. It's kind of idealistic, but it's inspiring for sure."

"Let's go for it, then," Denise replied, smiling outwardly and to herself that she had correctly spotted Josh's potential. She gave Josh a gentle clap on the shoulder. "Let's move back to the line."

According to Rother's current-state analysis Starter Kata, they were up to the step of creating what he called a block diagram. The idea was simply to outline each step in the process, with every step written inside a rectangle. The diagram showed the flow of the steps and you could also write in times for each step. Denise, Mark, and Josh began discussing just how they could create a block diagram of their process.

"With the line stopped right now, we could run ourselves two or three identical changeovers, measure how long each takes and observe if there are any differences," said Denise. "That's not exactly real world, though, so maybe we can observe an actual changeover at another line first and capture the steps, making sure we get a grasp of what really happens. Make sense?"

Josh and Mark nodded in agreement. All three of them walked over to a line that was just about to start a changeover. Denise asked Mark to do the recording of the times and take notes, and they all watched intently. The first thing the line's team members did was stop production and scatter for about 10 minutes, collecting tools and fixtures.

Denise explained that one of the most important things you can do to reduce changeover time is separate what is referred to as external setup from internal setup. External setup refers to all the things that can be done while the equipment is still running. Internal setup, on the other hand, can only be done while the equipment is shut down.

"We usually prepare all that external stuff beforehand," one of the team members explained a bit defensively.

"Yes we do, but there is always something missing. The lists we use for preparation are crappy," Josh said.

"Then we should definitely do something about that," Mark replied.

While they finished observing and writing down the changeover steps, they realized one of the other lines was just getting ready for a changeover, so they decided to observe that as well. They noticed the exact same pattern. The line was stopped, and this time it took even more than 10 minutes just to get stuff that could have been prepared while production was still going, which meant they lost more than 10 minutes of production. They also observed that changeover for the end-of-line testing station took the longest of all – this, they concluded, was a major bottleneck.

When they finished their observations, they walked back to the deserted line 3.

Josh turned to Denise. "You've been talking a lot about focusing and having a small next target condition," he said. "How about if we start by focusing only on reducing changeover time for end-of-line testing?"

"That's a great idea." Denise smiled. *Josh is naturally good at this. I wonder if there is such a thing as a natural scientific thinker.*

They decided to run three repetitions of changeover on end-of-line testing at line 3 with Josh performing them. The same thing happened. Josh prepared everything according to the list, but still some parts and tools were missing. And they made another interesting finding, too. Although the changeovers were theoretically identical, they actually differed each time and that was true even without the time spent searching for things. There was around three to four minutes difference each time, mainly due to the time Josh needed to properly align the fixtures. In addition, time was lost during two of the tries due to some quality issues.

"The design of the housing is crooked," growled Mark.

"Maybe," Denise replied, "but let's not draw any conclusions yet. For now, all we have to note is that it's one of our obstacles. Let's summarize what we've seen.

"The Starter Kata includes an 'obstacle parking lot'," she explained, leading them back to the flip chart. She flipped the page and grabbed a marker. "So, what obstacles did we see?" She wrote down the items as they called them out: looking for fixtures and tools, quality issues, and losing time for aligning fixtures (see Figure 5.1).

"But we can't just order new fixtures," Mark exclaimed, clearly exasperated.

FIGURE 5.1
Starting the obstacle parking lot.

"You are right Mark," Denise replied. "This is an obstacle and we should not make assumptions like we need to buy new fixtures. Thanks for pointing that out. At this point it is on the parking lot and I think we should address the obstacles one by one." She smiled to herself thinking how proud Maggie would be. Maybe she was starting to coach instead of telling Mark what to do or think.

"Oh, I get it," Josh said. "Parking obstacles like on a parking lot, parked there, waiting for us to address them. I like it. Cool visual."

Denis smiled again and gave herself another point for involving Josh.

Mark calmed down and agreed with Denise and Josh, "It makes sense to work on each obstacle. We will need some way to pick which to work on first."

"Absolutely Mark," Denise continued, "The next step of the Improvement Kata is to establish our first target condition that will get at that."

This is pretty cool, she thought. Now, *we're moving to step three of the Improvement Kata. This is a helpful pattern for establishing direction. We understood the challenge first, then grasped the current condition, which led to identifying a specific substep to focus on, testing, and now we can establish our next target condition – slicing the elephant. And Mark and Josh are engaged, working on real things, instead of listening to me spout theory and digging in their heels.*

She started a new page on the flip chart. "Let's list what we have observed and measured about end-of-line testing," she said. She drew a dark line from top to bottom underneath their challenge statement.

Over the left side she wrote, "current condition." Then she wrote:

- *Total changeover time line 3 for high-runners, 30 minutes.*
- *Searching for tools and fixtures, 10 minutes.*
- *Dismounting fixtures, 3 minutes.*
- *Loading software, 2 minutes.*
- *Mounting new fixtures, 10 minutes.*
- *Changing documents, 1 minute.*
- *Solving quality issues, 4 minutes.*

Underneath her notes, Denise sketched a block diagram of the current process pattern (see Figure 5.2). Then she wrote, "target condition," at the top on the right side of the vertical red line and a horizontal line beneath it across the whole page. The two thick lines formed a big T. Denise, Josh, and Mark each took a minute to look at the flip chart and then began discussing how they would like the changeover process to run.

"No time for searching, of course," Josh said. "And the time for mounting the new fixtures should be shorter too."

Denise started drawing a block diagram on the right side according to the process Josh and Mark described. *So that's the desired pattern for the process, depicting the condition part of our target condition,* Denise thought. *Just like Maggie described. Nice!*

Next, they calculated the target time each step would need to take if the total changeover was going to take 10 minutes and noted these numbers on the right side of the page.

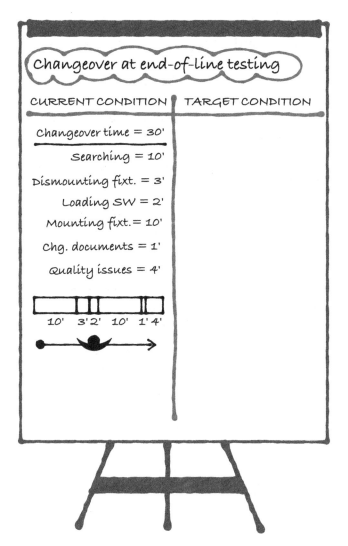

FIGURE 5.2
Visualizing the current condition.

"What would you like to work on first?" Denise asked.

"That searching time," Mark responded immediately. "That's a total waste."

"Great. And what would you like to achieve on searching time by the end of the week?" Denise asked.

Mark took a deep breath. "Well, honestly, I think we should completely eliminate having to search for anything while the line is stopped."

"I like it," Denise replied. She drew a box around "Searching = 0" and wrote "focus" and then the date one week out next to it. "So," Denise continued, "our next target condition is to reduce the time to search for tools during changeover to zero. But this is *only for the end-of-line test station*. Let's keep this very focused. We aim to achieve this by the end of this week, and it will contribute to reducing the overall changeover time of line 3" (see Figure 5.3).

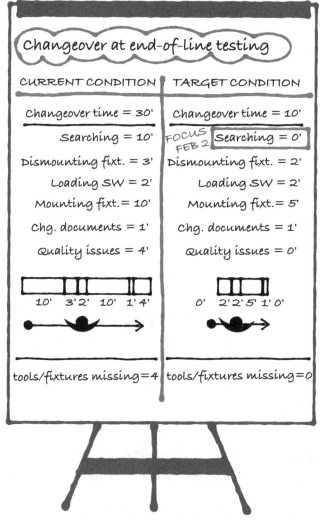

FIGURE 5.3
A first target condition.

"Cool," Mark said, "but how are we going to measure that? Our computer system will give us the overall time for the whole line, not specifically for the test station. And searching for stuff does not happen at just one point in the changeover process. We saw how Josh had to leave the line several times. It's going to be hard to measure the time for that for every changeover."

Josh spoke up. "Could we do a tally list?" he asked. "Whenever we have to get something, we just make a mark. That's easy to do, and we could limit it to the end-of-line test stand only. I don't think the actual amount of time we need for searching matters as much, or does it? Once there are no marks on the list anymore we've eliminated the time."

Denise smiled. "Brilliant," she said and added another row on the flip chart. They checked their observation record for the number of times Josh had left the line to get something for the end-of-line testing station changeover and added that number to the current condition on the flip chart. It now read: "Current condition tools/fixtures missing = 4; target condition tools/fixtures missing = 0."

Later that day, Denise sat at her desk basking in the success of her work with Josh and Mark. She felt the particular satisfaction that came from really working with her colleagues as a team. She opened her *Personal Learning Handbook* and thought about the target condition they had established. *It contains a metric for measuring our overall target, the changeover time for the whole line. And it links with our challenge. I'll call that the outcome metric.* She started writing. *Then there's the block diagram. That gives us a picture of the current and the desired operating pattern for the process. That's the condition part Maggie mentioned,* she realized.

Then how about the second metric that is part of our "target condition," the number of times tools/fixtures are missing? Well, that's a measurement we take at the process level. So maybe I'll call that the "process metric." Denise wrote that down. *That second metric is probably important to have,* she thought. *For this week, we'll only focus on the time needed searching for tools while changing over the end-of-line testing stand.*

Even if we get that down to zero, the impact on the total time for changing the whole line is small or can easily be counterbalanced by other effects occurring elsewhere. Focusing on the outcome only would become frustrating for Mark and Josh. With the process metric, we can measure precisely how much actual progress we are making at our focus point, Denise realized. *I could also call this our progress metric.* She added that to her list.

Elements of a target condition

☐ Outcome Metric - measuring the impact, links to challenge.

☐ Desired operating pattern - picture/description of the next desired condition.

☐ Process Metric - measuring progress at the chosen focus point (progress metric).

☐ Achieve-by date - short term!

FIGURE 5.4
Elements of a Target Condition, adapted from Mike Rother, *The Toyota Kata Practice Guide*, McGraw-Hill (New York), 2018.

How about the other metrics we have listed on the flip chart? I guess they're process metrics too. But it definitely seems better to focus on one to start. Let's address the others one by one with future target conditions. And then we needed a due date. It made sense to choose one week for that. That creates a clear focus and gives us a steady pace, just like Maggie said. Denise completed her list (see Figure 5.4).

I'll keep working on the recipe and show it to Maggie. I hope she'll be impressed. I felt resistant at first to Maggie's suggestion about the target condition, but now I can see how well it's working. One bite of the elephant at a time. And the guys are engaged for the first time, now that we are working on something real and specific and meaningful to them. And I feel myself making a shift from giving lectures like in the classroom to being a coach helping them achieve our goals. I have to remember not everybody enjoys abstract concepts like I do. People on the floor relate to specific observations and actions, what they can see and touch and hear. This really seems to be working now.

6

Storyboards and Experiments

FRIDAY, JANUARY 28, 5:30 PM,
THE GRASSHOPPER MAKES MAGGIE PROUD

DENISE WAS ON her way to the gym after an uplifting end to the week. It had been a gray and rainy January day and, as the evening grew colder, the raindrops became heavier, and the rain slowly transforming into slushy snowflakes. Denise flipped her windshield wipers up a level. Traffic was moving slowly. The heat was running full blast in her moss-green Mazda. She loved this sporty convertible, which she had been driving for several years, but it wasn't great in snow. As usual, Denise found herself thinking about her workweek. With everything going on at Goldberg, it had been a mix but definitely better than the week before.

Having the short-term target conditions in place had made a huge difference. Her team leaders were so much more engaged because they had a specific focus for their improvement work. The target condition involved just one piece of one particular process: searching for stuff during changeovers on the test station. *That's so much better than having only an outcome target. Working toward a condition for the process aligned our discussions. Now, it's more about how we can get there, rather than debating widely scattered suggestions*, Denise thought.

After her successful session with Mark and Josh, Denise had worked with Joe and established a target condition with him as well. They decided he would also work the same target condition, eliminating searching for tools and fixtures, but focus on a different workstation on the line.

Mark and Joe had become more active in contributing their ideas but were still hesitant to test their ideas. *They seem afraid to change things in their processes, probably because of bad experiences in the past*, Denise

DOI: 10.4324/9780429347023-7

thought. *I'll have to encourage them more to try things now that we are moving into the experiment phase of the Improvement Kata. It's their process, and they need to have control over it. And experimenting needs to be a safe space or we'll soon be back to a compliance mindset.*

Some of the operators in line 3 had joined in a bit as well. Denise had asked a few how it was going with the tally list.

"It's great that we are tracking this now," one operator had said. "It always annoys me when I have to go round and search for stuff while we do the changeover."

Denise got to the gym, changed clothes, and met up with Maggie for her training session. As she got on the treadmill, she gushed describing the big differences in Mark's and Joe's behavior. She also gushed over how quickly Josh was catching on and what a breath of fresh air he was.

Maggie was obviously proud of her grasshopper.

"I am so glad to hear that," Maggie said. "You are seeing the first signs of self-motivation and your team taking responsibility. You've obviously done well in creating psychological safety and giving your people autonomy for their area of responsibility. That's possible because they're now working on specific tasks they can control. Autonomy is one of the preconditions for self-motivation and getting into a flow state.[*]

"Another aspect is being challenged even slightly beyond what we are currently able to do. That's what you have created with the target conditions as well.

"Giving people autonomy requires us to coach, however. We need to support people so they succeed and achieve their goals, for their benefit and for the company."

Denise nodded. "That's why I'm checking in with Joe and Mark every day this week, sometimes even twice a day."

Denise also shared her list of elements that make a good target condition with Maggie. Maggie smiled approvingly when Denise explained her idea of having a focus process metric and calling it the "progress metric."

"That's what Chris McChesney and his coauthors[†] call their second discipline of strategy execution," Maggie said. "They explain it using a picture of a stone and the lever we press to move the stone. Where we

---

[*] Mihaly Csikszentmihaly, *Good Business. Leadership, Flow, and the Making of Meaning*, New York, Viking, 2003.

[†] Chris McChesney, Sean Covey, and Jim Huling, *The 4 Disciplines of Execution*, New York, Simon & Schuster, 2016.

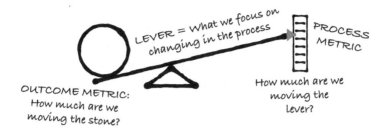

FIGURE 6.1
Stone and Lever, adapted from Chris McChesney at al, *The 4 Disciplines of Execution*, NY: Simon & Schuster, 2016.

want to move the stone to is the desired outcome, what you're calling 'the outcome metric'. The lever is what we focus our improvement efforts on to move the stone to that spot.

"Practicing Improvement Kata helps us find these levers, by investigating and observing firsthand the actual pattern of the underlying process. The focus you've chosen within your desired pattern of work, reducing the time spent searching for tools at the end-of-line test station, is the lever you are trying to move right now. With your focus process metric, you measure your progress in moving that lever."

Denise liked the idea of the picture of a stone and a lever and had made a mental note to sketch it into her *Personal Learning Handbook* later that evening (Figure 6.1).

After the workout, Denise described the challenge statement she and her team had devised.

"Wouldn't it be great if we could run six changeovers a day at 10 minutes each, enabling us to run through all 12 high runners every two days and giving us an extra hour of assembly time and so reduce our backlog to 0?" Denise proudly stated.

"And you know what? The team really has been talking about this challenge over and over," Denise continued. "And I can see how they are starting to play with it in their minds. Mark started talking about doing everything with one touch. Joe, he's a drummer in a local band, picked up the idea and coined the phrase 'changed in a touch'. He makes the last word sound like percussion. The team wrote that as a slogan on the flip chart with our challenge statement."

"Cool," Maggie exclaimed with genuine excitement. "Now you're getting somewhere. That's a challenge that inspires and will go beyond your six changeovers of 10 minutes per day."

Denise also described the flip chart with the obstacle parking lot and the T format she had used to describe the target condition. "Actually," Denise explained, "I got the idea for the T from Mike's book. It's super handy. I feel like I'm getting a handle on the Improvement Kata. It means having a clear longer-term direction, studying actual condition, and then focusing on bite-size chunks for a future state!"

"That is progress, and a good summary of the planning part," Maggie replied. "Soon, it will be time to run experiments. Come on, I'll show you something." She took Denise to the back-office room behind the entrance desk. There she showed her a board. It had all the elements Denise has used on her flip chart – and a few more (see Figure 6.2).

"Mike Rother calls this the learner's storyboard," Maggie had explained enthusiastically. "At the top, we wrote down our challenge. Up here, on the top left, you can see the target condition filled into the T template. In the middle, you have two charts, for the outcome and the process metrics, and here, bottom right, you can see our obstacle parking lot."

"And what's this up here on the right?" Denise asked, pointing to the top right corner.

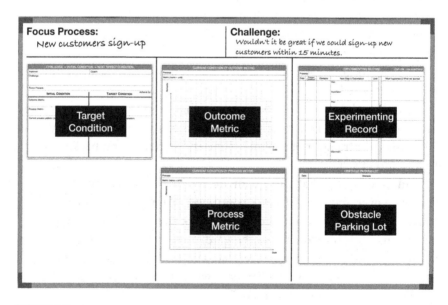

FIGURE 6.2
Improver's Storyboard, adapted from Mike Rother, *The Toyota Kata Practice Guide*, McGraw-Hill (New York), 2018.

"That's the experimenting record where we document our experiments," Maggie replied. "In fact, this is where I recommend you go next. You are now at the point where you can test ideas. Your team will love the action. Often, at this point, people are inclined to turn the team loose, brainstorm a bunch of 'solutions,' and implement them in parallel. But that's not very effective. If we do that, we won't know what's actually working. A scientific way of thinking means understanding that each idea is a hypothesis and should be tested. It's best to test the ideas in series rather than all in a confusing mess in parallel. We want to understand and be able to reflect on the results of each experiment, ideally one factor at a time, because this is how we learn.

"Be sure to take the time to coach your team, ask what they expect will happen when they try their idea, and then, after they've tried it, ask them what happened and what did they learn. That's all the info you write in the "experimenting record." Based on that, they can adapt their approach and come up with the next experiment. It's iterative, see, a repeating pattern? My storyboard has an actual version of that from a target condition we are working towards right now. See up here in the experimenting record."

"That sounds super helpful," Denise said, nodding her head. "I like the idea of viewing ideas as hypotheses to test. Maybe this will help my team leaders feel more comfortable trying things, even if they don't always work out as expected. I'll have Mark and Joe build their own storyboards."

"I promise it's super helpful," Maggie replied, "especially when you start coaching. I coach Jenny – you know Jenny, she oversees all our administration processes – I coach her each day using this board. Here's her storyboard," Maggie said, pointing to another board. "Her current challenge is '5-minute check in'.

"Our biggest revenue stream comes from our group classes where up to twenty people come for a class at a scheduled time with one coach. We rotate them through pieces of equipment and floor exercises, and they start at different stations. When we first opened, we asked members to come in 20 minutes ahead of time to check in, and then they would spend a long time sitting or standing in the lobby. It used to be that when we opened the door to the gym, it was like a herd of cattle charging to get to the station with their preferred piece of equipment. Most preferred the treadmill and the most aggressive got it, disappointing others.

"Practicing Improvement Kata, Jenny has almost reached her 5 minutes of waiting time challenge. They check in on apps on their phone and we have a process for assigning people to equipment so all get their fair share of first choices. They go directly to the equipment they are assigned. Satisfaction is way up, and I can see Jenny getting better and better at working towards her goals in a scientific way. Daily coaching with the storyboard is key."

"I'll do the same," Denise said. "I'm already doing my version of coaching Joe and Mark every day."

"That's great to hear," Maggie said encouragingly. "As we move on, I'll talk to you more about coaching. That's a whole skill set in and of itself. But, honestly Denise, you're advancing at lightning speed. And I'm learning so much as I coach you. Seriously, thank *you*!"

Denise thanked Maggie in turn, though she did not feel like she was moving at lightning speed. *Feels more like dragging through the mud*, she thought.

7

At Last, Experimenting!

ON MONDAY, DENISE had shown a picture of Maggie's storyboard to Mark and Joe, and together they had put up two boards, one for each of their target conditions. Then, they each began to plan their experiments using the experimenting record on the storyboard.

In the meantime, the world at Goldberg hadn't changed. They still had a huge backlog. There was more reprioritization of orders by sales. And after running out of parts, they had sent some of the assembly teams home. Two new contract workers arrived. Mark and Joe had to spend precious time training them. And then they had to send them home because of missing parts again, which at least freed up some time for her team leaders.

A bit of sunshine, though, was that Denise appreciated how having such a tiny and focused target condition helped them to at least do a small step every day. On Monday, they had managed to squeeze in updating the preparation lists for changeover. Within the next shift, they could already test the differences this change had made, and Denise had asked them to record the results and their reflections on the experimenting record.

Interesting, Denise had thought. *Probably it's easier to do a small step of improvement every day than finding time for running a huge project or workshop on a sporadic basis. Maybe doing one step a day could even become a habit. Eventually it might be everybody, every process, every day.* At least she could dream.

Having a short achieve-by date helped as well. They had recalibrated the target conditions to be Friday to Friday which seemed like a more natural approach – starting work on the next target condition on Monday. Mark and Joe were eager to reach their target conditions by Friday. They even had a bit of fun competition. They were more enthusiastic about Kata activities and even looked forward to the daily coaching sessions.

In her weekly meeting with David, Denise showed him what they had achieved lowering the changeover time by quickly testing small changes. David was interested, but he wanted faster results.

"At least something is happening," he said. "Still, these are baby steps and too slow for what we need right now. Keep improving production output and get that backlog down."

I understand the pressure and the need to achieve the outcomes the big bosses dictated, but David gave me no direction to act on in a focused and productive way, Denise thought. *If we had target conditions at all levels of our organization, it might go slow at first, but then improvement would accelerate exponentially.* Still, she sympathized with David. He looked like he had gotten very little sleep. He was pale and had dark rings underneath his eyes.

Thinking about her conversation with David, Denise recognized that there was a difference between small and slow. *Mark and Joe are making small improvements in relation to the overall impact, but they certainly aren't moving slowly. They're taking small, directed steps every day. And they are learning a lot. Although they have been working with their operating teams every day for years, they often are astonished at what people actually are doing or rather have to do to get things done in the assembly line. Seeing them come to better understand how things are working is kind of amazing. Their discussions have gained so much more depth and are deeply rooted in reality. When I first got here, they would discuss issues on a superficial level. "That's not possible because of the software," or the like. They were making assumptions without evidence but expressing them as facts.*

Denise couldn't help but compare the Kata approach of experimenting and learning fast to the five-day blitz workshops she did as a consultant. Her consultant life was pretty much as follows: Monday, a bit of training, then observe the process to create a list of wastes; Tuesday, come up with a litany of solutions, mostly things that worked somewhere in the past and mostly ones she suggested; Wednesday and Thursday, go crazy implementing as much as possible as fast as possible, hardly reflecting on anything; Friday morning, final cleanup and prepare presentation to management; and Friday early afternoon, present to management, then hit the bars for an early celebration.

The workshops made a big impact quickly, but we didn't learn about the underlying causes and how they impacted outcomes. We implemented seemingly obvious solutions fast, unaware of our assumptions. Come Friday, we celebrated the quick wins and then we'd be so surprised a few weeks later when things started failing because the underlying issues were not addressed. We of course blamed management.

The culture at Goldberg was obsessed with results. Get to the outcome fast, by any means necessary, seemed to be the motto.

Joe and Mark were slowly but steadily getting results, like the tortoise instead of the hare. *I think they'll ultimately win the race*, Denise thought, smiling at the analogy.

The day flew by, mostly putting out fires as usual, but with glimmers of hope during the short meetings she had with Joe and Mark. She was about to head home but decided to sit at her desk and write another entry into her notebook. It was quickly filling up with rich lessons from her experiences with Kata (see Figure 7.1).

February, 1st

Micro learnings from today

☐ Running small experiments helps accomplish something even when fighting fires in a crisis

☐ Achieving the target condition made the team leaders feel great satisfaction, intrinsic motivation

☐ It gave them something they could control in what seemed like a chaotic environment

☐ Small steps does not mean slow!

☐ Rapid, deliberate changes toward a target condition can actually speed improvement

FIGURE 7.1
Log February 1st.

8

May the Coaching Lessons Begin

WHAT A LONG day of work, Denise thought. She parked her car at the fitness studio, grabbed her duffel bag, and made her way to the changing room. She had met with Joe and Mark twice today to discuss the target conditions they were working on this week. It seemed that after an initial burst of energy early in the week, they had stalled. They had successfully reduced the waste of finding stuff and did all that preparation while the line was still producing, and now were on to the second target condition for their assigned workstations on line 3. Mark's next target condition focused on reducing the time to align the fixtures during changeover on the end-of-line test station. Joe took on a quality issue that had long plagued work at his assigned station. After the changeover, there were increased quality problems to fix before the line could start up again. Neither was getting traction, and they seemed to be avoiding working on their assignments.

Denise had tried to coach them using approaches she had learned during a training program at Francis & Drake. "What are you trying to achieve?"

"Getting that damn quality issue solved," Joe had said in frustration at one point.

"What options do you have?" was another question Denise had lobbed at him.

At first Joe and Mark had come up with suggestions. Denise had encouraged them to try them out right away. Unfortunately, they didn't work. They were further disillusioned.

"What other options can you think up?" was the question Denise had tried next.

DOI: 10.4324/9780429347023-9

Mark had just stared at her. "Nothing," he had said. "I've tried everything. It's just impossible."

Oh no, back to where we started, Denise had thought. She had tried to encourage them and also awaken their ambitions by asking, "how would it feel to be successful?"

"How would it feel?" Mark had replied. "I'd say relieved, because then we could stop these stupid interviews."

Then, she had tried yet another approach. "What is the real challenge here for you?"

"The real challenge is that I don't know how to solve the quality issue," Joe had snapped back at her.

"So, what options do you see?" Denise had asked him.

"I don't know," Joe had said, "I've tried everything. It just doesn't work. ""OK, what else could we do?"

"I don't know!" Joe had replied, even more annoyed than before. "These interrogations you call coaching are driving me crazy. Please just tell me what you want me to do!"

Denise had been just as frustrated as Joe. This had been exactly where she didn't want to go, but she knew she was running out of alternatives and had started making suggestions. Joe and Mark quickly shot each idea down. A litany of: "That doesn't work." "We've tried that already." "That doesn't work either, because..."

I need to talk to Maggie, desperately, Denise thought as she grabbed her towel and left the changing room. She entered the gym hall and walked over to the stationary bicycles, looking around for Maggie. But Denise couldn't see her anywhere. She started her workout. After 30 minutes, Maggie still hadn't arrived. Denise walked over to reception.

Jenny greeted her enthusiastically. "Hi Denise, how can I help you?" she said.

"Hi Jen, have you seen Maggie? I need to talk to her."

"Maggie hasn't been here all afternoon. I think she'll be here soon."

"Thanks, Jen," Denise said, trying to remain upbeat. She walked back to the gym floor and continued her workout. She was feeling anxious.

By the end of her workout, Maggie still hadn't appeared. Before she left, Denise stopped by the reception.

"Jenny, could you ask Maggie to call me, please?" Denise asked.

"Sure, does she have your cell?"

Denise thought for a second. "No," she said. "I don't think so." She was surprised to realize they had not gotten that far, despite all their workouts together.

"Give me your cell number, and I'll put a note on Maggie's desk. I bet she'll call you tomorrow."

Back in her loft, Denise was surprised that the workout had released some of the tension from her day after all, but now she felt incredibly tired. She made herself a cup of tea, lay down on the couch, and streamed her favorite Agatha Christie murder mystery series, Hercule Poirot. She loved his dry wit and calm brilliance as he put together clues to form a complete picture. When he cornered a suspect with questions during an interrogation, Denise winced. *I wonder if that was how Joe and Mark felt today?* When she finally got into bed, she quickly fell into a deep sleep.

FEBRUARY 3, THURSDAY 6:45 AM: A LOT OF SNOW AND A CALL FROM MAGGIE

Denise left her house at the wee hours to head to work. The night had been very cold, and the air was still chilly. Her car's windshield was completely frozen. When she opened the car door, she noticed that there was even ice on the inside of the glass. *That's probably from the humidity in the car last night because of my shower at the gym. That's going to take a while to remove.* She started the engine, turned on the heat to full blast, and began the arduous task of scraping off the ice. She always hated it when the windshield was frozen over inside. She was afraid that this was just the start of another frustrating day at Goldberg.

At 7:00 am, she was finally ready to make her way to work. She decided to avoid the highway. *In these conditions, there will be a traffic jam there for sure*, Denise thought as she turned left to take one of the back-country routes. While she drove up the road that crossed one of the nearby hills, her cell phone rang. Denise took the call on the car's speaker.

"Hi Denise, this is Maggie," the voice said. "I just found the note on my desk and thought I'd give you a call right away. How are you?"

Denise felt instantly relieved.

"Maggie! So great you're calling. Thank you, thank you. The answer is not well at all. I am really in trouble coaching Mark and Joe, if that is what you can call it." Then, she launched into a diatribe about what had happened so far this week, barely taking a breath throughout her whole explanation.

Maggie listened patiently for a long time. When Denise finally finished, Maggie spoke in an upbeat, even playful voice, "Well, it looks like you are ready to learn how to coach your team leaders now."

"But that's what I've been trying to do," Denise replied, somewhat defensively. "And I do have training in coaching from the consulting company I worked at."

"No, Denise," Maggie replied somewhat sternly, "what you've been doing is checking in with Joe and Mark every day, maybe even checking up on them, but that's not coaching. You're just checking how they are performing in pursuing their target conditions, and they're feeling overwhelmed. Done daily, that easily turns into micromanaging them, which is the opposite of giving true autonomy, especially if you start telling them what to do. It creates more pressure, tension, and maybe even fear. And fear and creativity don't go together.

"Listen, I've learned a few things about coaching since I left my old consulting firm. For example, many supposed coaches hide their orders behind suggestive questions," said Maggie. "'What do you think about trying X next?' Often they even use closed-ended questions, which makes matters worse. 'Don't you think we should try X now?' Mostly two things happen. Either people shut down their thinking and comply, or they oppose the suggestion explaining why it does not work. That's what happened to you with Mark and Joe."

"Yes, that's exactly what happened. So I should give them more autonomy to try things on their own and meet less frequently with them?" Denise interrupted Maggie while slowing down behind a snow plow cleaning the lane ahead of her and dispensing salt. *This is going to take a while*, Denise thought.

"Absolutely not!" replied Maggie. "If anything, the opposite. Ignoring them is not what autonomy means. That's just shirking your responsibility as a leader. They will feel, well, ignored, and likely stop experimenting. Coaching frequency matters for several reasons – but we'll get there later. For now, the problem you've run into is that Joe and Mark simply don't know how to remove the obstacles they face in order to reach their target conditions. They've run out of ideas because the target conditions for this week are outside of what Rother calls their 'known zone'.

"They could reach last week's target conditions with familiar solutions and ideas based on their experience. These target conditions were inside their known zone or at least close enough. We also call that the 'comfort zone.' So now, with this week's target conditions being outside, in the 'unknown zone,' that feels uncomfortable. They don't know how to get there and even admitting that feels uncomfortable for them.

"This is your next challenge as a coach, Denise. It is actually a positive development and an opportunity. You have to increase your team's capability, their ability to navigate unknown territory and master challenges that, right now, they don't have solutions for. That's what gives your team wings.

"There is a lot to effective coaching. In fact good coaching is an art, but there are some useful tips I can share with you and the method can be very precise. What you want as a coach is a precise method for asking questions and to be open to the ideas your learners come up with. They drive the content, you are focused on the process."

"That all makes sense in theory, but what does it mean in practice?" Denise asked, still stuck behind the snow plow.

Maggie went on and on about how people learn and what motivates them, and why most approaches to management coaching fail. Denise was more focused on getting out from behind the snow plow.

When Maggie's speech came to a close, Denise felt exhausted and it was only 7:30 a.m.

"Ok," Denise said, "so how can I do that?" As the snow plow thankfully turned left at the T-junction ahead, Denise turned right accelerating again.

"Sorry for the long lecture," said Maggie, laughing a little, "but as you can probably tell, coaching is a passion of mine, and so many people don't get it. Rother has another Starter Kata to help us begin to practice coaching, a set of five questions that, together with daily coaching cycles, he calls the Coaching Kata. You'll find them in his practice guide and on his website. These questions provide a starting point and framework for practicing a more effective kind of coaching. There is even a card you can print with the basic questions to use as a reference. Start by asking Mark and Joe these questions exactly in your daily coaching session. As you practice, you'll advance beyond simply asking the questions and learn to listen carefully to their responses and based on those you can ask further deepening questions. As I said, this is more an art than a science.

"Oh, and you might want to ask David to join your coaching cycles once in a while and observe. If you tell him about the questions and our discussion today, he can help you stay on track. It's always better to start practicing Coaching Kata with a partner. Who knows, over time David might pick up learning how to coach, too.

"I need to hang up now but keep in mind, frequency matters. Changing habits and ways of thinking is all about frequent practice, even in short bursts. You should start by coaching Joe and Mark every day. They will learn faster, and you will learn faster too. Also, that puts priority on working toward the next target condition.

"Find out about the Coaching Kata questions, I will email you the card Mike created. Print it out and start practicing. I'll see you at the gym."

With that, Maggie hung up.

Denise continued to make her way to work through the snow, her head spinning, and, occasionally, her tires, too.

Part II

Coaching as Learning

9

Starting to Coach (with Some Struggles)

THURSDAY, FEBRUARY 3, 7:45 AM, SORTING OUT MAGGIE'S BRAIN DUMP

DENISE SAT DOWN at her desk and picked up her notebook to summarize her takeaways from the call with Maggie. There was a lot to process, and she was having trouble even getting started. She found her mind wandering and suddenly recalled a nightmare she had the night before. She had called a meeting with Joe and Mark, but they had not shown up. She searched all over the assembly area to no avail. Then she heard some laughing and cheering coming from a conference room and entered it to find Joe and Mark and a few of their guys playing poker. As she entered, Mark pointed at her and they all laughed.

"There's the *woman who* thinks she's going to lead us!" Mark said. "Look at her, she's just a little *girl*."

At that, everyone laughed even louder. Denise had woken up in a sweat.

Wow, Denise thought, feeling sweat dripping down her forehead again. *I had forgotten that dream until now. My fears and insecurities must really be getting to me.*

She tried to shift her focus back to the notebook and took a deep breath. After a few minutes, she found she was able to organize her thoughts.

I guess Maggie's point is that in this management role I can't act like a consultant who comes in to save the day. I need to shift from telling to coaching. My job is not to have all the answers but to draw out the best of Joe and Mark and stimulate their thinking. And Maggie made clear that would happen if I asked the right questions. So, talk less and question more but try to ask good questions.

DOI: 10.4324/9780429347023-11

February, 3rd

Thoughts on Coaching

☐ Coaching for capability aims at developing the learner's skills and natural tendency to approach goals scientifically, helping them achieve their goals at the same time.

☐ The next target condition has to be in the learning zone of the improver. We learn through trying something new. Hit the sweet spot of difficulty, not too much or too little.

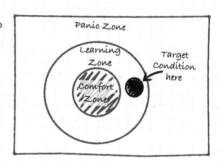

FIGURE 9.1
Place target condition in learning zone.

Denise began to formulate a summary in her notebook of what she learned about the target condition and her coaching role. She started to feel more relaxed almost immediately (see Figures 9.1 and 9.2).

As she was closing her notebook Denise recalled that Maggie had suggested, no, insisted, that she print out the Coaching Kata question card.

My challenge as a coach

☐ My challenge as a coach: Increase my team's ability to navigate unknown territory.

☐ Broader Challenge Statement: Learn to manage the business and develop people at the same time, like two sides of the same coin.

☐ Coaching for capability uses the Coaching Kata to develop the underlying thinking, regardless of the content. It is more than delegation and "empowerment."

☐ Coaching for capability = Precise on the method + open on the solutions.

FIGURE 9.2
My challenge as a coach.

She had looked at it online and was surprised to see how little was there. The questions seemed kind of rote and obvious (see Figure 9.3).

It feels like asking people to tell you what they did after you told them exactly how to do it. And the only coaching skill you need is reading the questions? Denise thought, feeling skeptical.

But then she recalled that Maggie referred to the Coaching Kata as a starting point for coaches. Maggie said these questions were only to start the conversation and see how the person you're coaching is thinking. Based on their answers, the next step was to ask questions that helped them reflect and deepened their thinking.

So, the higher-level coaching skill is to ask the right deepening question without "leading the witness?" Denise thought. *I guess the idea is to encourage thinking, not do the thinking. That kind of makes sense.*

Denise read through the information on the Toyota Kata homepage quickly and decided to try out the questions in her coaching sessions today. She printed out the card from the website as well, wondering if it was a waste of paper.

I'll take it along as Maggie suggested but I hope I don't have to read from the card. I think I have these questions memorized anyway from reading Mike's books, and they're pretty basic, she thought.

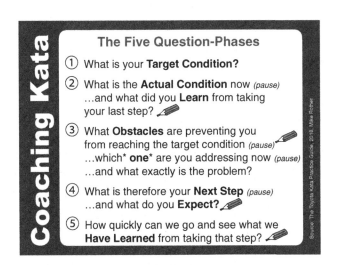

FIGURE 9.3
The Coaching Kata starter questions, adapted from Mike Rother, *The Toyota Kata Practice Guide*, McGraw-Hill (New York), 2018.

Denise got up from her desk and went to the plant floor for her coaching session with Mark, who was team leader on the first shift this week. She met him at his storyboard.

After greeting him, Denise asked, "is now still a good time for our coaching cycle?"

She had picked up the habit of checking if the time was still suitable at the beginning of each coaching session. It was a show of respect for their valuable time, a sign she recognized that sometimes urgent matters came up. If that happened, Denise shifted the coaching session to a later time the same day. As a consultant, she had seen too many managers force their schedule on their team, summoning them whenever it suited them. The message was "my time is important, but yours is not."

"Sure, let's start," said Mark, but he didn't seem particularly excited.

Suddenly, Denise was glad she had the card, she didn't want a repeat of what had happened the day before, when she and Mark had each gotten so frustrated. *I'll just play along and read what's on the card*, she thought. *But I should probably warn him first.*

"I might have mentioned my friend Maggie who runs the gym I go to," Denise said. "She told me about a way of coaching that involves reading questions from a card. It is part of the Kata thing we've been practicing. This is part of the Coaching Kata for me to learn to be a better coach. I would like to try it out now if that is okay."

Mark looked over her shoulder at the card.

"I could read the card myself, boss," he said. "But if you prefer to do the reading, then fire away."

She started with the first question. "What is your target condition?" she asked.

"Our goal is to reduce the changeover time of line 3 to 10 minutes or below. You know, change in a touch, as Joe would say," Mark shot back. He made the percussion sound and smiled. "Doing so would enable us to run six changeovers a day and so produce all our 12 high-runners every two days. In addition, reducing the changeover time would give us an extra hour of assembly time for each shift. That will help us to reduce our backlog," he added.

Hmmm, thought Denise. *Mark gave me the challenge and a great rationale. On the other hand, it was more about the challenge than the next target condition. Maybe he is confused about the difference, and I should explain it to him. But Maggie said I should be asking questions and not telling stuff. How do I give Mark feedback without hurting his pride and turning him off? I'll think about that later.* Denise made a mental note as Mark continued on a roll, obviously pleased by his clear, and lengthy, explanations.

"As you know, we've spent the past couple weeks working on eliminating searching time when doing a changeover. Now that that has been achieved, my next target condition is to reduce the time we need to change each workplace. The longest time for that is at workstation 5 because changing the fixtures there involves a lot of manual work. That's why my next target condition is to reduce the time needed for changing the fixtures at the workstation number 5 to 200 seconds. Of course, there are some boundaries like reducing time should not cause quality issues, and we also have a budget to think of, a budget you set …"

That was a mouthful. I'm glad we have set up the storyboard. Otherwise, I'd get lost. I'm not sure how I am supposed to respond as a coach, but I'll step outside the box and try to rephrase what I heard as a target condition. I think sometimes reflecting back what I've heard can help the learner.

"That's great, Mark," said Denise. "You sure have thought a lot about this. Am I correct that your next target condition is to reduce the time needed to change the fixtures at workstation 5 to 200 seconds?"

"I think I said that," Mark responded, a bit curtly, "but yes you heard me right."

Denise thanked Mark for his answer and then moved on to the next question. "So, what is the actual condition now?"

"Currently we need about 21 minutes for changeover and our backlog is still very high at 247 pieces as of today," Mark replied. "At workstation 5 we currently need around 380 seconds for changing all the fixtures, so we have ways to go. Oh, and by the way, we have even more quality issues probably because we do more changeovers now. Joe has that as his target condition, but I guess he's not making a lot of progress."

Again, that's too much information. We talk about the quality issues every day and what Joe is or is not doing is part of my coaching of Joe. I need to find a way to give Mark feedback without offending him. He did not seem to appreciate my rephrasing his target condition. I'll have to discuss this with Maggie. Ok, next question…

"What obstacles are preventing you from reaching your target condition?" Denise asked.

"There are several," Mark replied, "but first I'd really like to tell you about my last step."

Darn, he's right, I guess I missed that question. I got caught up in thinking about how to respond to Mark and forgot where I was on the card and then decided to wing it. I thought I had the questions memorized, but I guess I should look at the card while I am coaching, at least until I've really got the hang of it. Chalk that up to another one for Maggie.

"Good catch Mark," said Denise. "Please do that first."

Mark had a sly expression, and he winked with good humor. "I'm a quick reader, boss," he said, before launching into another detailed explanation that went beyond the question.

"My last step was to observe more closely what we do and what the steps are when we change the fixtures at workstation 5," he said. "What I found is that it sometimes takes a long time to align the fixtures before tightening the screws because operators measure several times from both sides of the table until they have the lower fixture in the correct position.

"Also, the position for each type of fixture for different pumps is different. The more experienced operators have created a list with measurements for each fixture so they know where to position it best. However, that's not ideal. If we had a mark on the table where to put each fixture we would save lots of time. A frame for containing the fixture probably would be even better, but I guess that's not our first step."

Denise was floored. *What do I even say to that? He gave me the step somewhere in there and the result and his speculation about the solution. It's way too much, and he is jumping to solutions prematurely, which is the opposite of scientific thinking. I really need him to focus. How can I reel Mark in?*

Denise felt defeated. She decided to wrap things up by asking Mark to write what he did and learned in the experimenting record which was now blank. To her surprise, it turned out to be just the right move. Mark realized he had explained too much and had to sort it out. He also realized he had not thought about a prediction, what he expected he would learn. He fumbled a bit but did an okay job filling in the boxes. His written responses were much clearer descriptions than his rambling verbal answers. Denise decided to move on.

"What obstacles are preventing you from reaching your target condition?" she asked. "I think we're ready for that one now," she added, laughing.

"Absolutely, boss," said Mark. "Well, as I said there is a mark missing on the table, which we should use to align the fixtures. Also, placing and tightening the screws takes a long time. And often the top part of the manual press has to be repositioned after the first piece. That takes time as well and often creates scrap. I guess that is also related to positioning the fixture on the table."

Mark is still winging it and did not write any obstacles on the parking lot.

"Good observations Mark. Could you write that list down on the obstacle parking lot?" After Mark was done writing, Denise asked, "which one are you addressing now?"

He looked at the parking lot and read, "the missing marking on the table."

Succinct answer. Answered the question. That worked. Denise immediately followed up before he had a chance to elaborate.

"And what will be your next step?" she said.

"I'll mark the correct position of the lower fixture on the table so operators know where to place it."

"And what do you expect will happen?"

Mark thought for a moment.

"Well, I guess operators won't have to measure and so they won't lose time when they're placing the lower fixture. That should save us at least 30 to 40 seconds."

"Great," Denise replied, "please add that to the next row on our experimenting record." After Mark finished writing, she asked, "how quickly can we go and see what we have learned from taking that step?"

"I guess I can manage to do that before our coaching session tomorrow."

Mark added the due date to the experimenting record as well. Denise thanked him for his time and great work and then walked back to her office (see Figure 9.4).

It was a bit of a rough start, but once we got rolling, it went quite well, she thought. *The change seemed to occur when I asked Mark to fill out the storyboard. Space there is limited, so he had to be succinct and precise and so his answers immediately became more focused. Next time, I'll use the Coaching Kata card and stick to the script. And I could sure use some tips from Maggie on what to do when the learner strays and does not directly answer the question. Maybe that is part of the more advanced deepening questions.*

She decided to study the card and start to really memorize the questions. *Oh, there's another question about the obstacle: "What exactly is the problem?" I guess I didn't ask that one. But why would you, since he already*

OBSTACLE PARKING LOT

Date	Obstacle
Feb 3	Marking missing on table for aligning fixtures
Feb 3	Placing and tightening screws takes too long
Feb 3	Repositioning of manual press takes extra time and creates scrap

EXPERIMENTING RECORD

(Each row = one experiment)

Process:

Date	Current Condition*	Obstacle	Next Step & Expectation	Until	What happened & What we learned
					CONDUCT THE EXPERIMENT
Feb 3	380 sec.	Missing marking on the table	Step: Mark correct position for lower fixture on table Expectation: Reduce changeover time by 30-40 sec.	Feb 4	Aligning new fixtures takes long Fixture pos. differs for each pump Experienced ops. have made list
			Step:		

FIGURE 9.4
Mark's storyboard forms, adapted from Mike Rother, *The Toyota Kata Practice Guide*, McGraw-Hill (New York), 2018.

QR CODE 9.1
Get a DIY print out.

stated the obstacle he is working on? Anyway, I'll take the card along to my coaching session with Joe this afternoon, so I don't miss items. I guess there was a reason Maggie asked me to start by simply asking the questions. Seems like she's always right, she thought, feeling a little envious.

Denise suddenly remembered Maggie's suggestion of inviting David to join and observe her coaching sessions. *I guess I'll wait to ask him. It puts too much pressure on Mark and Joe if David is around. And it's not like David knows anything about this Kata stuff. I'm not sure he'd really be able to give me any useful advice.*

THURSDAY, FEBRUARY 3, 3:00PM, A SECOND TRY AT COACHING

That afternoon, Denise met with Joe for their coaching session. She arrived at the storyboard a few minutes early and used the time to take a look at Joe's new target condition. The outcome metric was still the same: reduce changeover time on assembly line number 3 to 10 minutes. The focus of Joe's efforts though was different from his previous target condition. He was no longer working on eliminating searching time for tools, fixtures, and parts during changeover. Now he was working to reduce the quality issues they had after each changeover. His process metric now was to reduce the number of defects after the changeover to 0. Joe seemed to be more organized than Mark, or at least he had written more things down.

Denise could see Joe hurrying toward her. He looked preoccupied.

"Hi, Joe. Does this time still work for our coaching session?"

"Well, we have some urgent issues on line number 2, but if we're quick I can manage," he replied, a little out of breath.

"Ok, before we start, could I ask you for a favor?" She pulled out the card with the Coaching Kata questions. Joe looked at it quizzically, so she explained. "After our last coaching session you told me that my coaching attempts weren't really helping you. I talked to a more experienced coach and she gave me this coaching card. It's a checklist of questions, just so I don't miss anything important. If you don't mind I'll just read them one by one and you can answer. Is that okay?"

Joe seemed amused. "Whatever floats your boat Denise," he said. "Shoot."

Denise started with the first question. "Joe, what is your target condition?" she asked. For the whole session Denise kept the card in hand. The difference was night and day. It was a lot easier to stick to the questions. And it certainly helped that Joe had filled out the storyboard.

However, when the conversation got tricky, she again lost the thread. She looked down at her card. *Where are we? Right, I asked Joe about what one obstacle he was going to address. Then we got a bit off track because he had already explained what he wanted to change while we were still on the obstacle. So, I guess I need to go back to question 3 on obstacles. I'll put my thumb there so I know where we are.*

After completing the coaching cycle and thanking Joe, Denise felt satisfied but exhausted. *I need a break.* She walked over to the area with the vending machines and got herself a chocolate bar. *There goes my diet. But I desperately need some sugar now.*

Reflecting on the coaching cycle with Joe, she realized how much having the card in hand helped. It freed her brain from thinking about what questions to ask. But it was still hard to keep Joe on track, especially when they had discussed the obstacle. Joe had flooded her with too much information, just like Mark. She tried her hand at asking clarifying questions with the hopes of focusing Joe on succinct answers to the question, but it seemed to have the opposite effect. Joe went even further off topic speculating about future obstacles and solutions.

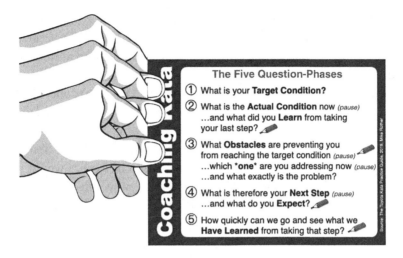

The Five Question-Phases

① What is your **Target Condition?**

② What is the **Actual Condition** now *(pause)*
...and what did you **Learn** from taking
your last step?

③ What **Obstacles** are preventing you
from reaching the target condition *(pause)*
...which *one* are you addressing now *(pause)*
...and what exactly is the problem?

④ What is therefore your **Next Step** *(pause)*
...and what do you **Expect?**

⑤ How quickly can we go and see what we
Have Learned from taking that step?

Coaching Kata

Source: The Toyota Kata Practice Guide, 2018, Mike Rother

My Rule of Thumb

Follow the questions on the card
with your thumb, always putting
it on the last question asked.

FIGURE 9.5
Rule of thumb. Tilo Schwarz, *Kata Coaching Dojo Handbook*, self-published, 2018.

Putting my thumb on the question I've asked and then moving along as I asked the next question really helped. Whenever Mark and Joe start to deviate from the topic at hand, I can look at the card and know exactly what question to focus on. I might have to restate the original question but that's OK. It'll get us back on track. I'll have to sketch that trick into my notebook when I return to my desk. Maybe I should call it "The Rule of Thumb," she thought with a smile. She returned to her desk to write (Figure 9.5).

"Hi Denise, how are you?"

Denise looked up, startled as David stepped into her office. He looked surprisingly good-humored.

Denise recovered from the surprise and responded pleasantly. "Fine," she said, "just a bit exhausted after my coaching session with Joe this afternoon. How about you?"

"Just had a meeting with Dick. He's still furious that we can't get the backlog down. I tried telling him that we've strangled our supply chain so much with the sudden increase in orders to reduce backlog so we keep running short of the parts we need. Of course he did not care. He demanded 'results, not excuses'. Honestly, he kind of yelled at me saying, 'I can hire anyone off the street right now and get excuses. You are in this position to get results'." David was imitating Dick's baritone, and still smiling. "The only good thing is that order income has improved and is back to the usual for this time of the year."

"You seem surprisingly cheerful after that beat down," Denise observed.

"If I got bent out of shape every time Dick criticized me, I would need somebody to take me away in a strait jacket. Anyway, I need a diversion from being a whipping boy. Tell me more about this coaching thing you're trying."

"Sure," Denise answered, pleased he was showing interest. "I've been meaning to talk to you about it, even invite you to a coaching session. Let's go over to one of our storyboards."

She took David over to Mark's storyboard and explained the structure to him.

David seemed to follow her explanation. "I can see how these boards, or 'storyboards' as you call them, help you to structure things," he said. "But don't we have enough boards in the plant? We have information boards, shop floor management boards, quality management boards, you name it. What's the difference here? I can't see how adding another board would help us. And by the way, how do these boards help us to reduce the backlog. Remember? That's the only thing Dick cares about and that is why I keep getting chewed out."

Denise didn't know what to say. She got the idea of the boards from Maggie. Should she tell David about her? Better not. Explaining that her fitness coach helped her with business might be difficult for David to get right now. Denise needed to draw on all the consulting skills she used with difficult clients.

"I see your point about all the boards we already have in the plant," she said. "But these boards are quite specific to the process I am using to help Joe and Mark work toward their goals, step by step, and each one is designed for them specifically. They are not generic information for a bunch of people to read in addition to all the other boards, but just for my team leaders and myself to help you meet your goal."

"Ok, but, seriously, Denise, this kind of seems excessive when our real problem is to reduce the backlog."

"David," Denise said in her best soothing voice, "I understand your frustration. I keep asking you for patience and I appreciate you letting me experiment when you are under so much pressure. We're headed toward solving the problem of backlog, but doing it systematically, so we actually solve the problem. As you can see from our challenge statement, we're focused on reducing changeover time. If we can reduce changeover time and make more changeovers each day, we will have more productive time, cycle through different products more quickly, and have the right ones our customers need when they need it. In Dick's last message, he made clear he didn't just want any products but the right products. Reducing changeover time will help us accomplish that.

"Let me backup a bit. What I'm practicing with my team is called Toyota Kata, a way of developing scientific thinking in our teams through practice. It was developed by Mike Rother from the University of Michigan. He had studied lean methods from Toyota and realized that they focused heavily on developing people by coaching them. Specifically, they coach them to work towards their goals and solve problems in a more scientific way instead of jumping to conclusions. For Toyota, scientific thinking is a central, enabling element in their system.

"They were a little vague about their approach, so Mike clarified it for others. He kind of described the key seed behavior of scientific thinking so we can practice it with people who know nothing about Toyota. The word kata comes from the martial arts, small practice routines to develop small skills eventually used for defending yourself."

"Oh, I know about kata," David said, jumping in enthusiastically. "When I was a kid, I studied karate, and the black belt explained he was teaching us one specific skill at a time and said each was a kata. The key was repetition and getting each small skill right."

"Yes, yes, that's exactly what we are talking about," said Denise, getting more and more excited. "As for the boards, they're there to help Mark and Joe practice Kata with the goal of getting them to think more scientifically. They reflect what Rother calls the Improvement Kata. By building and maintaining their boards, Mark and Joe practice the same approach over and over. At the top left is the target condition, a reminder of what we want to focus on. In the middle, there are the run charts for the current condition. The message there is to always get the actual facts first. And then there is the experimenting record. That's a pretty cool form. By filling in their next step, Joe and Mark practice how to conduct experiments in a more scientific way. What is it we want to test? What do we expect to happen? And then after the step, what did actually happen and what did we learn? As we go through repetitions, Mark and Joe learn to think more scientifically, based on facts, and view each step as an experiment, instead of jumping to conclusions. It frees them up to try things, whereas before they seemed to resist any change to the current practices, which they have known for so long and are completely comfortable with."

"Well, I can see how the boards you have created are nice for the level of detail you are working on and useful for developing your team leaders. *And* I can see how it would be more effective than just sitting them in a conference room and lecturing at them. But my world is so different," he said, shaking his head, his voice doubtful. "I can't imagine having boards all over our meeting rooms and spending time every day training every one of our leaders. And I hate to say it again, but all this effort results in what? Your backlog hasn't improved, right? I see you're convinced this scientific thinking seed is the right thing to practice with your team leaders and move, somewhat slowly, toward reducing backlog. But how do you even know you'll get there?"

Denise smiled. "David, I'm really happy with how focused and engaged Joe and Mark are. That is such a positive change from their running around fighting fires and refusing to work on any kind of improvement. They are tackling the beast piece by piece, scientifically. It all starts with having a focused target condition, and then the next one, and the next one. I can't explain how I know we'll reach the goal, but I have confidence in the process and in Joe and Mark."

"Okay, fine, I'll play along. It may get me fired, but at least it is kind of interesting. So what makes a good target condition?"

"I'm glad you asked, David. Three things," Denise replied. "You need an outcome metric, a desired pattern of work, and a process metric.

"Now in our case Dick has ordered us to eliminate the backlog, reasonable, but what he really wants is for us to ship what the customer wants on time. Shipping the right pumps on time is the desired outcome. To get there, he believes we should focus on eliminating the backlog – but having zero backlog is an outcome as well. That doesn't tell us anything about how to get there. We need to figure out what we need to change in our processes to reduce the backlog.

"From our analysis of the current condition, we realized that changeover time is taking away a lot of our possible production time and forcing us to make large batches of one type of motor, more than our customers actually ordered.

"Realizing that helped us to see our desired state. We should be able to produce every type of our largest-selling products every day. That of course requires much smaller batches – with the ideal batch size being 1. So, the desired pattern for the assembly is every main product every day.

"To do that, we'll need to reduce changeover time – otherwise the sheer amount of time spent on changeovers would kill us. Now to see if we're making progress, we've made changeover time our process metric.

"See, the three elements are desired outcome, satisfied customers – no backlog, desired pattern of work, every product every day, and process metric, changeover time. Together they tell us where to go and what to focus on for improvement."

"That's very interesting," said David, jumping in. "It does make me see how weak our current way of defining targets as a plant is. We only define high-level outcome targets. Even if we break them down, it's only to divide up the same outcome target among a group of managers. We say things like, 'we want a total of 10% cost reduction, therefore, each of you give us a 10% reduction in your area'. Then we send them off to chase the outcome. I guess that doesn't help teams understand exactly what to work on. Of course, there are multiple possible levers to move an outcome target. But focusing on one or two at a time does seem much better than trying to pull on all of them at the same time. It obviously creates more clarity. Once we get out of this backlog mess, we should try to do something like that for the whole plant."

Denise stared at David, stunned. *How did he figure all that out so quickly? I guess there's a reason he became plant manager at such a young age.*

"I have another question though," said David "When I saw you at the vending machine, you were playing with a little card in your hand. What's that about?"

"Oh, that's a card with questions to help me coach," Denise replied, as she pulled the card out of the back pocket of her jeans. "Here it is. It's a set of questions developed by Mike Rother and it's called Coaching Kata. Practicing these questions helps you to coach your people in a more scientific way of thinking and working toward their goals. The storyboard reflects the Improvement Kata that I want Mark and Joe to practice. This is my kata as a coach."

"You mean asking these questions is coaching? And you're even reading them from the card?" David frowned incredulously.

"Well, maybe it's more like a starting point," Denise replied hastily, feeling a little defensive. "What I've found is that they really help me to structure my coaching conversations in a positive way. As I practice more, I'll get better at asking further deepening questions and giving feedback. Rother calls these questions Starter Kata, to get me started until I develop the skills to ask further deepening questions that guide my team leaders without giving them the answers to the questions. I don't know, I was skeptical, too, but then I saw that it's kind of magical. Maybe you should give it a try and see for yourself."

"But this seems so robotic," David replied. "And also, how would I even use these questions in the situations I face every day? I'm not standing in front of such a nicely organized board, and we don't have these kinds of target conditions on our level."

Denise thought for a moment.

"I think you're correct that unless someone is practicing Improvement Kata and trying to follow the steps, then asking these questions may be confusing. Just going around asking the questions to people with no training might be putting the cart before the horse. Maybe you can observe some of my coaching sessions just to see what it's like. And I could use any feedback you have to offer. What do you think?"

"Alright, why not, if I can find the time I'll join you." David replied.

"That's easy," Denise responded with a smile. "I have an agreement with Mark and Joe to coach them at the same time every day. Just put the two time slots in your calendar and come over when you can. My only request is that you don't interfere while I coach. And I'll have to prepare Mark and Joe. They'll likely get nervous when you show up." Denise took out her cell phone and sent David an invite for both recurring meetings.

David checked his calendar.

"I can make it tomorrow," he said. "See you then."

After David left, Denise walked back to her office quietly humming to herself. *That went much better than I expected. He actually wants to come to sessions, even with all the pressure he is under. And boy is he sharp. Maybe I will get some useful feedback.*

Sitting at her desk, Denise thought about her two coaching sessions today and took another look at the card with the Coaching Kata questions. She realized that she had used the questions on the card but had also improvised some additional questions, and the ones she had come up with seemed to help get Mark and Joe on track. Suddenly, she felt completely energized and excited. *I think I discovered something new that I can teach Maggie.* Finally, she felt like she had a thing or two, however small, to offer in return.

As if by divine providence, her cell phone vibrated. It was a message from Maggie. "How did your coaching sessions go today? Want to join me for dinner? How about The Edamame?"

Denise hadn't realized how late it was. Catching up with Maggie and briefing her on her findings from today sounded great.

Plus, she'd been meaning to try The Edamame. It was the new sushi restaurant and it had just opened this week. It looked pretty classy, and she'd heard it had great food. Even her Japanese-American colleagues had positive things to say. *Not bad for a small town like Guilderville.*

She quickly texted Maggie back. "Yes. 7:30?"

Maggie replied with a thumbs-up emoji. Bing. Another message from Maggie. "Bring a photo of each of your storyboards."

Denise closed her laptop and grabbed her winter coat. On her way out, she took pictures of Mark's and Joe's storyboards with her cell phone, stopping to take a close up of their experimenting records, before running out the door.

10

Japanese Cuisine and a Lot of Learning

DENISE OPENED THE door to The Edamame, pushed aside the little Japanese-style curtains that hung behind it, and entered the restaurant. She had blasted through traffic to arrive on time. The place was buzzing, and all the tables were full. Denise looked around. Maggie was waving from one of the tables at the far end, and Denise rushed over to her.

"How are you?" Maggie asked, as Denise sat down.

Denise caught her breath.

"Excited and exhausted," she said, smiling. "I have so much to tell you. What a day. I had two very interesting coaching sessions and an inspiring conversation with David. I think he's getting interested. I want to tell you what happened and some of the things I think I learned, maybe even teach you something. But first, How are you?"

"I'm good. I also have some things to share. I just came back from a Coaching Kata workshop in Frankfurt led by Tilo Schwarz. Tilo is like an informal student of Mike Rother, and he picked up where Rother left off on the Coaching Kata. He has a lot of new insights into various problems that occur during coaching and how to deal with them. He sets up what he calls a *dojo*, which is what they call the training gym in Japanese martial arts, but his is a place to practice coaching not self-defense. I got a working copy of a book he wrote, and I have loads of notes.* So, yeah, lots to share. But first I want to hear more about your big day."

Denise glanced at the pot of green tea sitting in front of Maggie and the glasses of water set on the table.

---

* Stand on Red - Walk on Green, Tilo Schwarz, *Kata Coaching Dojo Handbook*, self-published, 2018.

"I think I need one of those famous Japanese beers first," Denise said. "Then we can dive into the nitty-gritty. I'm really looking forward to hearing all you have learned, but I have to admit I'm still very much of a beginner," she sighed.

The waiter came around and took their orders—A Kirin™ beer for Denise and some sashimi to share for starters. And, of course, they ordered a big bowl of the namesake Edamame, the warm soft shells you squeeze to get to the tasty soybeans inside. The February weather was wet and cold. *Some soup will warm me up*, Denise thought and ordered an udon soup as a main course. Once the waiter left, they continued their conversation.

"So what did you learn today?" Maggie asked after Denise's beer arrived.

Denise took a sip. "I coached Mark this morning. It took too long, and there were some struggles, but in the end it went pretty well. I had read about the Coaching Kata in Rother's book and studied the question card so I thought I could just wing it from memory. Boy was I wrong! At one point, Mark had stopped me to answer a question I forgot to ask. So, I guess one thing I learned today is that it's really helpful at first to stick to actually reading off the card."

Maggie nodded and smiled. "I remember making that mistake, too, at some point. I think as beginners we often overestimate our abilities. That's part of the point of the whole Starter Kata thing for beginners, so we can learn about our actual strengths and weaknesses through direct experience. We can theorize all we want, but it's not until you are actually there doing the coaching that you have a real opportunity to learn. Did you bring the pictures of your storyboards?"

"Yes mam, you ask I deliver." Denise took out her cell phone, opened the picture of Mark's storyboard, and passed it to Maggie. "I also took a close-up of the experimenting record. It's the next one. Actually, this was not what the storyboard looked like when I started the session. He had left a lot of things blank, like the experimenting record and the obstacle list. In fact, when I was asking him the questions his answers were all over the place, and he wasn't even really addressing the question I'd asked. I wasn't sure how to respond, and when I did make a suggestion, he got defensive. So, another big learning moment for me was when I asked him to write down the information on the storyboard. That really focused him."

"Good lesson," Maggie replied, still studying the pictures. "Hmm, that's interesting. Mark wrote down the obstacle and next step using nearly identical language. Here, have a look."

She passed the phone back to Denise. Indeed, the obstacle read: "missing marking on the table." The next step read: "mark the correct position of the lower fixture on the table (see figure 9.4)."

Denise was taken aback. "I didn't realize that during our session," she said. Maggie nodded.

"It's pretty common. When asked which obstacle to address to reach the target condition, people often answer prematurely with a next step. Or kind of an inverted next step or solution. Obstacle: position not marked. Next step: mark position. Obstacle: missing tools. Next step: buy new tools. Obstacle: missing software license. Next step: get a license. The problem is that that often means the improver is jumping to premature solutions. What did you ask Mark after he stated the obstacle he wanted to address?"

Denise thought about it trying to remember and replied, "I think I asked about the next step. Isn't that the next question on the card?"

"Nope, and that may explain what happened," Maggie responded. "Don't worry. That's a common trap for beginner coaches. They move too quickly to question 4 when they should dig more deeply into question 3. Remember that question 3 has three parts. What we're really trying to do is help the improver investigate the cause and effect of an obstacle before coming up with a countermeasure. We might even offer to go together to examine the actual process and discuss it there. Have you got your card? Take a look."

Denise reached for her back pocket. She felt relieved as she felt the card there. She took it out and skimmed it.

"Have a look at the question sequence about obstacles," Maggie said.

Denise looked again. "The third question there after asking about the obstacle they will work on next reads: And what exactly is the problem?"

"That additional question wasn't on the original question card by Rother. Tilo, the Kata expert who ran the workshop I just went to, added it to the starter set of questions to help beginner coaches avoid jumping prematurely to asking about the next step. If the improver reflects a bit on the obstacle, they are less likely to simply restate the obstacle as the next step."

"Oh, you know what, now I remember realizing after the session was over that I hadn't asked that question, and I was wondering why I should. It seemed redundant. I get it now, though. If I'd asked Mark what exactly the problem was, he might have said something like, 'losing time because the operators have to adjust the position of the fixture multiple times.'"

"Exactly!" Maggie exclaimed, "and that would have been a solution-open description of the obstacle that did not presume the next step. You'll find as you progress that you'll probably need to go beyond simply reading the initial questions or you might only get pro forma answers. To push Mark further you might have to ask deepening questions, like 'what exactly are operators doing when they adjust the position of the fixture?' "

"Wow, there's so much to learn," said Denise, jumping in. "But wait, we agreed that it's useful at first to have the card in your hand and read the questions in that order. Now, you're saying that if I just read the card I may get rote answers and not really understand how the improver is thinking. Honestly, that's kind of confusing."

Maggie didn't look deterred by Denise's question. In fact, she smiled, looking energized.

"It's still useful to use the card as a guide, but think about the questions as headings rather than the final word on what you should be asking. Plus, you've kind of answered your own question. The key words are 'at first'. Remember that Mike calls these 'Starter Kata', with the hope that as you gain experience and learn you will add your own take. Imagine that you ask, 'What did you learn from taking your last step?' Now, say the improver responds with something he or she learned from taking the last step, but the answer isn't related to what he or she said they expected to happen in the last coaching cycle. You then could throw in 'what did you expect to happen' as a deepening question. If they talk about expectations off the top of their head, you can refer them to the storyboard and what they had written down about the expectation. That way they can see the disconnect without you pointing it out. Now you have your improver thinking, which is the goal of the coaching session. Help your improver to think in a more scientific way.

Scan with your mobile to find out more about Maggie's card.

QR CODE 10.1
About Maggie's Card.

Of course, I may be getting ahead of myself because these are more advanced coaching skills, but you seem to be picking this all up super quick."

The waiter arrived with their udon soups and interrupted Maggie's lecture. Maggie had a large combination plate of sushi and sashimi that looked delicious, and so colorful. Denise was glad for the break. She understood that what Maggie explained was very helpful, but it had been a long day. *I have to put all this in my notebook tomorrow,* Denise thought. *Maybe this time I can do it without remembering a bad dream.* They ate in comfortable silence, and Denise could feel the warmth of the soup spreading through her body.

After a while, Denise felt restored and resumed the conversation.

"I noticed you've been using the term 'improver' for the person being coached. Rother's term refers to the 'learner', which is how I've been thinking about it. Why the difference?"

"Oh, that's such a good question. Another tip I got from Tilo. Most people use the term learner. I don't like it as much, though, because, to me, it implies a kind of hierarchy. The coach teaches and the learner learns. Personally, I feel more like both roles are all about learning. The person being coached learns about how to improve the process toward the next target condition in a more scientific way, so that's the 'improver,' while the coach learns how to coach in a better way."

"I like that distinction. Honestly, to me, it feels like the coaching part involves even more learning, and the learning you're doing is so complex," Denise replied. "I'll use 'improver' from now on, too."

Denise realized that distinction helped her feel less overwhelmed– it was kind of liberating to realize that she was *supposed* to be learning too. She told Maggie about her discovery that putting her thumb on the question card to mark where she was really helped and that she decided to call it her "rule of thumb."

Maggie laughed out loud, which was unusual for Maggie who was usually pretty staid.

"I love it. What a great tip," Maggie responded.

Denise moved on to her conversation with David.

"He still hasn't seen me coach," she said, "but I showed him the storyboard and the coaching card and he was both enthusiastic and skeptical. He liked the underlying structure we use for target conditions and how I've deployed them in my team. I think he likes the idea of setting goals and holding people accountable, like he's doing with me on production output targets.

He gets the value of having a process metric that is actionable rather than just an outcome metric, and he even thinks the target conditions could spread throughout the plant. He wasn't so enthusiastic about the Coaching Kata questions, though. He thought it sounded a bit robotic and said he couldn't transfer it to his daily work. I think he just doesn't get developing people to think scientifically."

"Mmm," said Maggie, "that's unfortunately a pretty common problem. Corporate cultures are often so focused on doing things quickly and getting immediate results, the opposite of scientific thinking. Honestly, it's the jumping to conclusions routine that Toyota Kata was designed to help us out of. The truth is, that in those kinds of corporate environments, developing people is low on the list of priorities. And even if it is prioritized, there's no model for scientific thinking and how to develop it. From what I've understood, that's one of the things that makes Toyota so unique – the focus on scientific thinking as the mindset that drives continuous improvement.

As for his observation that the question card is rote and mechanical, of course it is, but, as we discussed, reading the card is just the beginning, not the end game. Also, yes, he's right, you have to start by practicing the Coaching Kata in a very deliberate setting, like in front of a storyboard, but its use is in no way limited to that situation. Using the card in a controlled setting is just a way of getting started. Once using the Coaching Kata questions become intuitive, you can learn to use them in different settings and scenarios. Think of the karate example. You start out by learning the moves and practicing them in a very particular sequence, just to get good at them, to master them, but, eventually, you move beyond that and in a fight you can't use them in sequence. Once you've mastered them, you can do the kata in any sequence, use them in any applicable scenario.

"Really, what I want you to do is think of the Coaching Kata questions as stepping stones, each opening one of five phases for a coaching conversation." Maggie was getting really excited now, and she grabbed a napkin off the table and pulled out a pen from her bag. "Another trick I learned from Tilo. Think of it like this," she said, writing her thoughts down as she spoke.

Phase 1: Connect to the target condition.

Phase 2: Clarify the actual condition and reflect on what we have learned.

Phase 3: Identify obstacles and focus on one to address next. Understand cause.

Phase 4: Develop the next step and expectation.

Phase 5: Establish the first reflection point.

She paused after she finished writing and slid the napkin over to Denise's side of the table. "That," said Maggie, pointing at the napkin, "is the underlying coaching model you're learning to intuitively apply by practicing the Coaching Kata starter questions from the card. I promise you, this model offers a robust framework for coaching in many different situations."

Denise smiled. "I like that," she said.

"Yeah, it's nice, right? It takes something that should be intuitive, but isn't, and makes it simple, or simple enough. The intention of the Coaching Kata is to have a guideline, a recipe for the coach to structure the coaching conversation so it's actually helpful to the person being coached. It is helpful to the improver because it challenges their thinking and helps them to identify assumptions and blind spots without taking away their initiative.

"The five phases of the Coaching Kata are helpful in so many different settings, not just the office. I mean, I use it to help me coach people in achieving their life goals, like trying to reach a desired weight and fitness level. On the surface that couldn't be more different than what you're trying to do, but the same approach works. The beauty of the Coaching Kata is that you can always use the same five stepping stones for structuring the coaching conversation even if you might need to adapt the wording to match a distinct setting."

While Maggie was talking, Denise continued eating her udon soup. As she slurped her last noodle, she pushed the bowl to the side of the table so the waiter could pick it up on his next round. Maggie must have seen the tired look on her face, and she smiled apologetically.

"Sorry," Maggie said, "I feel like I'm doing a brain dump of everything I learned in Frankfurt from Tilo. Apologies for geeking out. I'm actually still processing everything I learned so this is helpful to me." She grinned sheepishly again. "If it's okay, though, there are a few more things I would like to try to explain, in summary form I promise."

Denise feigned enthusiasm in an attempt to show her appreciation, but the truth was her head was spinning.

"I know you're tired," Maggie said, "but this is pretty cool. Tilo found very visual and intuitive ways to explain things. In anticipation of this meeting, uh, I mean dinner," Maggie paused, laughing a little, and Denise echoed her laughter, "I made a copy of a page I got from Tilo."

She handed a piece of paper with a diagram on it to Denise (see Figure 10.1).

Denise looked at the complex diagram, feeling overwhelmed. "Wow, that's interesting, and complicated."

"It is simpler than it appears at first glance. I really just love this visual!" Maggie gushed. "Here the five questions are shown as stepping stones for the coaching cycle.

"In a well-run manufacturing plant you have quality gates throughout the process where the product is inspected and either is OK and proceeds or has defects and is stopped, right? Think of this the same way. In kata coaching, each of the questions opens the next phase of the coaching session. The coach starts a phase by asking the stepping-stone question from the card and then evaluates the answer. If the answer addresses the question in a precise way, the coach moves on to the next phase by asking the next stepping stone question. If the answer is imprecise, the coach helps the improver to clarify for themselves by asking deepening questions."

Suddenly, Denise didn't feel so tired anymore. This was exactly what she had been looking for.

"Wow," Denise said, "this is great. I had some similar thoughts as I tried to ask my own 'deepening questions'. I like the green check for go and the red X for stop. It's just like at a traffic light. Stand on red – walk on green. This is definitely going in my notebook."

Maggie looked hesitant.

"I'm worried I'm jumping ahead here," Maggie said. "I don't want to overwhelm you. But after you master the card, and then you master asking deepening questions, there comes a point where you may not even want to follow the steps linearly. I know you're somewhat familiar with Rother's concept of the 'threshold of knowledge'. Say the improver has gotten as far as they can based on what they know, and now they're starting to guess. This could happen at any phase.

"Perhaps they're describing the current condition, and you ask them a deepening question, and they just haven't observed the process enough to

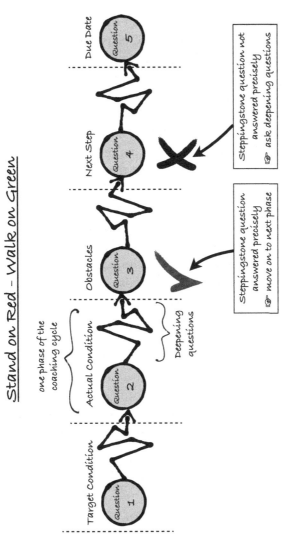

FIGURE 10.1

Stand on Red - Walk on Green, Tilo Schwarz, Kata Coaching Dojo Handbook (in italics), self-published, 2018.

know the answer. But then they fake it and give you an answer. At that point, they act like they're on green and ready to go ahead, but you realize they're really on red and should stop and learn something more. At this point, Tilo suggest you jump to question 4 and ask, 'What is therefore your next step to find out about the current condition?' This perhaps leads to more observation after the coaching session, and the next day you can return to the current condition, then move on to phase three, the obstacles. I'm probably getting ahead of myself, but you're picking things up so quickly."

Denise felt flattered.

"Thank you, Maggie," she said. "That makes me feel really good coming from you. This whole business of knowing when to stop and when to go is pretty tricky. How do I know when a phase is green so we can move on?"

"Okay, brace yourself for yet another concept. So, Tilo says that the coach needs a 'reference.' This really is more than just asking the questions. Anybody can read from a card. The more difficult part is learning how to evaluate the answer. How do we know when it's OK to move on and when it's not? Beginner coaches often move through the questions much too fast, prematurely setting each phase on green. That's OK at first to memorize the starter questions, but it's definitely not coaching."

"What do you mean by a reference?" Denise asked.

"You like to ski, right?" Maggie replied.

Denise nodded.

"Ok," said Maggie, "Think about a ski instructor. Step 1, they give a task, step 2, they observe, and then, step 3, they compare what they see, let's say me doing a right turn, to a picture in their mind of what my body and form should look like when doing a right turn. That picture is their reference. If the coach doesn't have a reference, they can't coach because they don't know what good looks like. Most people probably don't even realize they're doing this, but based on the coach's analysis of the differences between how I'm doing this right turn, say, and the reference picture in their mind, they'd move to step 4 and give me some feedback on how to do it better.

Now, let's transfer the four steps the skiing instructor is using to a coaching session. Step 1, give a task. That's what we're doing when we ask one of those stepping-stone questions from the card. They're open questions, and they provide a thinking task. Step 2, we listen to the answer. Now, that's difficult to learn. Listening without being biased by our own opinion and experience of the topic is not natural to most people. And now comes the crucial point in Step 3: What do you do with the answer? Are you on green or red? That's where you need a reference for what a good answer to the question would look like. Only then are you in a position to move to Step 4 and craft your next question."

"Hold on, though," said Denise, interrupting her, "then I need to know more about the topic or the process than my improver. Otherwise, how can I know if their answer is OK?"

Maggie shook her head vigorously.

"No, listen to me," Maggie said, "you don't. That's one of the big misconceptions about coaching, that you're there to get into the content and thereby evaluate the improver's answer. Remember, the improver is responsible for the content, you are teaching a *process*, a way of working towards the goal. We are asking questions to help the improver think, reflect and learn. The most fundamental thing here is to practice a mindset of honest curiosity. And then coaching is about developing people. So, we ask because we care. We ask them because we want them to learn to really think and then experiment for themselves, and we believe that they will come up with the best possible solution if they do. We believe in our heart of hearts that the best answers will come from the people who know the processes best and are themselves implementing them, not from above.

"Listen, it's like I said, you may not be aware of it but you have a reference already when you're asking these questions. Beginner coaches often use their experience or technical knowledge as their reference. They might say something like, 'I'm hearing the step you're proposing now, but from my experience it would be better to do it this way'. That's not coaching. It's giving advice. They might disguise that by asking questions, but they're guiding questions, often closed questions, to which the improver can only respond yes or no, like as 'are you sure this is the best way to do it?' or 'don't you think it would be better if we did X?'

"So, the question is what kind of reference do you need to truly be effective as a coach? This is where it's important to remember that you're coaching the improver in developing a more scientific way of thinking. So, what you should be asking yourself are questions like: Is the approach the improver is taking following a scientific way of understanding and exploring by experiment? Do they have a clear and complete target condition in place? Are they getting the facts first hand? Is the approach evidence based? Are they analyzing cause and effect, developing a hypothesis and testing it by experiment, and then learning and adapting?"

"Wow, ok, that's a lot, but I think I get it. It's pretty cool, really cool, actually," Denise said. "As a coach that enables me to stay away from the content. In fact, it sounds like it's my *job* to stay away from the content. I have to coach without injecting my own ideas and solutions and give autonomy to my team. That's good news since, honestly, I know so little about making pumps."

"Exactly," Maggie said, clearly delighted by Denise's response. "Using the Coaching Kata model as a coach is all about being open on the solutions but very precise on the method. Otherwise, it doesn't work. Injecting our ideas is just a different way of giving orders. It stifles people and kills creativity and initiative. On the other hand, *just* being solution open is laissez faire. Do anything you like. That's not gonna work. We need and want to achieve goals and, as a manager, you're responsible for the results. So, basically you're saying, 'here's the deal, you can do anything you like as long as it's aimed at getting closer to our target condition and you're following a scientific way of exploring the path'."

Denise thought for a moment. "I like it, but I still don't get how I develop my references as a coach?"

"I like that you used the word 'develop'," Maggie replied. "It *should* be a learning process. That's crucial. And, honestly, that's where some companies starting out with Kata have gotten off track. Mass training and just handing out the question cards to managers won't get the job done. Coaches need to build their references and the best way to do this is by being coached. You need to be an improver before you become a coach."

"So then how did you learn how to do it?"

"I am not sure I totally have yet," Maggie responded. "It is a process. And to some degree I need to unlearn some bad habits from my last job. You have no way of knowing this, but before starting the gym I also worked for Francis & Drake. I left about half a year before you started."

"What?" Denise cried, a bit too loudly, she realized, because people at the tables around them stopped their conversations and peered over their meals, staring at them. "I didn't know that. Wait, wait. I did hear people talk about a former superstar-partner, Margaret Petrikova. That's you?"

"Yup, you got it, though I am not sure about the superstar part," Maggie responded, laughing a little.

"So, then why did you leave?"

"It's a long story," Maggie responded, taking a sip of her green tea, "but bottom line I was getting burned out and wanted to do something on my own that was more focused on helping people."

QR CODE 10.2
The Kata Girl Geeks Website.

"Wow, ok."

"Sorry, I should have told you earlier – but I didn't really know how to bring it up. Anyway," Maggie took a breath, "let me get back to your question. It was a good one. You asked how I built up my references as a coach. After I happened upon the KataCon conference, where I met Mike Rother, I read his books. I felt like I finally understood why my clients at Francis & Drake weren't able to execute sustainable lean transformations. So, I started coaching my own staff and introduced them to Toyota Kata. I thought, 'I got this'."

"Then, I found a group of women who regularly connect online to practice Toyota Kata. They call themselves the Kata Girl Geeks.* It's pretty cool, a super-international group with members from all over the world. They have a rigid rule, though. You have to be an improver first. They ran me through, I think, a 4- or 6-week training period, where I was coached daily by one of the members of the group. Another group member, Tracy Defoe, was the second coach observing me coach and giving feedback.

"Later I became the coach for another new member while someone else was my second coach, observing me. I still think that's the best way to learn. Getting yourself an experienced coach."

"OK," Denise replied, "so can you be my coach?"

"I'm sorry, Denise," Maggie said, shaking her head vigorously, "but I just have too much on my plate right now. I can shadow coach you, like

---

* www.katagirlgeeks.com.

this, with meetings and even quick phone calls, but I can't come to your meetings and observe and give you feedback. We have to find a work-around. At least for now. I've been thinking about it, and I think the best solution is if you get someone from inside Goldberg to practice with you. Maybe David, your manager?"

"I actually asked him to observe my coaching sessions and he said yes," Denise replied somewhat skeptically. "We'll see if he actually shows up for a coaching session tomorrow. And I don't even know if that's a good move. Mark and Joe will definitely freak out. And David has no experience with Kata."

"Hmm, now ideally David would not only observe you but also let you observe him when he's coaching," said Maggie, thinking out loud. "Or even better, you coach David and he coaches you, while each of you works as an improver toward a next target condition. That way both of you can practice Improvement Kata and Coaching Kata at the same time. Actually, it's done best in a group of three because then you can take turns coaching and observing each other's coaching. Think of it as a Kata learning group."

"I can't see that happening in the near future with all the crises we are facing right now," Denise sighed. "I'm sorry to pressure you, but can't you just be my coach?"

Maggie again shook her head, "no.

"I promise to catch up with you regularly. And you can ask Mark and Joe if it would be OK to record your coaching sessions. Just the audio is enough, people can get squeamish with video. All you need to do is record them on your cell phone. That way we can review your sessions. I think this is a good makeshift solution. I commit to making it work."

"Thanks, Maggie," Denise said. "Seriously."

The waiter came by and asked if they wanted anything else. Both agreed that they were stuffed, thanked the waiter profusely for the wonderful food and for patiently letting them rant on, and asked for the check. Maggie reached for her purse, but Denise stopped her insisting on paying the bill. She added a big tip.

11

A Coach for the Coach

DENISE RETURNED TO her desk from her first-shift coaching session with Mark. Her head was still spinning from dinner with Maggie. *So much to digest. So much to learn.*

Denise had followed Maggie's advice, convincing David to train alongside her as "second coach." He coached Denise on her coaching. Of course, he was nowhere near knowledgeable or skilled enough to play this role, but David's time constraints, or more likely his ego, would not allow him to be subservient to Denise in any way. So, Denise played along. The good news was that he seemed to be getting on board, albeit slowly.

As she expected, having David in coaching sessions was intimidating for her team leaders. Before David joined for the first time, Denise had explained to Mark why he was joining them and that he would not be directly involved with Mark's project and coaching. Rather, David would focus on her coaching and give her feedback afterward. Still, Mark had been notably uncomfortable. After the session was over, Mark had left, and David had shared his observations and thoughts. Denise and David had been deep in conversation for over 10 minutes. Denise had noticed Mark looking in their direction several times. *He probably thought we were talking about him. That's not good. We have to do this differently,* Denise thought.

She was disappointed with David's "feedback." He acknowledged that the conversation seemed well structured but complained that it took much too long.

David was direct. "That coaching session took nearly 25 minutes," he said. "Next time, you should try to keep the conversation focused and be quicker. If I took that much time discussing every issue on my plate, I'd never get anywhere."

It was true. The coaching session had taken longer than the 10 to 15 minutes Maggie suggested was typical. Denise had noticed that herself. But David's feedback gave her no advice on how to improve. Was there something he saw that was wasting time or did he simply fail to appreciate the benefit of focusing on precision and spending the time to actually develop Mark?

Denise suspected David just saw the session as a means to quickly get the changeover reduction done, and he was right; it certainly was inefficient if that was the only goal. As a lean consultant, she had done changeover reductions in a few days. But that wasn't the point of practicing Kata. It was to develop scientific thinking and, in the process, get results. *How can I get David to understand what we are trying to do and perhaps even get some feedback that helps me instead of frustrates me and intimidates my team leaders? There has to be a way. Involving David was Maggie's idea, and she's been right about everything so far. Relax Denise. You can think more about David's role later.*

For now, Denise decided to try reflecting on the coaching session with Mark. She went through it in her mind phase by phase. *Oh wait, I can just listen to the recording on my cell phone*, she thought. *How convenient!* She took out her cell and pressed play. She set the volume down as low as possible. This was not for public consumption. Listening to it now, Denise realized they had spent a lot of unproductive time on the target condition. *Maybe David had a point after all. Mark clearly knew his target condition and just read from the storyboard. It was perfectly fine without all my clarifying questions. I think I overcooked this one.*

Next, she listened to their discussion of the actual condition, which again took lots of time. Mark explained each chart of his outcome and process metrics in great length, perhaps giving too much detail since they had gone through it all in a previous session when he had been developing the current condition.

Then, Mark explained that his step of putting a marking on the table so the operators would know where to place the fixture had not worked.

"You see, the problem is that I would need many different markings because the fixtures for each product type differ in size," he had said.

Mark had written his finding into the experimenting record, which was a positive step, but he was obviously disappointed that his plan hadn't worked as expected and seemed to take it as a personal failure. Denise tried to reassure him that it was good to have surprises – experiments that don't meet expectations. Otherwise, she argued, how can you learn? She had discussed with Maggie how a string of successes simply reinforces the learner's bias in assuming they're always right. Yet despite her best efforts, Mark was not happy with an unexpected outcome to his experiments. *Maybe it will take a few more tries to accept that some hypotheses are supported and some are not – and it's all useful information.*

One of the most interesting parts was phase 3, when they discussed obstacles.

"Which one obstacle are you addressing now?" she had asked.

"The obstacle is still the same," Mark had responded, "no marking on the table. However, I don't know how to solve this. We can't have a different marking for each fixture. Nobody would know which was which."

Denise appreciated that Mark now felt comfortable enough to actually admit there was something he didn't know, especially with David observing. She thought about her discussion with Maggie about the question card and so she had followed up with Tilo's additional question.

"Mark," Denise had said, "what exactly is the problem?"

"Well, the real problem is that the operators have to position the fixture on the table by measuring the position. And that takes a lot of time."

Cool, Denise thought, *now we have a much better definition of the obstacle. And we've broken the cycle of turning an obstacle into a solution without thinking it through. Maggie was right. "What exactly is the problem?" at this point helps.*

Feeling more confident, Denise had ad-libbed. "So," she had said, "what should happen ideally?"

"Well," Mark had replied, "ideally, the operators would put the fixture in the correct place right away, without measuring, and then tighten the screws."

Denise had decided to press further. "So," she had said, "what is the correct position for each fixture?"

Mark had paused. "That, I don't know."

Yes, threshold of knowledge, Denise had thought and asked "what, therefore, is your next step to find out?"

Mark had volunteered that he needed to go back to observe the process more deeply and Denise was thrilled. Unlike the previous session, she had moved from faithfully asking the questions in sequence to asking Mark what his next step would be after uncovering the threshold of his knowledge, and she hadn't been afraid to ad-lib a bit to get there. *So, Maggie was right. That does seem to be a good general strategy. When we reach the threshold of knowledge, instead of just blasting through red, we stopped and jumped to question 4, the next step. That got Mark to realize he needed to go back to observe to learn more.*

Denise opened her notebook and went to the page where she had drawn the diagram Maggie showed her with the five phases as stepping stones. Perhaps the key was to get to the threshold of knowledge, the point where it became clear the improver was just guessing and did not actually *know*, and then move to question 4. *In essence, what is it we don't know, and how can we find out?* Denise thought.

She took out her pen and wrote in her notebook, "Find the threshold of knowledge BEFORE asking question 4" (see Figure 11.1).

Probably that's not always the case, she thought, *but I think it makes sense. I'll try to confirm that with Maggie next time I talk to her. Maybe this is applicable to the earlier phases of the Coaching Kata as well? If we reach the threshold of knowledge say on question 2, current condition, I might want to jump ahead directly to question 4. That would mean skipping over question 3 temporarily, until the improver has a better understanding of the current condition.*

She added that tip to her notes as well.

In her second-shift coaching session with Joe, Denise again tried out the new concept Maggie had taught her, standing on red, walking on green. This time, it was more complicated though. Although she asked deepening questions whenever she felt the answer to the stepping-stone question was not good enough, she had to jump back several times. *Jumping back over my thumb,* Denise thought and smiled to herself. *Maggie will love that one. Maybe I can get another belly laugh out of her.*

Back at her desk, after a long day of coaching and the usual firefighting, Denise once again listened to her recording and reflected on what she heard. She took out her card with the Coaching Kata starter questions as a visual reminder about what had happened (see Figure 11.2).

After I asked Joe about his next step, phase 4, I had to jump back, over my thumb, to phase 3, discussing the obstacle again, she thought. *That's interesting. The problem was Joe had not analyzed the obstacle sufficiently*

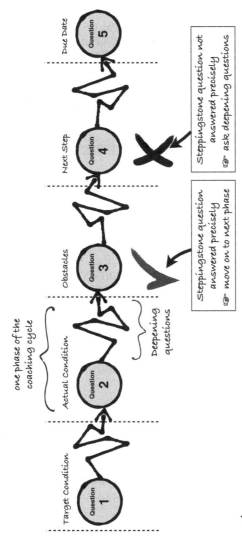

FIGURE 11.1

A task for the coach – finding the threshold of knowledge. Stand on Red - Walk on Green, Tilo Schwarz, *Kata Coaching Dojo Handbook*, self-published, 2018.

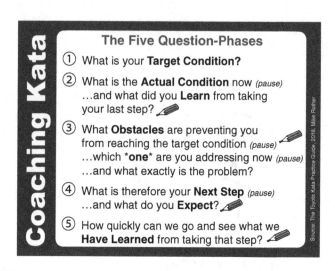

FIGURE 11.2
Coaching Kata Starter Kata, adapted from Mike Rother, *The Toyota Kata Practice Guide*, McGraw-Hill (New York), 2018.

to formulate a hypothesis for action. I followed the question card and asked 'what exactly is the problem?' on our first round of phase 3, but when Joe gave me a superficial answer, I just moved to question 4. So that's why we ended up with an imprecise step. In other words, I set phase 3 on green too early, moved on to 4, and that's why I had to jump back.

In general, that means that whenever I go on green too early, I will have to jump back. Or, put differently, in an ideal coaching session, when I get all the phases right, there are no jump backs. She adds to her notes: "Ideally a coaching cycle has no jump backs."

That's seriously a challenge. How do I realize when a stepping stone question has been answered precisely, and I can set the phase on green so we can move on to the next phase?

Denise remembered the ski coach example from Maggie and decided to sketch it, thinking about the idea of how a coach's reference model is so important. She tried to remember everything Maggie had said about references at the sushi place (see Figure 11.3).

As she drew, Denise realized she was learning a lot from her coaching experiences and all of Maggie's tips. She was excited to discover that she was already starting to advance beyond mindlessly reading the question card. Now she was doing real coaching, like the ski instructor. *If I'm being honest, I think I am learning more than Mark and Joe. While they're experimenting*

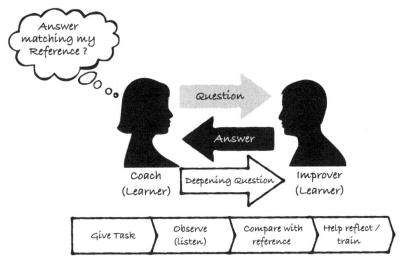

Coaching = Solution open + Precise about method

FIGURE 11.3
Coaching for skill needs a reference, Tilo Schwarz, *Kata Coaching Dojo Handbook*, self-published, 2018.

to reduce the changeover time, I'm experimenting with coaching techniques. Every coaching session is a chance to try out new ideas and then reflect on what happened. And this is also honing my scientific thinking skills. This is really starting to get fun! I'll have lots to talk about with Maggie.

Feeling energized, Denise called Maggie. She told her about jumping back over her thumb and got the belly laugh she had been hoping for. She told her, too, about finding the threshold of knowledge and her idea about moving to question 4 when that happened. To Denise's delight, Maggie told her that that was exactly what Tilo Schwarz recommended. While they were still on the phone, Denise emailed Maggie the "coaching needs a reference" diagram she made, and Maggie loved it.

"And how's it going with David?" Maggie asked.

Somewhat begrudgingly, Denise admitted that Maggie's idea of involving David as a second coach was a good one.

"Even though he had little understanding of the value of scientific thinking or Kata, he made commonsense observations that spurred my thinking and helped me improve my coaching," Denise explained. "And the more he learns the more valuable David will become as an ally and a coach. Thanks for the suggestion."

It was an energizing talk with Maggie, but Denise still felt almost desperate for the weekend. The progress she was making in coaching was amazing and exhilarating ... and exhausting. And while she enjoyed the coaching and was encouraged by her progress with David, production was still a struggle. Just before 5 pm, they realized that they had to contend with yet another unexpected parts shortage from a supplier. It affected two of her lines, so she had called off the second shift for the coming week. Not only did that affect morale, but it also added more backlog. Just when they had made enough improvement on changeover time to work down some of the backlog, things went south. Of course, this had nothing to do with the efforts of her team. But nonetheless they were being judged on *results, results, and results.*

Fortunately, that night she was heading off to a weekend ski trip with a group of colleagues. All the reports predicted fabulous conditions, and, indeed, when Denise hit the slopes on Saturday morning, the fresh powder was fantastic.

The icing on the cake was that Jason Wilson, the new head of sales administration, was also on the trip. He had started with Goldberg only a month before, and during his onboarding program, he had spent two days on Denise's team and worked on the assembly line to learn about the production processes firsthand. They had started talking about management approaches and realized they had similar ideas about how they wanted to lead their teams. As they skied together Saturday afternoon, it felt to Denise like they shared a spark.

The next morning over breakfast, Denise told Jason about her experiences practicing Toyota Kata. She felt like she was rambling on, but he seemed genuinely interested. He kept plying her with questions and saying how profound her coaching methods seemed. The pressures of the week quickly faded away as the weekend got better and better.

12

Minimum Viable Answer – A Reference for the Coach

AFTER HER MOST delightful weekend since joining the company, Denise started Monday with her daily shop-floor walk. David had joined her to do a coaching session with Mark. David would again play second coach, retaining his status as the boss. To prepare for the coaching session, she and David went through Mark's storyboard. Denise showed David the sketch of the five-phase concept and the stepping stones.

As usual, David was quick on the uptake and again had useful insights.

"So, in a way, the Coaching Kata question provides a framework for coaching. That's interesting. It might be more broadly applicable than I thought at first ... I may seem a little dense at times, but I think I'm starting to catch on. By practicing the same questions over and over, you get used to the underlying framework. That frees your mind to focus on the other person's way of thinking instead of indulging in discussing the content. Hmm ... maybe there is an upside to starting like a robot after all."

David smiled, and Denise smiled too. Inside, she felt like she was jumping with joy.

"David, honestly, it takes you minutes to grasp ideas that would take other people weeks or even months. That is such an incredible skill."

Denise couldn't have been more delighted. This was a 180-degree turn from David's previous attitude of "let's skip the questions and get to the results." He was starting to understand the value of Kata coaching to develop the improver. He was showing humility. He was opening up to her in a way she had not seen before.

DOI: 10.4324/9780429347023-14

It seemed to Denise that she had jumped to hasty conclusions about how rigid and defensive David was. She really liked this side of him. *Mental note,* she thought. *Try to avoid assumptions about other people based on initial impressions. Premature judgments are the opposite of scientific thinking.*

"David, can you do me a favor?" Denise asked, believing he really could be helpful now. "Please check how I follow the phases, especially if there are any jump backs or if I prematurely jump forward, going green when the answer should have been graded red. And, of course, let me know if I miss a phase. Hopefully, that won't happen. I'll stick to my rule of thumb. Maybe you could even measure the time for each phase? Remember your feedback yesterday? You said the coaching session took too long. What if we time the phases as if it were laps in a NASCAR race? Then I can find out where I spend too much time and maybe where I should spend more time."

"I like it," David replied. "I'll try to do that."

Denise smiled back at him. *I'm really feeling hopeful about the feedback he'll give me this way,* Denise thought, as they headed off to meet Mark. The session went pretty smoothly and she was pleased to see that Mark was more relaxed about David observing. Maybe David was more relaxed and that rubbed off on Mark.

And, indeed, after the coaching cycle, David offered much better feedback.

"I observed that you spent about four minutes on the first phase about the target condition," David said, reviewing his notes with Denise afterward. "From your body language, it seemed like you were feeling impatient during that phase. What exactly was the problem that bothered you?"

Denise sighed. "It's true," she said. "Mark always goes on for so long and into so much detail when he's explaining the challenge and each aspect of his target condition. I already know these details so well since we talk about them every session."

"Interesting point," David said, then paused for a few seconds, clearly thinking. "So, what's the reasoning behind asking about the target condition every day? What would be a productive way of answering the question from your point of view?"

Denise was floored. *How could David ask such good reflection questions without Maggie coaching him?* She thought for a while, then finally gathered her thoughts.

"Well," she said, "when I first started coaching Mark and Joe, I realized that they were struggling to focus on their improvement targets in addition to their daily tasks. So, it was helpful to start our coaching sessions with a recap of the challenge and discussion of the different aspects of their target conditions, the metrics as well as the pattern of work. It got them focused and reminded them of the 'why' behind the details of the improvement process.

"Now, they're doing so much better, though, and I think all they really need to do is read what is on the board about the next target condition. What is the desired outcome and what is the target on the process metric?"

Denise thought of the stone and lever picture Maggie had mentioned and continued, "the outcome target reminds them of what they are trying to achieve on the way to the challenge and the process metric target tells them what specifically they are trying to work on to affect the outcome. Remember that the process metric is measuring how much progress they are making toward the desired pattern of work. This way they have the context of their process and outcome targets when we discuss the actual condition in phase 2. You know what? You got me thinking. I think I'll test that right away, in my coaching session with Joe this afternoon."

"I like that. Come up with an idea and then quickly test it," said David. "I'll be curious to see how it goes."

"Actually," said Denise, "now that I think about it, the same structure also applies for phase 2. What I really want to hear is how the actual condition relates to the target condition they are working on. The rest of the detail is kind of extra. So, the question I should be asking is, 'how does the actual condition relate to the outcome metric and the process metric?' So if Mark and Joe just read that off the board that should be sufficient to frame our caching cycle, and we'll move much more quickly through the session."

"Nicely done," said David. "I like how you're thinking."

"Thank you, and wow, David, seriously, that was such useful feedback. Now I have another hypothesis to test in my next coaching session. I feel like I'm thinking scientifically about my own coaching."

David gave Denise the timing for the different phases and shared a few more observations and then they wrapped up. Denise returned to her office feeling like she was walking on air. *What a turnaround. David is becoming a helpful observer. And it was useful that I asked him to time the phases. That extra structure was kind of like a Starter Kata for the second coach.*

Denise sat down at her desk and pulled out her notebook. She started thinking about the difference between an answer that is somewhat broad and scattered, like the answers Mark had been giving her, and an answer that was spot on for what they need to discuss. *Why not call it the minimum viable answer? That would give me the kind of reference that Maggie was talking about. The minimum viable answer for question 1 would be this. My target condition is (target value of outcome metric); therefore, we have to reach (target value process metric). "Therefore" is a nice linking word here.*

And then how about a minimum viable answer for question 2? Maybe it's something like this: The actual condition is (current value of outcome metric). And, in this case, "because" is an excellent linking word. That gets the improver thinking about the causal connection between the process characteristics and the desired outcome. So, a great answer would be: The actual condition is (present value of outcome metric) because the (process metric) is at (current value of process metric).

"Therefore" and "because" are easy cues in this context. I'll ask Mark and Joe if they can use these two key words in their answers for phases 1 and 2. Let's see if we move more quickly than. These can be what Maggie calls "references" for the coach (see Figure 12.1).

In the afternoon, Denise met with David again and thanked him for his excellent feedback. She described how it got her thinking about what she really hoped for out of the improvers' answers. That spurred her to

Minimum viable answer Question 1

My target condition is (outcome metric + target) THEREFORE
we are currently focusing on reaching (focus process metric + target).

Minimum viable answer Question 2

The actual condition is (outcome metric) BECAUSE
the (focus process metric) is at...

FIGURE 12.1

Minimum viable answers for questions 1 and 2.

consider what a "spot-on" answer would be. She knew if she had that, then she could explain to Joe and Mark what she expected and point out deviations from the spot-on answers while she was coaching them.

David liked the idea and suggested she try it in her next coaching sessions. He couldn't attend but would be interested in how it went.

During her coaching session with Joe, Denise explained the concept, and Joe seemed to understand and said he would try responding as she suggested. And, indeed, phases 1 and 2 took less time, and Joe's answers were much more precise.

So, questions 1 and 2 were working now, but Denise still found herself struggling in phase 3, when they talked about the obstacles. She thought about the concept of "stand on red – walk on green" and her experience with having to jump back to a prior stage of the coaching cycle, "over her thumb."

Maybe if I struggle in any one phase, the cause originates before that. So, if I struggle when talking about the obstacles, perhaps the problem is with how I'm discussing the actual condition. Something about that answer was red, but I thought it was green. But what exactly is causing it? I'll ask David to observe phases 2 and 3 more closely when he joins me next. I kind of like this partnership forming with David. I was starting to dread having him at coaching sessions. Now, I look forward to sharing my ideas and getting his feedback. And I think David is enjoying it too, especially when he is giving me useful feedback and advice.

13

Digging Deeper into the Obstacles

TUESDAY, FEBRUARY 8, 8:00 AM, A MORE THAN PLEASANT SURPRISE AND MORE LEARNING

DENISE WAS BUSY replying to emails at her desk when she looked up, startled. Standing there was Jason the new head of sales administration.

"Hi, Jason," she said, trying to recover from the surprise, "I didn't expect to see you this morning."

"Sorry I frightened you," he said, somewhat apologetically. "I kept thinking about our weekend on the ski trip, and, well, I really enjoyed it, by the way, you know talking with you," he paused, blushing a little. "I mean, I kept thinking about Kata. It was fascinating. I've never heard of anything like that. And to tell you the truth, it was the most stimulating discussion I've had since joining the company."

He paused. Denise couldn't tell if he was interested in kata, or in her, or both. He was obviously uncomfortable. She flashed her best professional smile, and tried to sound reassuring.

"I'm glad you enjoyed our conversation," she said. "I did, too."

"Yeah," Jason replied. "I really did. In sales circles we rarely talk about improving our processes. In fact I am not sure many sales people even think about what they do as having processes. And you know, on my team, continuous improvement is like a foreign language. It's all about sell, sell, sell. Maybe Toyota Kata can help me to get my team to start thinking of what they do as having processes that can be improved. Even with all my management experience in sales, the books I have read, the leadership courses I have attended, I realize now that I've never been very good at coaching. But my team has so much potential – I don't want to let them down."

DOI: 10.4324/9780429347023-15

As Jason spoke, Denise couldn't help but think how much she also enjoyed exchanging ideas with him, too, and that he was a good skier, tall, athletic, good looking, and … single. *But, hey, stop dreaming*, she scolded herself. *You are at work.*

"That's great, Jason," said Denise. "But is there something I can help you with? I need to run to a coaching session with one of my team leaders."

"Oh yes, sure, Denise," Jason replied, seeming even more apologetic. "I was trying to lead up to that. I was wondering, if you could help me with my sales team, maybe even coach me a bit. Would that be possible?"

"Of course, Jason," said Denise, smiling. "I would love to do that. I'm very interested in spreading Kata beyond manufacturing. And sales would be a great next step. Maybe we can talk about it more over lunch."

They politely said their goodbyes, and Denise started to think about the coaching sessions she had planned for the day. They were still running one shift because of lack of parts, but that had an upside. Now both of Denise's team leaders worked the first shift, and she could coach them both in the morning. *Our productivity will plunge this week but at least we can get some improvement work done. Let's go for a week of power coaching.*

As soon as Jason left, David walked into her office. Despite the increased backlog resulting from the parts' shortage, he was still on board with kata – a great sign. He was joining her again today to observe her coaching sessions. After greeting him, Denise told David what she wanted him to focus his observation on today.

"David, I've been struggling a lot in phase 3 when we investigate the obstacles. I don't know why, but I hypothesize that it might be something I do not realize I am doing in phase 2. Could you please pay special attention to those two phases today?"

"Of course, I will," he replied cheerfully, as they left the office to meet with Joe for the first session.

After the two sessions were complete, Denise nervously awaited David's feedback, especially about the coaching cycle with Joe which had been painful. Joe was working on technical quality issues, which were more complex than changeover issues. He needed to figure out why defects were occurring after changeover, causing scrap and rework. This was no longer about time wasted searching for things. He had struggled to identify obstacles despite the clear gap between his current condition and his target condition. He had described general issues and issued excuses for why they had a higher scrap rate after a changeover. Denise had suggested he observe another changeover.

Joe had not been pleased.

"I've seen that a thousand times," Joe had said. "But if you want me to see it a thousand and one times, I'll have another look. It's always the same. Sometimes we get defects, sometimes we don't."

Now, David looked at his notes and started in with his feedback.

"You asked me to pay special attention to phases 2 and 3 because you often struggle when discussing the obstacles," he said. "Today's coaching cycle with Joe was short in phase 1 and 2, only 30 seconds each. I can see how your new approach of just focusing on the values of the outcome metric and process metric is efficient. But then you needed almost 5 minutes to discuss the obstacles. I also got the impression that Joe wasn't systematically picking one obstacle to address. He was struggling."

"I had the same feeling," said Denise, reaffirming David's observation, "but I didn't know what to do."

"Ok, so you told me that your idea is that when you struggle as a coach, the problem might originate in the previous phase. So, now we know that during your session with Joe, you struggled during phase 3. So, following your idea, the reason for that might be in phase 2. Let's see." David paused to take another look at his notes. "Ok, so I noticed that in answering question 2, Joe used the wording you expected about the current situation. I heard Joe say: 'My current condition for my outcome metric, changeover time on assembly line number 3, is at an average of around 23 minutes over the last two weeks because my process metric of the number of defects after the changeover is just too high'.

I noted that Joe formulated the outcome metric as an average of the last two weeks and did not mention actual numbers regarding the process metric. His understanding of the process metric related to defects was vague at best. I have the impression that because of that it was challenging to detect actual obstacles."

"Wow, David, what an insight! Can you tell me more?" Denise asked excitedly, her misgivings fading.

"Well, Joe is currently working on reducing the number of defects after the changeover, so that's his process metric, the number of defects, I mean. Obstacles express themselves by having a negative impact on the process metric, right? In Joe's case, obstacles will create a certain amount of defects after the changeover. So more or bigger obstacles produce more defects.

That means he should be focusing on obstacles with an observable impact on the process metric."

Denise followed the thought. "That means ideally Joe's focus and observations should be only on obstacles with an undesirable impact on the process metric. So, that's another kind of reference."

"Exactly," said David. "So, there are two ways to find obstacles. On the one hand, you can directly recognize obstacles through process observation, which is basically what we've been doing so far, and, on the other hand, you can recognize them indirectly, by measuring the process metric for each cycle – in this case, the number of defects after a changeover. So if one cycle has a significantly worse value for the process metric, i.e. more defects, there must be one or more important obstacles in that cycle. We can then search to try to identify what exactly caused this difference in the process. It reminds me of my old training in finding the root cause of a problem, or in this case causes."

"I get it. The problem is that Joe was looking at average defects over a period, and that left him to speculate about obstacles. Instead, I should coach him to look at individual cases where there are defects and then in each case try to identify the obstacle," Denise said, becoming visibly excited. "Then we can look for the obstacles with big impact or that appear often. Now, I understand what the problem was today. In current condition, step 2, Joe only gave me a general statement about the process metric. In retrospect, my desire to have a short and efficient answer about the current condition worked against me."

"Yes, and I think this means that, in general, we should ensure that there are always current figures for the process metric from which outliers and trends can be identified – we could probably display that as a run chart," David cut in. "As a coach, you can then ask for the reason for these outliers and help the person you're coaching identify obstacles." Now, David was matching Denise's excitement, his voice rising. "The coaching session with Joe just shows again what we already thought, that each phase prepares the next. Stand on red, walk on green. See, I'm not so dumb about this Kata stuff after all."

Denise laughed. "Dumb is never an adjective I would use to describe you, David," she said. "I like where we're going with this. I think it's going to help guide Joe, while giving him the freedom to think for himself. Thank you so much, again, for the great feedback! It's so helpful to have someone else to collaborate with instead of trying to figure all this stuff out on my own."

When Denise returned to her office, she sat down at her desk, opened her little notebook, and began reflecting on what she had learned from the morning's coaching cycles. She wrote, "Focus on obstacles that generate a measurable, unwanted effect on the process metric. So, Obstacle = Unwanted Effect."

She reflected further: *To eliminate an obstacle, we have to understand not only its effect but its cause. If we know the cause and remove it, the unwanted effect disappears, and the process metric should improve by the amount of the unwanted effect.* Denise started writing again and specified her formula: *Obstacle = Unwanted Effect × Cause.*

This way the formula is even better, Denise thought. *Also, if direct observation of individual cycles does not help us identify obstacles, we can look for variation and outliers on the process metric and investigate the reasons, the underlying obstacles.*

Denise's mind then wandered to her secret passion, watching murder mysteries.

Hercule Poirot would never find the murdered if he only looked at averages on data charts. He had to discover the facts one by one, and put the pieces together into a mosaic. She smiled inwardly at the analogy.

For Joe's target condition, this means we need single event data, not averaged data, Denise thought. *If we do this, outliers will show themselves. I don't want Joe or Mark to print out new charts every day anyway. A run chart can easily be filled in by hand. And we can draw a red line on the chart that shows the target value. Then we would easily understand the current condition versus target at a glance.*

Denise summarized her new trick in her notebook, "We have to spot outliers, trends, and patterns immediately," she wrote. "Use run charts with individual data points, not averages!" (see Figure 13.1). Suddenly she had an idea for a name for her new trick: "Love at first sight." She smiled and, she couldn't help it, she thought about dreamy Jason from sales again – or maybe she had already been thinking of him.

Focus, Denise thought to herself, and turned her attention to reviewing the morning's coaching cycle with Mark. He was all over the place when discussing the current condition. He had put up several sketches on the storyboard – a block diagram of the process, a new run chart, and a figure called a spaghetti diagram that showed the movement of the operators. Every time the operators moved, he drew their walk pattern on a layout of the area and it ended up looking like a plate of spaghetti. There was so much unnecessary motion.

(a)   The Obstacle Formula

OBSTACLE = UNWANTED EFFECT × CAUSE

↳ On Process Metric

Love at first sight ♡
We have to be able to spot outliers, trends, and patterns immediately.
Use run charts and individual data points to do so. No average!

(b)

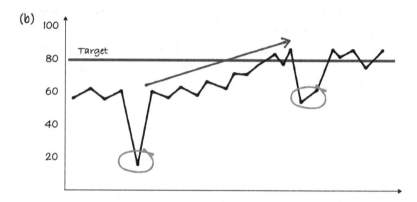

(c)

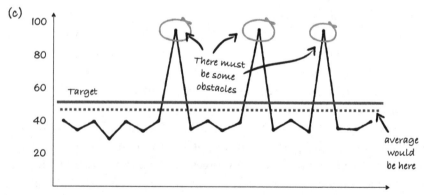

FIGURE 13.1
The Obstacle Formula and Love at first sight, Tilo Schwarz, *Kata Coaching Dojo Handbook*, self-published, 2018.

It was all good information, but he had jumped back and forth between these diagrams and the target condition form. Denise struggled to orient herself on the board. *Somehow we have to bring some structure to the storyboard,* she thought. *I'll discuss that with Maggie when I meet her at the gym tonight. Then, maybe I can take another look at the storyboard in her back office.*

A knock at Denise's door, and then Jason looked in.

"Hey, time for lunch," he said. "Did you forget me?" He laughed.

"How could I forget you?" Denise replied with a big smile. She closed her notebook, got up from the desk, and they made their way to a gourmet (she wished) lunch in the canteen.

Over an okay lunch they had another rousing discussion of Kata. But then Jason admitted he was concerned that it would be hard to apply it in sales since there were so few repeating activities compared to manufacturing. Denise countered that Kata was about practicing a meta skill to help achieve any goal and gave Maggie's gym as an example. They agreed that Jason would think about what process he could pick for practicing Improvement Kata and also start looking into the current state of that process collecting some data. Denise did not expect that Jason would do a great job understanding the current condition on his own, but at least it would be a start. They finally said their goodbyes politely, agreeing to do lunch again soon.

14

A Green Drink, and Fresh Look at Storyboards

AFTER ANOTHER INTENSE workout, Denise sat at the bar inside the gym and ordered her usual green smoothie. She tried to avoid all thoughts of what made it green. She didn't even like looking at it, it sort of looked like a Halloween prank, but it tasted okay and was, apparently, very healthy. As she was sipping gingerly, she saw Maggie walk by.

"Hey, Maggie, can I see the storyboard in your back office again? I realized how hard it was in my coaching cycles today to follow Mark's and Joe's explanations. Their storyboards have become a mish-mash of charts, drawings, and several templates."

"Sure, let's go right now," Maggie replied.

When they entered the back office, Denise was shocked to see how orderly Maggie's storyboard was. *Now I am embarrassed. I would hate to show her mine.*

"Wow, this is so organized. I have to learn how to replicate this. Can you walk me through the templates one more time?" Denise asked.

Maggie started to explain. "There is no hard-and-fast rule on which forms to use and what they should look like. I am a bit of a fanatic about neatness, but neatness doesn't really count. Mostly I printed the forms right out of Mike's book making some slight adaptations that I find helpful. There are two main purposes for using these forms, especially when a new coach and improver are just starting out. First, they focus and amplify the aspects of scientific thinking we aim to develop. They are like guide rails for the improver, who is forced to focus to put the right information in the right place. Second, they provide helpful guidance for the coach. Think of them as kind of a cheat sheet, so you can see what the improver is also seeing, and get an idea how they are thinking.

"Ok, so, take a look. The T-template is helpful for describing the next target condition. At the top, there's room for describing the challenge or longer-term direction which, as you know, should come first when starting to coach somebody. Perhaps the challenge is one year out. Sometimes when discussing a long-term challenge like this, we realize it is too broad and we have to slice it even in step 1 to come up with a helpful objective giving direction for the next say 3 months. For example, in your case, we need to give the customer what they want when they want it; therefore we have to eliminate the backlog. You even have a third level of focusing on reducing changeover time across your high-runner lines, so you could add, therefore we have to reduce overall changeover time.

"Below that is the T. It separates the page into a left side, describing the current condition, and a right side describing the target condition we are striving for. The form reminds us of the three elements for a good target condition. The outcome metric, the process or what you call the progress metric, and a picture of the current and desired state – we might also call that the pattern of work (see Figure 14.1).

"As you know, you can easily sketch this structure when doing some impromptu coaching on a white sheet of paper or a flip chart, as you did in the beginning with Joe and Mark."

Denise nodded, taking it all in.

"Now," Maggie continued, "in the middle of the storyboard, we have at least two charts about the actual condition. One for the outcome metric and one for the process metric that we're currently focusing on (see Figure 14.2).

"Having current data about the actual condition is essential for finding and understanding obstacles and learning from experiments, as well as checking our progress," said Maggie.

Now, she tells me, Denise thought to herself, but continued following along carefully.

"Of course," Maggie continued, "any format can do. However, using run charts and being clear about units and the date is very helpful for the coach. It's like your 'love at first sight' idea, which I love by the way. I've been thinking about it ever since you told me about it at the beginning of your workout today. Ok, so, anyway, I use this standard form for the run chart.

CHALLENGE ⇒ INITIAL CONDITION ⇒ NEXT TARGET CONDITION		
Improver:	Coach:	
Challenge:		
Focus Process:		
INITIAL CONDITION	**TARGET CONDITION**	Achieve by:
Outcome Metric:		
Process Metric:		
Current process pattern / process parameters	Desired process pattern / process parameters	

FIGURE 14.1

Target Condition Form, adapted from Mike Rother, *The Toyota Kata Practice Guide*, McGraw-Hill (New York), 2018.

I always draw the target condition as a line across the run chart so the improver and I can see the gap to the current condition."

"I was thinking of doing that, too!" replied Denise. "But this is so much better organized than what we have right now."

"That's ok. You'll get there. The organization is the easy part," Maggie replied.

"At least for you it is, Maggie," said Denise.

Maggie laughed. "Ok, here's another tiny tip. At the top, it says metric, name plus unit. Make sure to be specific. For example, speed can be measured in kilometers per hour. So speed is the metric name while kilometers per hour is the unit which tells us how to measure it – at least every hour. I know it sounds simple enough but people often forget to do it. I've seen so many storyboards where the metric and how to measure isn't specified at all.

"And then there is my favorite form, the experimenting record (see Figure 14.3). As you know, it helps us to keep track of our experiments as well as helping us to reflect and learn. I think it is important to make clear the

(a)

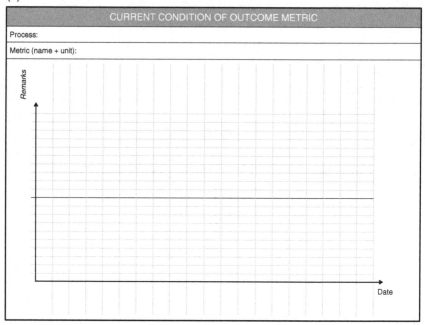

(b)

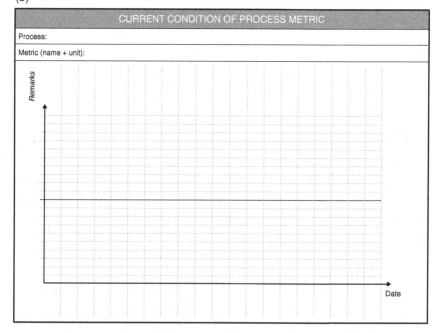

FIGURE 14.2
Current Condition Forms.

EXPERIMENTING RECORD						*(Each row = one experiment)*

Process:

Date	Current Condition*	Obstacle	Next Step & Expectation	Until		What happened & What we learned
			Step: - - - - - - - - - - - - - - - Expectation:			
			Step: - - - - - - - - - - - - - - - Expectation:		CONDUCT THE EXPERIMENT	
			Step: - - - - - - - - - - - - - - - Expectation:			
			Step: - - - - - - - - - - - - - - - Expectation:			

*Current condition of process metric

FIGURE 14.3
Experimenting Record, adapted from Mike Rother, *The Toyota Kata Practice Guide*, McGraw-Hill (New York), 2018.

obstacle we are experimenting against to improve. I usually like to make a new form for each obstacle as we go along. It helps keep the improver focused on the particular obstacle and visually see when we are moving on to another. Then the 'plan' part is just a short, simple description of the step we're testing, as well as what we expect will occur. From there, the steps are simple: Do the experiment, check your findings after the experiment is complete, and, here's the one people tend to forget, reflect on what you've learned – that's the 'Act,' though I don't really like that term in this case. The act in PDCA should be a reflection. One company I visited used 'Plan–Do–Study–Learn'. I really like that.

Adding the date of the coaching cycle, the current condition of the process metric and the date we have agreed on for our next coaching cycle is also helpful."

"Why?" asked Denise, working hard to keep up. "Seems like extra writing."

"You'll find out," Maggie replied.

Denise tried not to roll her eyes. She so appreciated everything Maggie was doing for her, but she was getting a little tired of Maggie's mystic sensei act.

It's a little like she's imitating a Buddhist priest, Denise thought. *Be patient, grasshopper.*

Maggie took a breath. "Ok, last but not least, the obstacle parking lot, which, as you know, is basically a white sheet of paper for listing the obstacles you encounter along the way."

"So, why have you arranged the forms on the storyboard the way you have?" Denise asked at last (see Figure 14.4).

"Good question," Maggie replied. "Again, there are a lot of ways to do it, and my way certainly isn't law, but here's how I like to think of it. We read left to right, right? Basically I am following what Rother laid out in the *Practice Guide*. I put the target condition on the left side, that's what you're trying to achieve. The charts visualizing the actual condition of outcome and process metrics are in the middle. The obstacle parking lot and the experimenting record are on the right side – what you are actually doing to try to achieve the target condition. That order makes the conversation

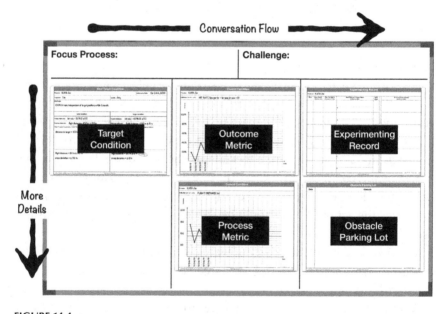

FIGURE 14.4

Improver's Storyboard, adapted from Mike Rother, *The Toyota Kata Practice Guide*, McGraw-Hill (New York), 2018.

during a coaching cycle move from left to right which is the sequence we are used to reading in and it matches the sequence of the Coaching Kata questions. In addition, the further down you go on the board, the more detail you go into, another logical progression. Outcome metric at the top, process metric below, and further data from let's say individual experiments below that.

"Now, look at how the storyboard resembles the steps of the Improvement Kata (see Figure 14.5). On the left side of the board are the first three steps," Maggie said, tapping the board as she spoke. "Understand the challenge, grasp the current condition, and establish the next target condition. You can find all three on the T-template.

"Now, the rest of the board is dedicated to step 4: Conducting experiments toward the next target condition. That's where we should be focusing most of our coaching energies anyway.

"But, honestly, don't overthink this. The storyboard is a Starter Kata – and it's an important one, for the improver as well as for the coach. But

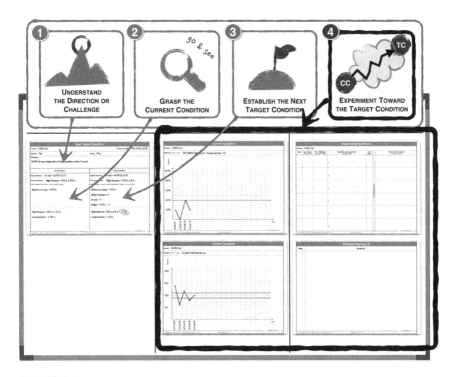

FIGURE 14.5
Improvement Kata steps resembled on the storyboard.

you don't have to understand every aspect of a Starter Kata before you begin practicing it. Remember, that in this process, you learn by doing, and over time things will click. You know the expression 'perfect is the enemy of good?' In this case, good is enough.

"And also, sorry to go on for so long, but this is important, keep in mind that the storyboard and the forms are owned by the person that is working toward the target condition. Hence the improver does the writing not the coach. Don't take away ownership by taking over the writing. In practice, that means don't take away the pen or pencil. Writing yourself is another way to tell a person what to do."

"Ok, wait though, then when should I ask Mark and Joe to write something on the storyboard? Before our coaching cycle? Or after each question?" Denise asked.

Maggie responded. "Ideally, they would have updated the current condition here", Maggie pointed at the two charts in the middle of the storyboard, "*before* the coaching cycle. It's their responsibility to prepare for the session. For the experimenting record though, I find it helpful to discuss and let them fill it out during the coaching cycle.

"However, try to avoid interrupting the conversation by asking them to write things down while they are still talking. Thinking, talking, and writing at the same time is hard for anybody. It's better to have distinct points in the coaching cycle when they can pause to write down anything that needs to be added.

"There are natural places where you can do this. The first one occurs after reflecting on the last step. Once the improver is done discussing what they have learned, you could ask them to summarize and write down their main findings on the experimenting record. That also adds value to the coaching cycle as it helps the other person to distill a conclusion."

Denise frowned. "Hold on, wouldn't it be even better if they filled that in prior to the coaching cycle, as a kind of preparation, like with the other information?"

Maggie took a deep breath. "Well, look, probably there is not a yes or no here. It's very likely that over time your improvers will start to prefill their experimenting record, at least about their findings and maybe even their next step.

"In my experience, though, it's better to do all the writing on the experimenting record during the coaching cycle for several reasons. I've seen too many coaches not even bother to read the experimenting record that the learner filled out in advance. Obviously, not good.

"In addition, writing in advance takes away at least one round of thinking during the coaching cycle. I'll give you an example. Let's say you ask, 'What did you learn from taking your last step?' And, as you yourself have experienced, your improver swamps you with heaps of information. After listening, you might follow up with, 'Could you please write down the main points of your finding on the experimenting record?' Now, your improver has to think about how to summarize their findings with a few main points. That's good. And then writing serves as a trigger for rethinking. 'Ink makes us think,' as Lord Byron put it.

Also, the time it takes to write their thoughts down gives you, the coach, some time to digest what you have just heard."

"OK, that makes sense," Denise said, nodding. "I'll practice that with Joe and Mark."

"Great, so, the next point in the conversation when you could naturally break to write something down is when you open phase three by asking, 'What obstacles are preventing you from reaching the target condition?' The improver comes up with a list of obstacles and you say, ok, great, add them to the parking lot.

"Some coaches start asking about individual obstacles as they are added to the obstacle parking lot. They want their improvers to write down a good description of the obstacle, maybe even effect and cause. Personally, I feel like that's jumping the gun. 'It takes away a lot of time and you don't yet know what obstacle you're going to focus on – it can influence the process in a negative way, too. If the coach asks about a particular obstacle at that point it subconsciously primes the improver to think that the coach wants them to focus on that obstacle. Now, you might not get their spontaneous answer to 'Which one obstacle are you addressing now?' but the one they think you want to hear.

"When you wait for the discussion to take its natural course, then select the one obstacle to focus on, it seems like you get a better obstacle and a better description of that obstacle. Then, the improver can write down the better description on the experimenting record."

"Hold on, I'm not sure I understand what you mean," Denise said, frowning again.

"Ok, no worries. Let's go back a bit," Maggie replied. "Last week we talked about the way Mark offered you an obstacle that already contained

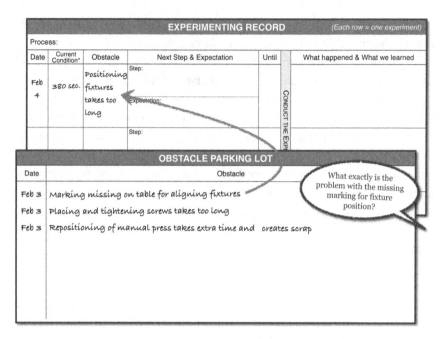

FIGURE 14.6

Specify the obstacle when moving it to the Experimenting Record.

a solution. He said the obstacle was the missing marking for fixture position on the table, remember? We know now that that's not a good way of describing an obstacle because it already implies a specific next step. What I'm saying is, if I were you, I would still let Mark add that description to the obstacle parking lot and just make a mental note (see Figure 14.6). Then, I might follow-up by asking, 'What further obstacles exist?' That way I keep the conversation flowing, invite him to identify more obstacles, rather than prematurely zooming in on one obstacle.

"Once, we'd finished listing obstacles in the parking lot, I'd say: 'Mark, which one are you addressing now?' And let's imagine he picks 'missing marking for fixture position on the table,' just like he did, right? *Now* is the time to get into the details. I can easily do so by asking, 'What exactly is the problem with the missing marking for fixture position on the table?'

"So, now, Mark might answer, 'The operators have to position the fixture on the table by measuring the position. And that takes a lot of time'. You said this is how he rephrased it when you asked them what exactly is the problem, which was a good move. Then, you can ask Mark to write down the better description of that to the experimenting record. And the result is so, so much better."

"Wow, that's really subtle," Denise exclaimed. "It's astonishing how easily you shift someone's thinking when you're coaching them and might not even realize it. I guess I have to be very deliberate about what I ask, even about what words I use."

"Yup, spot on," Maggie replied. "Good coaching is an art. I feel I'll never stop learning how to do it better. That's what makes it so inspiring to me."

Maggie paused for a second, took a breath, and then continued. "The rest of phase 3 and phase 4 are probably best to conduct without interruptions. It's often better to wait until you have agreed on a next step and developed the expectation before you ask them to fill in the experimenting record.

"Often, you might even go and see the process during this phase, while the improver explains it. Then, you can return to the storyboard and document what you have discussed as a next step and the expectation associated with it.

"I know that sounds like it will slow things down, but when I do it this way I find the writing adds value again as the improver has to summarize what the next step and expectation will be. If you fill out the final pieces of the experimenting record, then you're benefiting from the discussion that occurs during the coaching session itself and the time you've taken to go and see the improver's idea for his next step. I bet just about anything that the next step and expectation will often be different from what the improver had in mind before the coaching session. So, if they wait to fill out the experimenting record, there's no rework, and the improver can write down the new and improved version – ultimately, you've saved time, because you've devised a better experiment and hypothesis.

"This has been a lot, but we are almost done. Final step is we add the date of our next coaching cycle. Also," Maggie said, taking her Coaching Kata card out of her pocket, "as you can see, I've added little pencils to my card as a reminder for when to ask for writing things down, so I don't forget" (see Figure 14.7).

Denise took a deep breath. "Wow, ok, this is so organized and it makes so much sense. Once again I'm in your debt. I learn so much from these sessions that I can directly relate to my coaching."

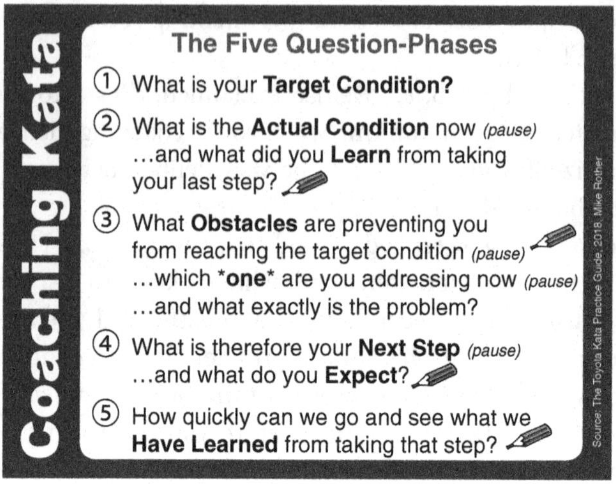

The Five Question-Phases

Coaching Kata

① What is your **Target Condition?**

② What is the **Actual Condition** now *(pause)* ...and what did you **Learn** from taking your last step?

③ What **Obstacles** are preventing you from reaching the target condition *(pause)* ...which *one* are you addressing now *(pause)* ...and what exactly is the problem?

④ What is therefore your **Next Step** *(pause)* ...and what do you **Expect?**

⑤ How quickly can we go and see what we **Have Learned** from taking that step?

Source: The Toyota Kata Practice Guide, 2018, Mike Rother

FIGURE 14.7

Coaching Kata starter questions, adapted from Mike Rother, *The Toyota Kata Practice Guide*, McGraw-Hill (New York), 2018.

"Don't worry," said Maggie, smiling. "I'll cash in on that favor some time. Maybe I'll make you buy more smoothies. Right now I'm just getting a kick out of watching you pretend to enjoy that horrible-looking green stuff we make. I mean, we've been talking for nearly an hour, and you *still* haven't finished."

15

Clever Experiments then Stuck in the Mud

WEDNESDAY, FEBRUARY 9, 1:00 PM, ANOTHER DAY, MORE COACHING EXPERIMENTS

AFTER THE EXCITEMENT of seeing Maggie's extraordinarily well-organized storyboard and feeling like she had learned so much, Denise found it a bit deflating to be back at the grind at the office the next day. After her usual morning of putting out fires, and a quick lunch at her desk, Denise was looking forward to her coaching sessions with Mark and then with Joe, who was still working the day shift.

Just then Mark popped his head in.

"Ready for our coaching session. I am excited about it," he said.

Wow, Mark is excited about a coaching session? Something must have happened.

"Sure Mark," Denise replied. "Let's go to the storyboard and get started right away."

They made their way to the storyboard. Denise asked the usual questions, and Mark answered every one of them in a clear and concise way. Mark was still working on the positioning of the fixture obstacle from last week. When Denise asked him about his last experiment, Mark seemed to be bursting with excitement.

"Well, Denise I know I am not supposed to go off script, but you remember in our session yesterday I talked about drawing a bunch of markings for where each of the different fixtures should go. They are different sizes, so each has to be placed differently. It was a disaster. The operators were so confused by all the different markings. My reflection was, I felt really bad about the whole thing. After all, that was my big idea."

DOI: 10.4324/9780429347023-17

"That night I remembered that the obstacle was not missing markings, but that it took them time to position the fixtures. That got me thinking about different ways they might be able to position the fixture correctly the first time with little time and effort. And then it hit me. If there was the right-sized frame in the right place, they could simply insert the fixture and as long as the frame was in the correct position, bingo, they would have it. So, yesterday in my home shop I rigged up some frames, the right size for each fixture. I figured out a way that they could slide each frame into another gadget attached to the table and easily slide them out. Bingo the fixture is in the right position, no fuss, no muss. We tried it out this morning. Worked perfectly, and I met my target condition." Mark was beaming.

Denise couldn't help it, she was beaming, too.

"Wow, Mark. That's incredible. My goal is not to always ask and answer the questions in exactly the right order but to get you to think scientifically and use your creativity to find innovative solutions. I gotta say, what you did was genius. And I love that you built it at home in your workshop. Honestly, good for you! You made my day, maybe my week. Thanks so much."

Mark took in the praise. "I won't let it go to my head boss. The light bulbs won't always go on like this, but it sure is fun when they do."

Denise was walking on air, as she walked to meet Joe at his storyboard. She was not expecting any big breakthroughs on his tough project. Their current target condition focused on reducing defects when inserting the pump piston. For some types of pumps, it often happened after changeover that the piston jammed, especially for the standard highest volume pumps. Joe had agreed to observe the process in detail to learn what exactly was causing this. During the coaching session, Denise discovered that Joe had not yet done this, despite saying that he would. *Here we go again,* she thought.

"Listen, it's actually really not my fault," Joe said. "It's the reprioritization of orders again. Production planning has put in an urgent order for centrifugal pumps. There's no piston jamming problem post-changeover with those pumps. That's why I haven't been able to complete the process observation yet."

Denise chastised herself again for jumping to conclusions. It clearly wasn't Joe's fault – how could he observe a process that wasn't running? She decided to proceed with the next question: "What obstacles are preventing you from reaching your target condition?"

"Still the same," Joe replied, pointing to the obstacle parking lot. "Besides, I can't observe the problem right now." He added this new obstacle to the obstacle parking lot.

"Which one are you addressing now?" Denise continued.

"That piston-type pumps are not assembled correctly," Joe replied.

"And what exactly is the problem?" Denise asked after looking down at her thumb on her card.

"That I do not know. The question is when will they next schedule the piston pumps," Joe explained again, a little annoyed.

"So what's your next step?"

"My next step is to speak with production planning."

"And what do you expect?" Denise asked.

"To know when I will be able to conduct my process observation," Joe answered. He filled out the experimenting record on his storyboard with his next step. They arranged the next coaching cycle for the following day.

As they were finishing up, Joe said, "Listen, Denise, I told you I couldn't observe the right engine because of production control at the beginning of the session. We could have agreed that I would talk to production control without all these roundabout questions."

With that Joe left, but Denise stayed at the storyboard to reflect on their coaching cycle.

I followed all the questions, but still Joe didn't really make progress today toward his target condition, she concluded. *That happens quite often. And, I have to admit, he was correct that the questions I asked did not really help him.*

Denise began to flip through the old experimenting records feeling stumped. She repeatedly found obstacles similar to the one Joe had written down today. Examples were: needed data is missing, waiting on colleagues from department X to do the next step, product to observe not produced right now, no time to take the step, and necessary measuring equipment missing for measuring parameter Y.

These are not obstacles in the process, Denise thought. *They all have no direct effect on our process metric. They only stop us from implementing the next step. That doesn't mean we can ignore them, but only when we eliminate obstacles in the process will we get closer to our next target condition.*

Denise formed the idea of distinguishing between two types of obstacles in the future: process obstacles and implementation obstacles (see Figure 15.1).

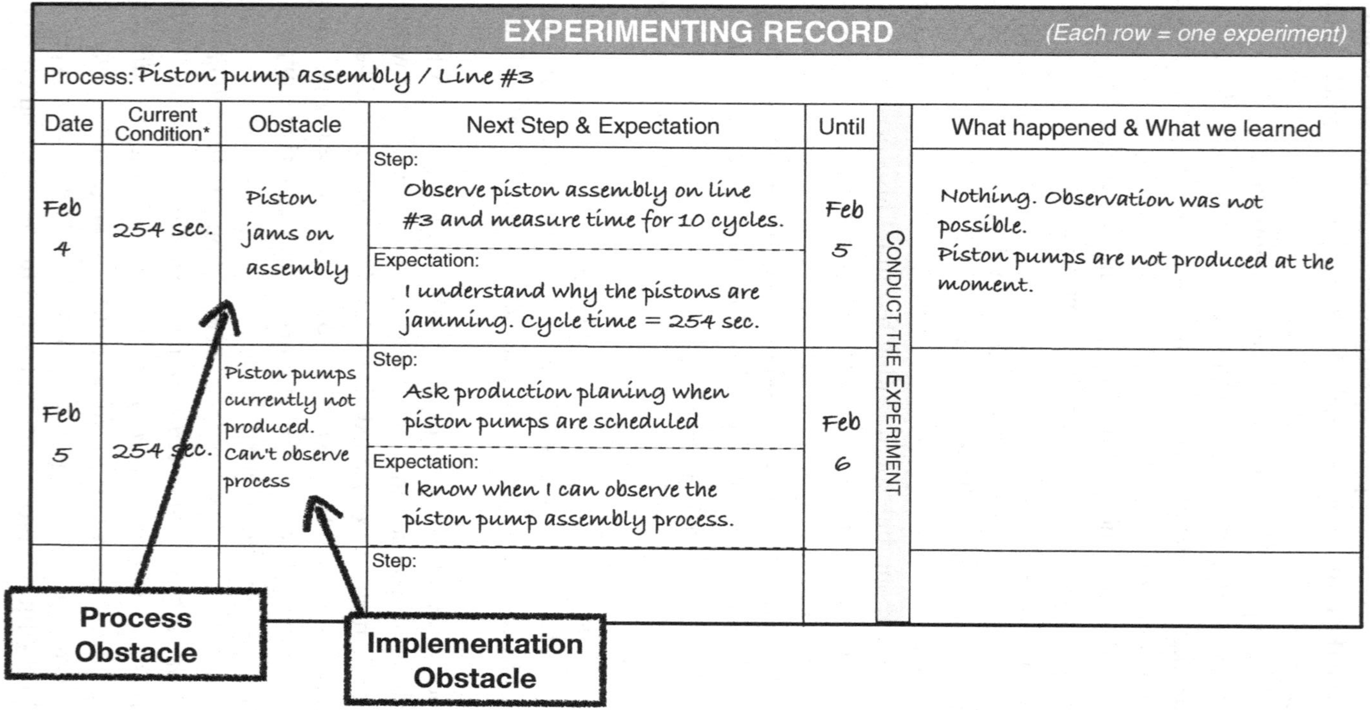

EXPERIMENTING RECORD				*(Each row = one experiment)*
Process: Piston pump assembly / Line #3				
Date	Current Condition*	Obstacle	Next Step & Expectation	Until	What happened & What we learned
				CONDUCT THE EXPERIMENT	
Feb 4	254 sec.	Piston jams on assembly	Step: Observe piston assembly on line #3 and measure time for 10 cycles. Expectation: I understand why the pistons are jamming. Cycle time = 254 sec.	Feb 5	Nothing. Observation was not possible. Piston pumps are not produced at the moment.
Feb 5	254 sec.	Piston pumps currently not produced. Can't observe process	Step: Ask production planing when piston pumps are scheduled Expectation: I know when I can observe the piston pump assembly process.	Feb 6	
			Step:		

Implementation Obstacle

Process Obstacle

FIGURE 15.1

The Two Types of Obstacles, Tilo Schwarz, *Kata Coaching Dojo Handbook*, self-published, 2018.

When Denise reviewed the experimenting record a second time, she discovered that the obstacle column contained an alternating mixture of process obstacles and implementation obstacles.

This makes things very confusing, Denise thought. *From a distance, it looks like we are performing many coaching cycles and steps to improve the process. In fact, we are just spinning our wheels, removing one implementation obstacle after the other. The obstacle parking lot is also full of both kinds of obstacles.*

In addition, she discovered obstacles still listed in the parking lot that Joe had worked on and removed long ago. Denise walked back to her office, took out her notebook, and started to write down what she had learned this morning:

Distinguish between two types of obstacles.

So, if we always write down the "process obstacle," we are currently working on, even when an "implementation obstacle" occurs, we'll know if we're making progress.

She added to her notes:

Note the current process obstacle in the experimenting record.

She paused her writing to puzzle this out further. *This will leave the obstacle in the obstacle column on the experimenting record unchanged until it is removed,* she thought. *The result will be a much clearer picture of where we are, and we will easily recognize if we are not making progress as line after line on the experimenting record will address the same obstacle.*

Denise recalled Maggie saying she used a separate experimenting record for every new process obstacle and decided to make a note of that as well in her notebook.

Use a separate experimenting record for each process obstacle, not for implementation obstacles.

Addressing implementation obstacles should happen fast, she thought. *It would be best to take the step immediately. Today, in the coaching session, we could have called production planning right away to find out when Joe will be able to observe the piston pump assembly. I'll push for that in the future instead of waiting for information until the next coaching cycle.*

Perhaps I should even be more proactive and check on any implementation obstacles with the improver during my regular rounds. Then, maybe I can use my limited authority as a manager to try to overcome the obstacle, like even asking production planning to schedule the pump we need for a short run. Hmm, I guess the risk is I take responsibility away from the improver. I have to think about that.

Also, the obstacle parking lot needs to be more concise. In the future, we should cross out obstacles we successfully remove. Suddenly she remembered that in Rother's *Practice Guide*, he highlighted the obstacle that was currently being worked on with an arrow. *Maybe we can use a sticky arrow and move it as the current obstacle changes.*

If Mark and Joe find it challenging to prioritize obstacles and choose the next obstacle to address, a well-structured obstacle parking lot might be helpful. We could create a column with the unwanted effect of the obstacles or add a tally list with the frequency of occurrence. Then it would be so easy to prioritize what obstacle to address next.

Feeling energized by her new ideas, Denise picked up her pen and summarized the rest of her thoughts in her notebook. She decided to discuss and test them with Joe and Mark the next day.

THURSDAY, FEBRUARY 10, 9:00 AM, NEW IDEAS TO TEST AT WORK

As usual, Denise and Joe met at 9 am for their daily coaching cycle. Before she began asking the questions, Denise talked with Joe, gushing about her thoughts on the two types of obstacles, explaining the logic and what she was proposing.

Joe listened patiently and when Denise paused simply said:

"Sure boss. That makes sense. Let's try it."

They set about cleaning up the obstacle parking lot and marked the process obstacle they were working on with a self-adhesive arrow (see Figure 15.2).

OBSTACLE PARKING LOT	
Date	Obstacle
~~Feb 3~~	~~Marking missing on table for aligning fixtures~~
~~Feb 3~~	~~Placing and tightening screws takes too long~~
Feb 3	Pistons jam during assembly ⬅
Feb 3	Repositioning of manual press takes extra time and creates scrap

FIGURE 15.2
Marking the currently addressed obstacle.

When they scanned the experimenting records, they found that the last four steps only addressed implementation obstacles.

"No wonder we're moving so slowly," Joe said, thinking aloud.

They replaced the implementation obstacles on the latest experimenting record with the process obstacle "piston jams," which Joe was currently addressing.

"From now on let's use a separate experimenting record for each process obstacle we address," said Denise. "Then, we won't lose track and can identify if we have truly removed the obstacle."

"I like that," Joe said, "now the experimenting record makes much more sense to me."

In their coaching session, Joe explained he had checked with production planning to find out when the next batch of piston pumps was planned for assembly. To his surprise, he had discovered that the next batch was scheduled for this morning. In fact he had already done his observations in preparation for the coaching session.

"I talked with Leah from production planning who's doing all the scheduling for our department. She's really nice," he said.

Denise smiled. She knew that many of the guys on her production team had a bit of a crush on Leah. Joe must have forgotten he was speaking with Denise and not one of his buddies. *That's the first time I have seen him so relaxed with me during a coaching session. Maybe it's because we're working together to improve the coaching process, which makes it less hierarchical.*

"Now, listen to this, Leah told me that she has drastically reduced batch size for the production orders she puts into the system for us," Joe continued, clearly proud. "She said that the reduction in changeover time we have achieved so far makes planning so much easier. She can now run a higher model mix and follow custom demand more closely. She said – get this – If we keep up our efforts, she said, we'll be out of our backlog way earlier than the other teams. I was blown away. I had no idea we were having that kind of positive impact." He paused. "Leah was so happy," he added, blushing a little.

Denise was delighted to see that Joe was really on a roll getting more energetic as he spoke.

"When I mentioned that with the current supply situation it was going to be hard to reach our goal, Leah said, 'don't worry. I have your back'. So it seems like our improvements are earning us some fans who want to help us. Who would have thought it?" Joe said, positively beaming now.

Hmm, thought Denise, deep in the middle of her own aha moment, *I sure am glad I didn't intervene with Leah and try to solve the problem for Joe. He got so much out of taking responsibility for his own project. I have to add that to my notebook. And he clearly doesn't mind an excuse to talk to Leah.*

Denise then proceeded with the coaching session. She skipped ahead a bit to Joe's observation of the assembly process. Joe explained that during his observation, the piston had jammed three times.

Denise was so proud of Joe for showing so much initiative. *Wow, he's on fire,* she thought. *He's really growing as a leader. Daily coaching sessions seem like they're finally paying off.*

"What did you learn from your last step about the obstacle with the jammed pistons?" Denise asked Joe, trying to hide her excitement. She didn't want to throw him off.

"The solution is easy. The operators simply have to insert the piston with a straight, vertical move. Then it doesn't jam. They just don't do it correctly for the first pumps after the changeover. I don't think they were aware of how important it is."

Denise noticed that Joe had jumped to a conclusion about why the operators were not doing it right and then leaped to a solution, one that she suspected was not very helpful. When she first arrived at Goldberg, she had done some assembly to familiarize herself with her team's process. She knew, therefore, that to tell the operators to insert the piston with a straight, vertical movement wasn't very helpful advice because the piston was inserted by hand and it was difficult, especially with the long pistons, to keep them precisely straight. If they really wanted to solve this problem, they first had to better understand the cause.

Once again, I find myself in the coaching dilemma of wanting to guide Joe but needing to let him stay in control. What can I do within the coaching framework? Identify obstacles and pick one to address. Then understand the cause. Only then should we test a solution, she thought. *There is a logical sequence.*

Then Denise remembered her formula: Obstacle = Cause × Unwanted Effect. She decided to follow it by investigating the unwanted effect first.

"Joe," she asked, "what is the unwanted effect of this obstacle on your process metric?"

"As I explained during my observation this morning the problem has occurred three times. Our records show that this happened on average about six times per changeover. If the piston jams, we lose at least 10 minutes loosening it. That means a loss of 60 extra minutes of production time per changeover," Joe replied.

Denise suggested adding this data in the obstacle column on the experimenting record. Joe wrote with a pencil: "Piston jammed/60 minutes per changeover."

Denise thought: *That is a good way of describing process obstacles. Piston jamming leads to 60 minutes of lost time. This corresponded precisely to the first and last part of the obstacle formula.* She made a mental note to sketch this in her notebook later.

"Joe," Denise asked, "what exactly happens in the process that causes the piston to jam?"

"I'm not sure," Joe replied sheepishly. "The operators need to insert the piston as straight as possible into the suction cylinder of the pump."

Ah, our old friend, the threshold of knowledge has been reached, Denise thought. *Let's go to question 4.*

"Don't worry if you don't know exactly," she replied. "In fact, we shouldn't expect that you know everything. That's why this is a scientific process of discovery. So, what's your next step to finding out?"

Joe brightened. "I'll have to take a closer look and do another observation on what exactly the team members do when they insert the piston. I guess I'll need to talk to Leah again about scheduling," he added with a sly look.

"And what do you expect to learn from that step?" Denise prompted.

"That I'll better understand the reason the piston is jamming," Joe replied.

Yes, we've identified the obstacle. Now, the next logical step is to understand its cause, which means going back to the current condition. Only then will finding a sustainable solution become possible. Would this process apply to any obstacle? she wondered.

Joe pulled her out of her thoughts.

"Should I write this down on the experimenting record?" he asked.

Denise nodded. They finished the session, and Denise walked cheerily back to her office, softly singing one of her favorite Fleetwood Mac songs. "Don't stop thinking about tomorrow .... It'll be better than before...," she sang, barely audible to anyone but her.

Arriving at her desk, she sat down and picked up her notebook to write down what she learned. In general, the steps might look like this, she thought: one, identify an obstacle, two, determine its cause, three, test a possible solution. So there were three basic types of experiments. She started writing (see Figure 15.3).

The 3 Types of Experiments:

(1) Experiment for identifying or quantifying obstacles.

(2) Experiment for understanding the cause.

(3) Experiment for testing a hypothesis or solution.

FIGURE 15.3
The three types of experiments.

Scan with your mobile and find out how Denise discovers the Fortuneteller's Crystal Ball.

QR CODE 15.1
Denise discovers the Fortuneteller's crystal ball.

16

We Deliver Same Day

DENISE WAS HAPPY when she ran into Jason at the canteen at lunchtime.

"Hi, Jason," she said. "It's been a little while. I've been so busy with Kata since we last chatted, and, you know what, we are finally getting results." She paused. "Sorry. Let me back up. How was your weekend?"

"Honestly, I had two very quiet days," Jason replied, looking up at her. "Please. Sit," he said, and she did. "So, I took the opportunity this weekend to read through the *Toyota Kata Practice Guide*. I can't say I memorized it or even understood all the concepts. But in general, I love the ideas and I am anxious to give it a try in the sales support group."

Wow, that's cool, Denise thought. *It's spreading.*

"My main problem, though," Jason continued, "is that my team works on so many different tasks during the course of a day. In production, you guys have it so much easier. Your teams always do the same things throughout a shift."

"I wish that was true," Denise replied, "but that's what we are trying to get closer to – stable, quality processes. Of course, sales is definitely different from manufacturing. I'm a little embarrassed by this question, but what is sales support and what exactly do you do?"

"That's a perfectly reasonable question Denise," Jason replied. "In fact, even though I was hired to run this department, sometimes I feel like I'm still trying to figure it out. Most people think of sales and imagine knocking on doors and calling consumers at their homes to try to convince them to buy your product or service. Goldberg's customers are other companies, mostly manufacturing. These companies use the pumps to support their production processes, such as sending liquids to machines to cool equipment or piping chemicals used to make paint. They need our products to be absolutely reliable and to arrive on time, or it shuts down their production. There are many different versions of our pumps which are used for different purposes.

"In some cases, we sell one-off pumps out of a catalog, but in many cases, customers are custom ordering a set of pumps for specific technical purposes. This can also include installation by our service people. That's where my group comes in. Sales needs us to specify the right pumps and supporting equipment and give them an overall proposal for the product and whatever service we think they need. We are the back-office tech folk who develop the technical solutions for our customers and write up a proposal including a quote for our sales people to use. Then the sales group takes over again to pitch the proposal and try to close the deal. Often after the purchase the customers have technical questions and sales refers them directly to us."

"Great explanation, Jason. I get it," said Denise. "It also gives me a different window into what our company does. Thanks for that. So, what are your main processes to do this?"

Jason and Denise had already discussed the need to be clear on the team's main processes before starting with practicing Kata at their lunch the week before. To find out, Jason explained, he had conducted his own rough current-state analysis. Everyone in his team had tracked, over several days, how much time they spent on different types of activities.

Wow, that was fast, Denise thought.

"So, here's what we found," Jason said. "On average, my team spends about one-third of their time on the phone with customers. Mostly these are requests for quotes or queries about a previous offer we've sent them.

"How they spend the rest of the time differs between the team members. For three team members, updating the online catalog and system data is the second most time-consuming task, requiring one-thirds of their time.

"Two other team members spend about 25% of their time on scheduling and managing installations of our equipment. One other team member supports the sales force when they have technical questions.

"I've also noticed that everyone in my team spends about 5% of their time writing and pricing offers. Given the current size of my team, this means that it is as though we have one person doing this half-time. Some of our most important sales are a large number of pumps and installations to a single customer. We think of that as a 'project' as opposed to a one-off sale.

Remember, that includes a whole system of pumps and often connecting pipes and we offer to do installation as well. These are big jobs for us to manage, like a project, and involve many of our different specialties as a company. When the sales team is working on selling a project, they need quotes from us which they often complain take too long. Since revenue in the project business accounts for 20% of total revenue, we need to do better to win those projects and support our sales force.

"Based on that, and our earlier discussion about practicing Kata on a manageable, defined topic that matters to us, I want to begin with the process of quoting in the project business. An initial quick and dirty look at the situation today showed the time from when sales requests a written proposal from us to when they get it takes 5 to 8 days. We would like to reduce that to 3 days in the next six months."

"I'm impressed!" Denise replied. "You've really thought about this. You've collected data, and have even started defining a challenge. You're seriously off and running."

Denise reflected back on her skepticism that Jason would do much of a current state analysis on his own. *Note to self 100, stop prejudging people!* She came out of her daze as Jason responded.

"Thanks," Jason said. "One thing, though, I'm concerned about is that the time for a quote is not completely under our control. To create an offer, you can think of it as three steps. First, we identify the pumps and services we are selling to the customer, including some custom designs; second, we pass it on to the finance department for the final pricing. It can be held up in finance for a few days. Third, we finish the offer and put it in writing. I worry that it will be hard to achieve a 3-day turnaround, if, right now, we sometimes spend 3 days waiting for finance to get back to us."

Denise suddenly remembered her summer job working at a bank in the months before she began college. There, she had learned about same-day processing which was a federal requirement for banks. In earlier times, this had been a serious challenge, especially on busy days. Now, with the high level of automation, this was easily possible.

"Jason, I worked for a summer in a bank where we did same-day processing. In your case that would mean that every new task your team gets today would be completed today," she said with growing excitement (see Figure 16.1).

"So, you could start by measuring the same-day processing rate for the two process steps your team controls, before and after they go out to

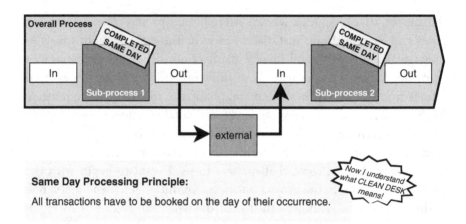

Same Day Processing Principle:

All transactions have to be booked on the day of their occurrence.

FIGURE 16.1

Same-day processing principle.

finance. That will give you the percentage of inquiries that are completed on the same day they arrive for each process step."

"Hmm," Jason said, a thoughtful smile on his face. "I think I like that. You said we should start with a challenge, one that can be clearly stated to the team. That would certainly be a challenge.

If we achieve a 100% same-day rate for our quotes in both process steps, that would be two days in lead time. If I can convince the finance team to strive to reach the same for their process steps, we would have a total lead time of three days. That's exactly where I want to go. How can I develop a target condition for that?"

Denise's mind raced. *We're jumping ahead,* she thought. *I have to get Jason to understand the current condition first.*

"The first step of the Improvement Kata is to agree on the process and the challenge," Denise said. "It sounds like you've done that. Now, we need a target completion date for the challenge."

"I think three months is good. I'm supposed to state it as a question that starts, 'Wouldn't it be great…' right?" Jason asked.

Denise nodded amazed by how quickly he had read and absorbed the Practice Guide.

"Ok," Jason said, "So…. Wouldn't it be great if we reduced the lead time for delivering quotes in the project business to three days within the next three months? Uh, now that I say that aloud though, it sounds pretty daunting. I don't know if it's realistic."

"I understand, but don't worry, through practicing Kata your team will build the skills to achieve even seemingly impossible challenges. Even though the challenge is big and will almost certainly by definition seem a bit daunting, you don't need to go after it all at once. In fact, you're almost certainly bound to fail if you do. What you want to do instead is break the problem into smaller pieces and then take on one at a time. Those are your target conditions. For example, we might focus at first on gathering the technical information needed for the proposal."

"OK, I get that," Jason replied. "Makes sense. In that case, we can keep the due date of three months from now for our challenge. So, to break it down, I need to establish my first target condition, right? That's what I am struggling to understand."

Jason clearly is enthusiastic, too enthusiastic maybe because he's still getting ahead of himself, Denise thought.

"Let's back up a bit before jumping into the first target condition," she said. "The next step is to understand the current condition. That's key to developing a solid next target condition. We need to understand the process and the current pattern of work first."

"But I've already done that," Jason said, interrupting her. "I know what my team is working on, what process I want to improve, and we've measured that the current lead time is 5 to 8 days. So, we know the current condition."

Denise tried her best to be patient, just as Maggie had done with her.

"You certainly have a great start," she said. "But unfortunately there's a little more to it. We need to go deeper, starting with understanding customer demand and then the process steps and sequences. Otherwise, we will just be flailing around in the dark in setting a target condition."

"OK, OK," Jason said, lifting both his hands. "I don't quite get it, but if you say so, we'll do it. So, then tell me, how do I grasp the current condition?"

"The starting point is customer demand," Denise explained. "How often do you need to produce a complete proposal for your customers?"

"Wait a second Denise," Jason protested. "How could I possibly calculate that? It varies every day. One proposal takes us 2 hours to complete, another 6 days. It's not like the automotive industry, where I understand they produce a car every minute."

This led to a lengthy discussion during which they finished their lunch. They decided to continue their discussion in Denise's office where it would be quieter. As they made their way from the canteen to the assembly department Denise explained that the customer demand rate is different from how much time it takes to create a proposal. They sat down at Denise's desk and worked through the nitty-gritties. In the end they agreed that on average, roughly speaking, they needed to produce a proposal every 80 minutes. Jason was shocked at how little time they had and could see why their customers were so unhappy.

"Okay, Jason, now let's look at how you produce these proposals," Denise continued. "According to the *Kata Practice Guide*, it helps to develop a big-picture run chart. Take a random sample of proposals and figure out the time it took to produce each one, start to finish, and plot those times so you can see the variation. Another key step is to develop a block diagram. That is simply the steps in the current process and can also include timing. I understand the steps, sequence, and timing vary across different proposals. Still, drawing a block diagram will help us to have a general understanding of your process. It's similar to what you might think of as a process-flow diagram. When you look at the time it takes and the steps, you'll be able to get a sense of what to focus on for your first target condition. It is all about focus. Break the elephant into small bite-sized pieces."

"Ok, this is great, I can do that," Jason said, getting excited. "I can work with my people and develop a block diagram and also time our process cycles. I see that's measuring several quotations to see how long we currently need and how frequently we ship a proposal compared to the 80 minutes. I'll add that to my homework list. This has been really helpful, Denise. I have a clear idea of what to do next."

Scan with your mobile and read how Denise and Jason discuss grasping current condition.

QR CODE 16.1
Find out more about grasping current condition.

"Wow, Jason, you're really flying through this. I guess I am not surprised. There are more steps in Rother's Starter Kata, but I think we have enough to work with now," Denise said.

Jason nodded confidently. "Now, I think I can start coaching my team."

But Denise shook her head. "To be honest, I don't think that's a good idea. We don't want to put the cart before the horse. Maggie pointed out how important it is to first practice the Improvement Kata ourselves, with the help of a coach, before we start coaching others. Maybe you can start by building your storyboard and then I'll coach you?"

"Well," Jason paused, "I guess a storyboard might be a good idea. Maybe you can show me one of yours and then I can take it from there.

"And, I'll think about the coaching. I'm not sure if I need that. I think I could start on my own with my team." They left Denise's glass cubicle and went to Joe's storyboard where Denise explained what it contained and how to set it up. She promised to send him the forms so he could print them out. They agreed to meet the next day.

As Denise walked back to her office, she had mixed feelings. She could not help but be impressed with how quickly Jason was learning, yet she was concerned by how he was getting ahead of himself. *Jason is certainly quick, and motivated, but he is a bit head strong, and then there's that male ego. I don't like him starting to coach his team with no practice in scientific thinking himself. I'll discuss that with Maggie.*

Scan with your mobile to
find out how Denise
discovers the Kata Cycle

QR CODE 16.2
Denise discovers the Kata Cycle.

TUESDAY, FEBRUARY 15, 12:00 PM, A GREAT LUNCH CAPPED OFF BY A BEAT DOWN FROM DICK

Another busy day, little sleep, and a morning of coaching where Denise had a true light-bulb moment. But she couldn't reflect as the morning meeting with the other department managers came first. David wasn't in a good mood today as Dick had given the management team another of his dreaded sense of urgency speeches.

At noon, Denise finally had a chance to talk to Maggie about her coaching session with Jason. They met for lunch at the local pub, and Denise dove right in. She shared what they had worked on and how quickly he caught on and then her struggles with explaining how the concepts applied to his sales support work and her disappointment that Jason insisted on coaching by himself. She was concerned he was not ready for coaching his team and disappointed she could not persuade him to accept her as his coach.

Maggie took a deep breath. "That's usual for administrative processes," Maggie explained. "There's a lot more variability of tasks compared to the production line. And it is more difficult for managers to even see that the seemingly random actions of their people are processes at all. What you and Jason accomplished in one meeting, defining processes, prioritizing, developing a challenge, doing an initial current condition analysis, calculating the customer demand rate, is actually pretty remarkable. Honestly, it seems like this collaboration is working out quite well. Jason seems to have an intuitive sense of process improvement, even though that does not seem to be a big thing in sales.

"In fact, Jason may be the best learning partner you have. He sounds very bright and receptive to the ideas of Kata. He reads voraciously and has been one step ahead of you in collecting data and defining his focus. And the fact that he leads an administrative team is interesting. It gives you the opportunity to practice coaching under circumstances that are different from manufacturing. I suggest you talk to Jason about forming a learning group. Remember I talked to you about the group of women I have been working with? It's been amazing. We have learned so much from one another. We all take turns coaching each other – so it feels more egalitarian. Jason and one other person, perhaps someone from his team, and you could form a great learning group. His ego may be able to accept that better than being the improver to your coach."

Once again, Maggie's calm and reassuring explanations recharged Denise's battery. After returning to the plant from her lunch with Maggie her mind was buzzing with ideas about how to help Jason the next time they met. As usual, when she arrived at her desk, Denise checked her email first thing.

Date: February 15, 1:05 pm
To: All Managers Plant Guilderville, Sarah Burlow, Head of Quality Management, David Meyers, Plant Manager Plant Guilderville
From: Dick Murdoch
Subject: DELIVERY PERFORMANCE
Priority: Highest
Cc: Roger Deng, Roland Palmer, Sam Watson, Pete Cheng

To All Managers at Goldberg Plant Guilderville:

The current delivery situation is still unacceptable. Thus far, we have only reduced the backlog for a very few products. I really wonder if some of us understand the magnitude of the situation we are in.

I just learned about the quality issues in our motor fabrication. For many years, we've excelled at quality and now it seems management has forgotten what quality is. This is unacceptable, particularly for our newest, most high-end product.

This pump has all the functionality and technology to bring us back to number one with our customers. But if we've lost the ability or will to produce with the quality required, we have to seriously consider options.

I expect all of you to get your teams back to their stations and make sure everybody has a clear understanding that quality is not up for debate.

Our head of quality, Sarah Burlow, along with David Meyers, will give my executive team a daily status update on your progress.

—Dick

Oh no, not another stunt from Dick, thought Denise. *He's bypassed David again. I wonder if that guy has any idea how much damage he causes. I pity his wife. He must be a train wreck at home.*

Denise was relieved that at least her team wasn't in the doghouse this time. Her assembly department had made further progress on their backlog and were close to getting ahead. Still, the fabrication department that machined the precision motor parts, the heart of the pump, was clearly struggling. Denise knew from their plant-management meetings with David that this was related to the new HX-1000 pump. Parts of the engine housing had super-high-precision requirements, which demanded a high degree of accuracy, prior to painting the parts.

Then, to make matters worse, the pumps went to an external supplier to be coated and, after returning, the motors department had to perform some more operations with the coating applied. *That's one of the dumbest ways to design a value stream*, Denise had thought when she'd first heard about the process.

And, indeed, it created many quality issues. The high-precision areas of the parts got damaged at the supplier. There was further damage on the second run through the motors department. Scrap costs skyrocketed, parts were piling up because the coating supplier was running large batches, and, as a result of all the rework and poor logistics, late deliveries were the norm. Since Guilderville was the global source for motors, shipping to all the overseas operations, these process issues had global implications.

Maybe this does not make me the greatest team player, but I'm just glad it's not my team in trouble this time, Denise thought to herself. *I do not expect any praise from Dick, but at least he is not beating us up.*

TUESDAY, FEBRUARY 14, 8 PM, REFLECTING ON MAGGIE'S MIND DUMP

The rest of the day was jam packed with meetings and putting out fires Joe brought to her attention. When she finally managed to leave, it was nearly 8 pm. *I'm now officially married to the factory*, Denise thought, as she pulled out of her parking space. *It's not like I had much of a personal life to begin with, I guess.*

Driving her usual route home, Denise realized she had not managed to write down in her *Personal Learning Handbook* all the great stuff Maggie

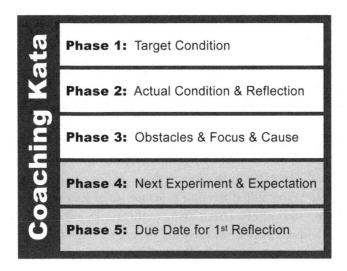

FIGURE 16.2
The Coaching Kata five-phase model, Tilo Schwarz, *Kata Coaching Dojo Handbook*, self-published, 2018.

had shared with her over lunch. She couldn't help but replay it from memory. Maggie had once again reminded her of the importance of the five questions or actually phases (see Figure 16.2).

In phase 1, Denise recalled, *we clarify and connect to the objective the person or team we are coaching is striving to achieve. That serves as a point of reference throughout the coaching conversation.*

Phase 2 then focuses on making sure we have current facts and data. In this phase, we have to avoid opinions, assumptions, and outdated experiences, to truly grasp the actual condition. This phase also includes reflecting on the last step and what we have learned from it.

Phase 3 was about obstacles and focus. That phase of our coaching conversation focuses on identifying obstacles that hinder us from reaching our target condition and selecting the next one to address. Slice and analyze you could say. Hmmm, I kind of like that, especially since I am such a bad cook. We want to identify the next one that will hinder us from reaching our target condition. And this phase also includes analyzing the one obstacle we are addressing to understand the effect and cause. Understanding the causes can even open our perspective to new possibilities, she thought excitedly.

Phase 4 is about experimenting. An experiment starts with a hypothesis; a hypothesis that should evolve from our analysis in phase 3, she thought.

What is, THEREFORE, your next step? Then we make explicit the hypothesis by stating our expectation. I predict this will happen.

    And then finally in phase 5, we have the due date. We run experiments to gain new knowledge, explore the obstacles and territory ahead, learn regarding our hypothesis, and adapt accordingly. To do so, we need a fast feedback loop. How quickly can we get the next feedback to adapt if necessary?

When Denise eventually arrived home, she parked her car in the garage. *Finally, they're done with the construction work down here,* Denise thought as she took the elevator to the fourth floor. *Having to park outside is a pain in winter; especially if you had to scrape ice of your windshield every morning.* For a year, she had been living in this funky loft apartment in the city center, and she liked it. By the time she got through the door, she was too tired to cook. She grabbed a bowl of cereal, added some yogurt, sat down on the sofa, and turned on the TV.

Scan with your mobile to
find out how Denise
discovers the cause funnel.

QR CODE 16.3
Denise discovers the Cause Funnel while watching a crime series on TV.

17

Fun in the Learning Group?

THE LAST TWO weeks had passed with lightning speed. At least, that was how Denise felt. Lots had happened in that short time.

As Maggie had suggested, Denise had spoken with Jason about forming a learning group where they would coach each other, while each of them worked on a series of target conditions as well. That way, they would experience both roles: improver and coach.

As they worked together, Denise realized more and more how important it was to have experience as an improver before starting to coach. She had skipped over that step – Maggie had been coaching her informally but she had never done the process herself. Just like it was impossible to be a good piano teacher if you had never played the piano, a good coach had to have practiced Improvement Kata first to teach someone else. Even if it was possible, maybe, to coach someone without having been an improver first, it would take longer and the coach would probably be more vague about their reference model. By now, Denise was also convinced that having a reference model to identify gaps between ideal and actual was one of the keys to good coaching. That is, she needed a reference for good scientific logic, not for the specific content of the problem being worked on. That was the domain of the improver (see QR code 17.1).

Scan with your mobile to
find out how Denise
discovers Go West.

QR CODE 17.1
Denise discovers the Logic Links and Go West.

When she last met with Jason, she explained the concept of a learning group consisting of three or four people. Each of them, she said, would pick a target condition to work on and then coach each other so they were both improvers and coaches. Jason had happily agreed to join.

It turned out Jason had tried to use the Coaching Kata questions a number of times with improvers he selected from his team. That had been a sobering experience for him.

"You think: it's super easy," he told Denise. "Hey, you say to yourself, anyone can read questions from a card. And I'm a manager, so I know how to coach my team. But then you realize how hard it really is in the heat of the moment – and that, guess what, you're a lousy coach."

Denise really appreciated Jason's humility. It was a new side of him. She was so glad Maggie had encouraged her to work more closely with him … for various reasons.

Then Jason perked up.

"You know Denise," he said, "we have made some serious progress on reducing the time to develop our proposals, despite my terrible coaching. Remember how our process had three steps? Step 1, my team figures out what pumps we should propose and writes the initial proposal. Step 2, the proposal goes to finance to get the price we'll quote to our customer, and Step 3, we finalize the proposal. The challenge was to do each step the same day we got the information, so three days total.

So far, we've focused on step 1. My team collected a ton of data on the current state. Then, they came up with a current process flow and a future desired process flow. They've gone through a couple of target conditions and have run a bunch of experiments. For example, they developed some creative stuff with the software group that greatly simplifies searching for information. Now, we're close to doing the first step in one day. And it's all thanks to Kata and to you Denise. So thank you. Our team members are so excited. They were certainly not engaged like this when I first joined the company. And we are about to launch our next project, reducing the time it takes to respond to requests from customers on maintenance and repair of pumps. There is a ton of low hanging fruit there."

While Jason spoke, Denise just sat there quietly taking it all in.

"Jason," she said at last, "that's fantastic. And I highly doubt you could have accomplished so much so quickly if you were a lousy coach. You underestimate yourself."

Jason turned slightly red and deflected the compliment.

"I doubt I am a good coach yet, but I owe a lot of our success so far to my team member Mary," he said. "She is so attuned to scientific thinking. It seems to be how she thinks naturally. In fact, she is my choice for the third member of our learning group.

"You know, in sales we have a very flat hierarchy," he continued. "That means I would be the only coach and coaching everyone on my team. And that would make me the bottleneck for our improvement work. I don't want to add an extra level in the org chart but maybe Mary could become a coach as well and coach others in the team."

They agreed that Denise would coach Jason who would coach Mary who would coach Denise. Whoever was not a coach or improver would quietly observe and give feedback immediately afterward. Denise had picked a personal challenge to be coached on: improving her eating habits. They had degraded horribly from the stress of her job, and, for the first time in her life, she found herself binge eating. After examining her current condition, she had derived a small target condition and Mary coached her on that.

They tried to meet daily for their learning group coaching sessions. It usually took 50 to 60 minutes to complete the three coaching cycles. That was a lot of time because, in addition, Denise had her daily coaching sessions with Mark and Joe which together usually took another 30 to 40 minutes. That meant Denise needed around 90 minutes a day for her coaching. *It's a lot, but in the long term, it's actually a good way to invest my time*, she thought, *developing my team's ability through coaching.*

After Denise had completed her sessions with Mark and Joe, she would make her way to the sales administration department to meet Mary and Jason for their learning group coaching cycles. When Denise first observed Jason coaching Mary, she had not taken notes. However, she soon noticed that without detailed notes she had a hard time giving good feedback. Precise feedback as second coach, Denise realized, required accurate observation. She made up a version of a form Maggie had shown her at the gym. It contained five horizontal rows, each one corresponding to one of the five phases of the Coaching Kata and then a column for notes on the coach and one for the improver (see Figure 17.1).

She even developed the habit of timing the duration of each phase, as David had done for her. Timekeeping forced her to pay close attention to the individual phases of the conversation. It was a good mental exercise, and it allowed her to learn how to parse the session and helped her stay focused throughout, too.

To give feedback, Denise used a structure she had learned during her time as a consultant at Francis & Drake. There were three stages for the feedback based on delivering first-person messages. She had just recently written it into her notebook (see Figure 17.2).

Observing the Coaching-Cycle		
Process:	Date:	
Coach:	Improver:	Duration:
Q 1		
Q 2		
Q 3		
Q 4		
Q 5		

FIGURE 17.1

Coaching observation form. Adapted from Mike Rother, *The Toyota Kata Practice Guide*, McGraw-Hill (New York), 2018.

<u>3 Steps for giving Feedback:</u>

1) I have observed...

2) I have the impression that...

3) From my perspective, it would be helpful...

FIGURE 17.2
3 Steps for giving Feedback.

A knock on the door of her office pulled Denise out of her thoughts. It was Jason. "Hey, how about some lunch?"

"Great idea," Denise replied, "let's go."

Scan with your mobile to find out how Denise and Jason develop deepening questions.

QR CODE 17.2
Denise and Jason develop deepening questions over lunch.

FRIDAY, MARCH 3, 10:45 AM, A FUN JAUNT TO SALES ... SHE THOUGHT

After making her daily round through assembly, and dealing with the usual fires, Denise arrived at her desk and checked her emails. David had dropped her a note apologizing that he hadn't joined her for her coaching cycles for so long. He also congratulated her on how her team's backlog had diminished. *Ah, he's seen the February reports, right, it's the beginning of March already,* Denise thought. *I was a bit concerned that our approach of small steps, experimenting and learning and coaching, would slow us down and we would not meet our objectives. I guess I have to trust the process.*

With her little self-pat on the back, she got up to meet Joe for their first coaching cycle today. Afterward, she excitedly made her way to the sales administration department to meet Mary and Jason for their learning group coaching cycles.

QR CODE 17.3
Coaching cycle with Joe.

Denise crossed the yard toward the main office building where the sales team resided. It was the newest building at Goldberg, just one year old. She admired the sleek, modern design, lots of glass and wood. She climbed a long winding stairway snaked around the open atrium at the building's center and looked up and down seeing all the floors in between. It made for a lofty feeling, but Denise could not help contrasting the pennies they worked to save in production with this expensive state-of-art building for executives and office workers. It showed something of the values of senior management. *Come to the castle of the overlords*, she thought.

Still, she secretly appreciated the high-end, automatic Swiss espresso machine on every floor. *What a difference from our pale brown seventies style drip-grind coffee makers in the production offices and meeting rooms*, Denise thought. *It's good that my team doesn't spend any time here, or even*

---

4 Questions for observing as a 2nd coach

(1) How does the conversation flow through the five phases?

(2) Where is the improver's threshold of knowledge?

(3) Where does the improver make assumptions or jumps to conclusions?

(4) Where does the conversation become unstructured?

FIGURE 17.3
Four questions for the second coach while observing a coaching cycle.

know what it's like. It would be so deflating for them. Whenever I'm here, I feel like a peasant who has snuck in.

Denise reached the level where Jason's team was located, and she could see him and Mary already standing at a storyboard. They would start with Jason coaching Mary, while Denise observed. She took out a new card she had created and wanted to test. On the card were four questions to aid her observations and Denise quickly went through them in her mind (see Figure 17.3).

When Denise arrived at the board, she greeted Mary and Jason. Jason flashed her a warm smile. "Hi Denise, great to see you," he said.

Denise was happy to see him, too, but was wary of showing it too much in this setting. She responded casually, "nice to see you too Jason."

Mary jumped in, her usual upbeat self. "Hi Denise, how are you, ready to go?"

"Yeah, let's go," she said and readied her observation record and stopwatch.

Jason looked quizzically at Denise's tools for observation but began coaching Mary.

"What's your target condition?" he asked.

Denise started her stopwatch.

"I want to reduce the time needed for processing new orders from 30 to 20 minutes," Mary replied, "Therefore, I have to reduce the time needed for entering the basic order data to 4 minutes."

"And what is the actual condition now?"

Mary pointed to the charts on her board. "At the moment," she said, "we need between 26 and 35 minutes for order processing because typing in the basic data just takes too long."

Jason ad-libbed, "What does 'too long' mean in numbers?"

Hey, cool, he's doubling down on that, Denise marveled and quickly wrote it on her form.

"The last few days were really busy," Mary said, "so I didn't remeasure the time for the step 'enter basic data' with every order. But when we measured it two weeks ago, it always took between eight and ten minutes."

Jason thought about this, but then moved on to phase 3.

"What obstacles are preventing you from reaching the target condition?" he asked.

Mary pondered for a second, then replied. "Inserting the basic data for an order is simply too complicated." She then paused to think and added, "on other occasions typing in the items ordered takes too long."

This time, instead of moving on, Jason dug deeper into the obstacles.

"And what exactly is the problem that keeps you from reaching the target condition?" Jason added.

Denise grinned to herself and took more notes. *He is stopping on red. Way to go Jason.*

Mary shrugged. "Actually," she admitted, "I don't know exactly. It varies every time because every new order is different."

Denise noticed that Mary was at her threshold of knowledge. *I wonder where Jason will go with this*, she thought.

"Well what could it be that makes the data entry take so long?" Jason persisted.

Mary cocked her head as she considered this. "I think that the whole manual entry of the data takes a lot of time and also cross checking the item numbers." She quickly added, "that could easily be automated by our IT guys, I think."

Jason paused and looked down at his card with the Coaching Kata questions using the rule of thumb, then continued.

"So what, therefore, is your next step?" he asked

Jason assumed Mary was back on track.

"I'll talk to Randy from IT and ask him to take a look," she said. "Maybe we can find a way to speed up the input by automating it."

"And what do you expect?" asked Jason.

"I expect I'll learn which steps can be automated in order processing," Mary replied.

Jason continued with the script.

"How quickly can we go and see what we've learned from taking that step?" Jason asked, the final question.

"If I get a hold of Randy today, maybe tomorrow or the day after, somebody from his team could take a look. Today is Monday. To be safe I will say, I'll have something for you by Friday," said Mary.

Jason nodded. "OK, let's write down what we just discussed."

Mary wrote down the agreed step and what she expected on her experimenting record. That completed the coaching cycle. Immediately Mary and Jason turned toward Denise who was in the middle of finishing her notes on her observation record.

After a few seconds, Jason spoke up, clearly a little impatient.

"Well you sure had a lot to write," he said. "I hope some of it was good. What do you think, how did I do?"

Feeling pressure to give Jason a grade, Denise scanned her notes.

"You did some good things, like trying your hand at some deepening questions. I made a note of that." Denise looked up and smiled. "But still you kind of skimmed over the discussion of obstacles and kept going," she blurted out, somewhat thoughtlessly. "Sure, you added a deepening question, asking Mary what she thought might make the data entry take so long, and Mary's response was vague and then she jumped to a solution – automating the process – which would take most of the week to investigate. She was at her threshold of knowledge and guessing, but you just went on reading the card. Right now, we don't know what is causing the long time for data entry, or whether automation is the solution for time reduction. I think it would be helpful to define a smaller step so you can meet again by tomorrow."

Jason looked deflated, but also seemed to be reflecting on what Denise had said.

"I noticed that too," he replied. "That was exactly the problem. Mary did not understand the process deeply enough and, therefore, did not come up with actual obstacles. Recognizing that, I tried to work out at least one obstacle, and Mary jumped to a solution. And then, the action step somehow got too big. I realized that, too, but didn't know what to do as a coach in that situation without being overly directive. As I learned from you, I wanted to be in coaching mode not telling mode."

Jason sighed and then continued. "First, I asked the question about the obstacles. Then, I recalled a tip I think you got from Maggie. You told me when their answer is too vague and I want them to focus more I should try 'repeat and add'. I took that as repeat the question but add a specific qualifier. In this case after Mary gave me a vague answer about the obstacle to the target condition I followed up with: 'and what exactly is the problem that keeps you from reaching the target condition?' Next, I tried, 'but what could it be that makes the data entry take so long?' and still Mary was not giving me more precise obstacles.

"At that point, I also had the impression that Mary was feeling cornered by my questions. I really didn't know what to do and just went to the next question on the card, asking about the next step. In other words, I agree with your feedback and you make some good points. What I don't know is what to do about it. To be honest Denise, your feedback reinforced what I had already noticed, but it's not helping me to improve."

"I understand," Denise said, feeling tense, but trying to appear calm. "For what it is worth I did make a note of your use of the repeat and add. You did that well and I agree that I still have a lot to learn when observing and giving feedback. I had good notes, but my process kind of fell apart when I was trying to figure out how to use my observations. Maybe we can discuss this over lunch and figure out what we can learn from it. How about we continue with the next coaching session?"

"Agreed," said Jason. "Let's move on."

Next, Denise coached Jason with Mary acting as second coach. Mary noted a few items for improvement, but overall Denise and Jason were both comfortable with the process and the coaching session went very smoothly.

Then, they switched roles with Mary coaching Denise about her weight loss goals. Denise had tracked her calories and eating and exercise patterns for two weeks to get her current state. This week's target condition was to cut out all junk food, and she predicted a modest 1 pound weight loss on the outcome measure. Jason did not have a lot to say as second coach since Denise answered each question precisely, and he seemed to still be mulling over her critique of his coaching. It was all a bit stilted, but there was no visible conflict.

Later, Denise and Jason were sitting in the canteen picking at their food. Both had opted for the Hawaiian-style poke bowl that was the special of the day. There was a different special every day, and it usually cost a little more than what the company covered but was a lot better than the standard options.

Sitting over their bowls, Jason picked up the conversation about his coaching session.

"You know," he said, "your feedback about what happened was spot on. The problem was that I noticed the same issues myself during the coaching cycle and, still, I struggled. Honestly, it felt like you were jumping in and attacking me as if I was unaware of what had happened. I just didn't know how to deal with it. I wanted some feedback on how to do better" Jason paused and smiled at Denise. "Sorry for pushing back in front of Mary. I know that made things worse."

Denise was relieved that Jason seemed to be relaxing and was sharing his thoughts honestly without being defensive.

"You don't have to apologize Jason. I am not real proud of how I gave feedback. This is all about learning together, including from our mistakes. What you're telling me makes me think that the feedback should address the key point of difficulty during the conversation, the coaching obstacle so to speak, and provide specific help for the coach," she said. "But I'm not sure that if I had jumped in with solutions right away that would have been helpful, and it certainly would not be acting very scientifically. Perhaps there is a way for me to open with listening instead of firing off my observations? Let's try it now. What do you think was the one big obstacle in your coaching session?"

Jason thought for a few moments.

"I think," he said at last, "that somehow, the points I was struggling with during the coaching cycle are all related. We didn't have a clear and measurable obstacle, so we couldn't define a precise next step. That, in turn, led to Mary jumping to a quick-fix technical solution, which would take a long time to test. Automating the process seems like a go-to solution in administrative work when the problem has not been thought through."

"So actually the threshold of knowledge was at question 3, the obstacles?" asked Denise.

"Exactly," Jason replied, "and at that point I should have immediately gone to asking her about her next step, to question 4, instead of continuing to drill for obstacles which only drove her to make assumptions. You taught me that at the threshold of knowledge, we go to question four, which encourages the improver to go and find out the information that is beyond their threshold of knowledge. Encouraging closer observation on Mary's part would have been the right thing to do. That was the key point in the conversation."

"You know I like what just happened here," Denise said. "I asked you about the obstacle, and you gave me your observation in your words, instead of me jumping in with my outside observation telling you what went wrong. There was no defensiveness, and your observation was richer than mine." Denise kept thinking as she stirred her bowl to mix some of the cashew nuts with the sauce and rice.

"What I found is when I encounter a problem at a phase, often the cause lies even earlier in the conversation where I skimmed over a previous phase," she said at last. "The data and the chart for the actual condition were not up-to-date today. The last measurements took place two weeks ago. Mary mentioned that. So today, you didn't have the opportunity to point out outliers and trends to help Mary identify individual obstacles and then do a more detailed analysis of these outliers. You know, my 'love at first sight' tip I shared with you the other day?"

Jason had continued eating while Denise was talking. Once he swallowed, he picked up her line of thought.

"That's right," he said. "That was another key point. Frankly, that was one that I didn't even notice. Now we have two points for the second coach to give feedback on: 'having up-to-date data' and 'taking the next step at the threshold of knowledge'. Maybe, though, that is too much for the coach to process? Maybe more effective feedback focuses on one, right? Otherwise, it will be hard for the coach to put things into practice."

Denise and Jason concluded that good feedback should ideally focus on only one point. That way the coach wouldn't be overwhelmed and would be more inspired and better able to practice. It also gave the second coach the opportunity to see if the coach was making progress on that point or was constantly struggling with the same problem – in a way, this was a kind of scientific thinking, too. The coach and second coach were only studying one area at a time.

Denise and Jason also reasoned that, if possible, the feedback should refer to the key point that came first in the conversation. In this case, the first obstacle was up-to-date data and that should have been the focus of Denise's feedback to Jason. That was the point where Jason needed to jump to question 4 and ask Mary how she could learn more about the actual condition right now. After all, the five phases of the Coaching Kata build on each other. If there was a threshold of knowledge in the foundation, things wouldn't get better later on. Denise opened her notebook to record this (see Figure 17.4).

"Having the improver come up with imprecise obstacles has happened to me quite often," Jason said, looking over at Denise's notes. "That seems to

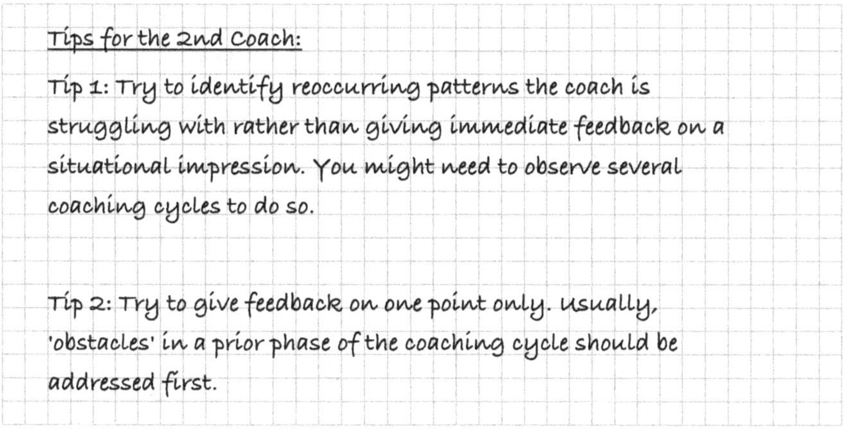

> Tips for the 2nd Coach:
>
> Tip 1: Try to identify reoccurring patterns the coach is struggling with rather than giving immediate feedback on a situational impression. You might need to observe several coaching cycles to do so.
>
> Tip 2: Try to give feedback on one point only. Usually, 'obstacles' in a prior phase of the coaching cycle should be addressed first.

FIGURE 17.4
Tips for the second coach.

be a pattern. And it's true, we regularly don't have up-to-date data. So, that is a connection I wasn't aware of. Good feedback would point out exactly what key point I should watch for in my coaching cycles and give concrete instructions on what to do as a coach. What do you think?"

"Hmm, maybe it's like this: Helpful feedback should give not only helpful advice on what to do but also name a trigger that indicates when to use the advice, thus helping the coach to recognize when to act," said Denise, building on Jason's thoughts. "That's a good trick (see Figure 17.5)."

"Let's try that for your coaching cycle we observed today," Denise continued. "I have observed that the data for the current condition was not up-to-date. I have the impression that it was, therefore, difficult to identify obstacles precisely.

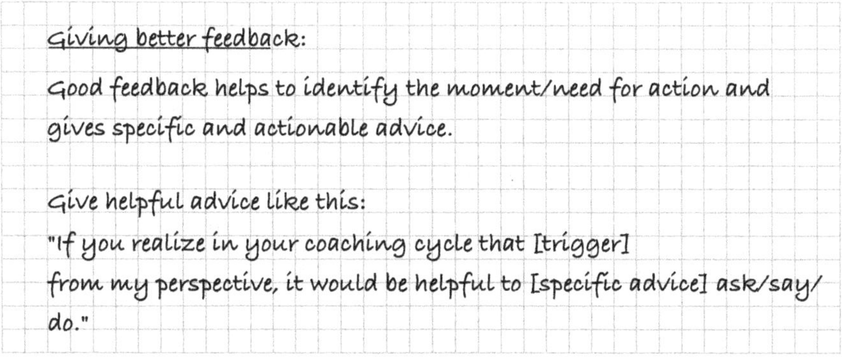

> Giving better feedback:
>
> Good feedback helps to identify the moment/need for action and gives specific and actionable advice.
>
> Give helpful advice like this:
> "If you realize in your coaching cycle that [trigger] from my perspective, it would be helpful to [specific advice] ask/say/do."

FIGURE 17.5
Giving better feedback.

"From my perspective, it would be helpful to try the following: If, in phase 2, you notice that the data on the chart for the current condition is not up to date, repeat question 2 with a time constraint like, 'what is the actual condition today?' Then, if the threshold of knowledge is uncovered, go to question 4 defining the next step such as getting up-to-date data."

"Hey, that's really helpful now," Jason replied, "that's a version of 'Repeat and Add'. I like that feedback, especially because it not only helps me with the coaching session from this morning but actually addresses a pattern I frequently struggle with. I'll share this feedback structure with Mary so we can test it in our learning group."

"Let's see if we can find a better way to give the initial feedback, too," Denise said, "to avoid situations where I fire away at you and you get defensive."

"OK, let's see," Jason replied, "how about coming up with some questions you could have asked me after the coaching cycle before you gave your feedback."

They started discussing questions and then sketching them on a napkin (see Figure 17.6).

"Wow, that's cool," Denise said with excitement. "After asking these questions, a second coach could start the feedback with something like, 'That's similar to what I put in my notes. I also noticed this. I'll try to give you some feedback on this point. Would that be okay?' That would create a totally different and open atmosphere for the feedback."

"Yes!" Jason agreed enthusiastically. "I like that."

They finished their lunch. Denise returned to her desk and reflected on everything she had learned, flipping through her notebook. She started doodling with a figure to summarize how her feedback as second coach could connect to the coach's own self-assessment (see Figure 17.7). She

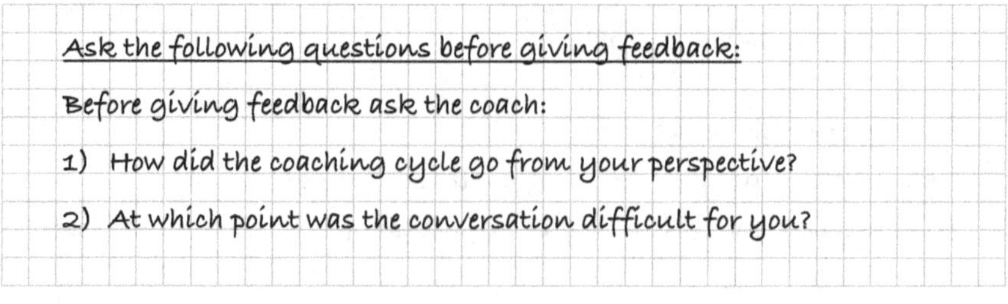

> *Ask the following questions before giving feedback:*
>
> Before giving feedback ask the coach:
>
> 1) How did the coaching cycle go from your perspective?
>
> 2) At which point was the conversation difficult for you?

FIGURE 17.6
Question for the 2nd coach to ask the coach before giving feedback.

kind of liked it. *By asking Jason for his perspective on his coaching session, I could have avoided the conflict we had. I think we resolved that conflict well and I love working with him, but I do keep hoping that at some point we can move beyond talking about coaching.*

After the start of the second shift, Denise made her way to meet Mark for their daily coaching cycle. During that coaching cycle, she discovered a better way to specify the next step. *Every coaching session is an experiment to learn from*, she reminded herself.

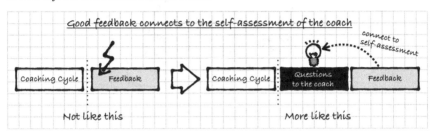

FIGURE 17.7
Good feedback connects two self-assessment.

Back in the office, she wrote down what she had learned in her notebook and also updated her card with the deepening questions. Then she finished reading and responding to her emails and called it a day. *This has been another exhausting, though productive week*, she thought when she left her office to start the weekend.

QR CODE 17.4
Denise's coaching cycle with Mark.

QR CODE 17.5
Coaching for smaller steps.

18

A Big Surprise – Twice

IT WAS FINALLY time for Denise's first semi-annual feedback meeting with David, and she was determined to make it productive. She believed she had a strong report card but hoped they could accomplish something useful. She stepped into his office. David was sitting behind his desk with papers scattered in front of him.

He was looking at the figures on the performance of the assembly department, glanced up, and said, "Please, sit down."

David was smiling, but in a somewhat guarded way. *I wonder what's going on. I thought this would be a slam dunk. I even hoped for a bit of a raise,* Denise thought.

"I was just looking at your key performance indicators, particularly on-time delivery," David began. "You killed them all. Between you and me, you made the rest of our departments look bad. Nobody came close to your performance. Congratulations," he said, as he walked around his desk and shook her hand.

Denise perked up. "Thank you, David, and especially, thank you, for all your support. I know there has been pressure, lots of it. And you stuck with me when I wanted to work on actually improving our processes, instead of papering over the problems and trying to pressure struggling people to improve productivity in a bad system. I know it got a little dicey when I learned about kata and took the time to coach Joe and Mark. I hope that you can now see the benefits."

"Actually Denise, I am not sure how much credit I deserve for supporting you," David admitted. He looked surprisingly sheepish compared to his usual confident, take-charge persona. "I was getting pretty impatient with Kata and coaching and what looked like a go-slow approach. I wanted you to grab the bull by the horns and go for quick results. More than once, I thought about pulling the plug on the Kata stuff. I was wrong. Your results proved me wrong. And I really have learned a lot from watching you coach, and even helping you on occasion, but I must admit I'm a real novice. In fact, I was hoping you could teach me more about Kata, and perhaps, together, we can spread it further than just assembly."

Denise was delighted. *Now this is more like it*, she thought. She explained to David about what was happening in Jason's sales team thanks to their learning group, how he was working to reduce the time to get quotes to customers. She was becoming increasingly excited, saying how she thought there was a big opportunity to spread scientific thinking through the company, making it a core part of their culture. She was even thinking about creating a learning group in manufacturing with David participating as part of the first triad. She found herself gushing non-stop about all the possibilities.

David seemed to be trying to listen as she went into detail about some of her ideas for how to spread the Kata, but at the same time looked distracted. His eyes kept shifting down to some document in front of him.

Denise had not noticed it at first, but he was showing definite signs of stress. *David's brow is furrowed, his mind seems to be wandering as I talk, and he looks just plain tired out.*

Finally, David interrupted her. "Denise, I really appreciate your excitement about Kata and coaching, and I fully support you on that. But there is something important I need to talk to you about, something that could change this whole company, and not in a good way.

I need this to stay strictly confidential. You probably noticed that I haven't been around much. You may recall that in one of Dick's famous memos in the middle of February, he called out the motor-fabrication department. As you know, that department does a lot of high-precision machining of components that make up the motor and we often have quality issues. You know how Dick seems to obsess over one thing at a time, and it usually leads to finding a guilty party to be the object of his wrath. Motors is his new whipping boy. By the way, around here we often refer to it with a kind of slang as 'motors." Dick is the kind of guy who acts first and thinks second, if at all. Without consulting or informing me, he asked our purchasing director to meet with the head of finance and investigate outsourcing the whole operation. He's convinced we don't have the capability inhouse to build quality components or to be cost competitive. He wants suppliers to make all the parts and then we just slap them together in assembly. No offense. That's not to say quality assembly is unimportant, but our core competence is the precision of our machining, and that is where most of our people are."

Denise was shocked. This was not what she expected from her performance review. *Dick is at it again*, she thought. *He seems to make only big-scale decisions and based on little information at that. You would have hoped that when he noticed the problem, he'd call David in for a conversation, perhaps ask him some questions. David could have investigated the current condition of the process, like I would have done through coaching. But that just isn't Dick's mindset or style. Jumping to conclusions is his default, the opposite of scientific thinking. I saw this so many times as a consultant. If you don't want to do the hard work of solving the real, underlying problems, outsource it to a subcontractor to figure it out.*

As David went into more detail, Denise became increasingly aware of how much pressure he had been under. *It must have been a nightmare. I'm not sure if I could have taken it.* Dick had a series of meetings with David and Eric Miller, who was the department manager for motors. In the last meeting Dick yelled at and threatened them, saying that either they would solve the quality issues and rescue cost at the speed of light or he would make sure motor-components were sourced from outside. Last week, Eric had cracked under the pressure and resigned.

David pulled himself together, and, suddenly, he looked like his usual confident self.

"I finally convinced Dick that his pressure tactics just aren't working," he said. "I said that we need a fair shot, or he should just outsource right away. Then, I built up an alliance of other executives to persuade Dick to at least give us a fair chance. We agreed on a not insignificant target to reduce the total cost of our motor parts fabrication by 30% within the next 3 months. That is supposedly the difference between our cost and what he could get in pricing from the outside supplier – though I have my doubts that it would actually cost that little on the outside. Suppliers often low ball then find ways to ratchet up price."

"What?" Denise exclaimed interrupting David. "That's called a fair chance? I'd assume that at least half of the cost is material-related, so reducing total cost by 30% is more like reducing our internal cost by 60%."

But before Denise could continue, she stopped herself. She was making assumptions, the opposite of scientific thinking. *Keep calm, breathe, practice Kata*, she told herself. *I haven't grasped the current condition, yet. But three months, is that possible?* Her skepticism felt overwhelming.

David took a deep breath and looked her straight in the eyes. "This is going to be the number one project for the plant over the next three months, and it will have the full attention and support of the management team. However, with Eric resigning, we need a new motors department manager to lead this initiative. There is no one better than you to do it, Denise."

Denise froze and couldn't speak. *This was the reward for doing a great job in assembly?* She could feel her heart racing and wondered if David could hear it too.

David ignored her flabbergasted expression and continued.

"Your current team is quite small," he said matter-of-factly. "You have organized pump assembly well, and the results speak for themselves. You are ready to take on more responsibility. That's what we promised you when we hired you, after all. And now, in this new role, you have the opportunity to bring your way of coaching beyond your department. You said you wanted to spread Kata throughout the plant. Here is your chance."

To Denise, it sounded like David's voice was coming from far away, dampened almost, as if she were standing under a waterfall and he were on the other side. The whole thing felt surreal. *Is this a panic attack?* She could barely hear, let alone process what he was saying. It was true that assembly was small. And yes, it was also true that she was anxious to expand the coaching approach. Taking on another department of 120 people, however, and starting off with an impossible challenge, was not quite what she had had in mind. And she only had six months of experience as a manager.

She tried to pull herself together and respond rationally.

"I'm proud of what my team has accomplished in assembly," she said. "And practicing Toyota Kata has increased my confidence that with a good team and good coaching, and time to develop people, we can accomplish seemingly impossible challenges. But I need the people I'm coaching to open up and get involved in developing new ideas. I need them to conduct experiments that might not turn out exactly as expected. Psychological safety is key to that. People don't experiment when they fear getting fired if things go differently than expected. And even though the possibility of outsourcing has not been discussed publicly, news travels fast here–the rumor mill turns just as quickly as at any other workplace. My team will know they are fighting for their livelihood. To be honest, David, it seems like I am being set up to fail and then get shown the door. I appreciate your thinking of me, but I don't think I'm ready for this."

At first David looked taken aback, like he had expected Denise to jump at the opportunity, but then, his face softened.

"I know this is going to be a rocky ride," he said gently, clearly changing his approach, "but I believe in you. I know I've been distracted and have more often than not issued demands rather than providing real commitment and support, but this really will be my top priority. I'll do everything I can to make this project a success. We need to keep motor fabrication in the plant. Otherwise, we'll be hobbling with one leg amputated. And a lot of good people will lose their jobs. I realize this is a big step up in responsibility for you, and it's coming earlier than either of us expected, but the motors team needs you now, Denise, not later. Or there may not be a later."

Denise felt her resistance weakening. David had correctly intuited that it was difficult for her to refuse a request to help people, in this case, a lot of people. She had always felt that in a leadership role you owed the ranks as much job security as possible. They did their best today to deliver quality products to the customer, and they believed management should reciprocate by making sure they still had a job tomorrow. That was the deal, or at least that was what Denise felt it should be—mutual commitment and support.

"Give me two days to think about it," she said. "OK?"

David was clearly trying to appear calm, but it was obvious to her that he wasn't happy with her answer. "Alright," he said after collecting himself. "I understand you need a little time. But Dick pressed me to come up with a name right away, and I told him you were my number one pick and that I didn't have a second. Dick agreed, but he demanded I get back to him with confirmation by the end of business today."

"Oh, come on David!" said Denise. "Now you're just passing on the pressure you're under from Dick to me. That's not your style. And, anyway, I'm pretty sure it's already way after 5 o'clock so business has ended."

David looked both anxious and a little guilty. "You're right, Denise," he said. "I do hate to pressure you like this. You know that isn't me. I realize Dick is being unreasonable, but I am backed into a corner here, and I need you to say yes. I have no plan b. Come on, please help me out."

"I'll think about it. At least give me a few hours to clear my mind. I'll text you tonight, I promise. I do want to help, especially for the sake of our people, and, if I do agree, know that I'm going to have some conditions about how we take care of them. They need to be treated with respect, unlike the way Dick is treating you and me."

David still looked desperate, but what he said next surprised and pleased Denise.

"You know, Denise," he said, sighing, "I have to say I'm impressed your focus is on how best to support the team. You're not haggling with me about money, you're asking to be able to really support your employees."

"Thanks, David."

"And I promise, it will be your show. You'll decide how to deal with your team."

MONDAY, MARCH 6 – 6:30 PM, DESPERATELY TRYING TO UNWIND

On her way home, Denise passed the stadium where the local track and field club was doing their after-work training. It was brightly lit with people scattered about, running in groups. Denise had planned to go to the gym tonight after work. Even before her performance review, she was hoping to have one of her great discussions with Maggie, but her talk with David had taken so long that she did not want to bother Maggie. At least she had her exercise clothes in the trunk. *I need to clear my mind*, she thought. *I'll go for a run around the track.*

After talking to one of the coaches and asking if it was OK for her to run a few laps, she changed discreetly in her car and began her workout. She ran and ran, attempting to think through her predicament rationally, to calm her racing mind with racing feet.

Eventually, the brisk air did begin to clear her mind, and the adrenaline and endorphins from running started to take effect too. Denise found she was feeling increasingly positive about the challenge. After 45 minutes of maintaining a good pace, she did an all-out sprint. Still panting, she stopped to stretch.

I think I'll do it. Why not? It could be a great challenge, and it's a chance to help the frontline workers. Plus, there's so much low-hanging fruit, getting quick wins should be easy. The worst thing that could happen is I'll fail, pick myself up, and find another job. That doesn't sound great, but if I say no I'm likely looking for a new job anyway. I'll ask Maggie to help me pull it off. Maybe I can convince her to come in as a paid consultant. There must be some budget allocated for this project. That could be one of my demands. Interesting that David commended me for not demanding a big raise. It had not occurred to me. Maybe I should have also thought more about myself.

Denise grabbed her bag, walked back to her car, and drove home. After a hot shower, she texted David.

"I'm in," she wrote, "but I need a few commitments from you. Number one, you and I need to communicate this to the staff together, my way, before they hear it from anyone else."

That's done, she thought, turning off her cell phone for the evening. She went to the kitchen, prepared herself a bowl of her favorite coffee yogurt and granola, sat down on the couch, and switched on *True Detective*.

When she went to bed, she felt tired but in a good way. As she faded off to sleep, she thought, *I hope I made the right decision. I'll talk to Maggie tomorrow...*

MONDAY, MARCH 6 – 11:46 PM, IT HITS THE FAN, BIG TIME!

Date: March 6, 11:46 pm
To: All Managers Plant Guilderville, David Meyers, Plant Manager Guilderville
From: Dick Murdoch
Subject: FUTURE OF MOTOR PRODUCTION
Priority: Highest
Cc: Roger Deng, Roland Palmer, Sam Watson, Pete Cheng

Managers,

The executive team has been reviewing the data on our motor fabrication. Major quality problems, cost overruns, and customer backlogs due to motor parts are an existential threat to the business. Thus far, the targets we have set have not led to any measurable improvements. To deal with this crisis, we decided to seriously examine the option of outsourcing motor production to a competent source with a competitive cost basis. Pete Cheng and his purchasing team have done a remarkable job of identifying a reliable source within a very short time.

We have made no final decisions about outsourcing, but we have set aggressive targets for improvement that must be met within the next three months. At that point, we will make a go-no-go decision on outsourcing. We need to solve the quality problems in motor design and production and reduce costs within our Guilderville operation quickly. We are providing you with an opportunity to maintain production in this plant. We believe we can succeed at this if we work as a team.

To meet the challenges of lowering cost and improving quality, effective immediately, Denise Shelsky will be promoted to take over the motor fabrication department, in addition to her duties running assembly. Denise has proven to be an exceptional manager of change in assembly, and we are confident she can straighten out our issues with motors. And if the inevitable consequence is outsourcing, Denise will help lead the transition to an outside supplier. I am placing great faith in Denise.

I am sure there is no need to explain that this project is of the utmost importance. I expect all of you to fully support Denise and her leadership to return our production to its former glory.

– Dick

Part III

Scaling Up against the Odds

Some New Faces:

Sarah Burlow, Head of Quality Management
Sam Wheeler, Team Leader, Motors
Doug Laundry, Team Leader, Motors
Betty Preston, Team Leader, Motors
Drew Bolton, Team Leader, Motors
Phil Lowe, Senior Production Engineer
Jennifer Billington, Senior Product Engineer, Motors
Randolph Cunningham, Senior Analyst, Plant Accounting
Derek Menlo, Senior Expert, Scheduling
Luther Ropes, Team Leader, Plant Logistics
Ray Diaz, Senior Expert, Purchasing
Jack Van de Berg, President of Workers' Union

19

A Confrontation, Then a Way Forward

TUESDAY, MARCH 7 – 6:00 AM, AN EXPLOSIVE START

DENISE AWOKE IN a surprisingly good mood. *Another day, another dollar. Come on Denise. Your job is so much more than that. After all, I have a chance to really save some jobs here.*

She dragged herself out of bed. After a refreshing shower, she headed to the kitchen. *This is an egg and toast day. I've certainly earned it, or I'm about to.* She started cooking two eggs over easy and cut off a few thick slices of bread from a fresh loaf she had purchased from the new bakery down the street. She popped them in the toaster. She then plopped the eggs on the toast. It all tasted wonderful, much more satisfying than her usual bowl of Cheerios ™.

Then, she decided to check her email, opening the app on her phone. It was her rule to wait to check her email until she got to her office, but she was curious to see if anything new had popped up. *Why not? Nothing could be worse than the big reveal yesterday from David.* Or so she thought. She spent minutes staring at Dick's memo in shock and thinking about what damage she could do to his car with a crow bar. Any semblance of her credibility destroyed, she charged to her car and angrily drove to work, narrowly avoiding a major accident.

On the way, she cursed David, then Dick, then herself for accepting this new role in the first place, and then back to David. And on top of violating the *one* condition she had set out in her text to David last night, Dick's memo suggested there was a high chance her efforts might fail and claimed she had already agreed to lead the outsourcing efforts. How could she possibly gain the trust of her new team now?

DOI: 10.4324/9780429347023-22

David, being plant manager, should have taken the lead on a project this crucial to the survival of the plant, Denise thought. *He thinks that's too risky and wants me to take the bullet for him. And he knew* exactly *how to get me to buy-in by emphasizing that the team needs me to keep motors inhouse and therefore keep their jobs. And that we would work together to spread Kata. He was playing me completely.*

When she arrived at Goldberg, Denise did not even stop by her office. She charged straight into David's.

"David, what kind of crap is this?" she said, pushing his door open. "I told you I wanted to tell the team first and communicate the news my way. And the first thing Dick does is send out an email to everyone. And he lies on top of it claiming I agreed to lead the outsourcing effort if we fail. Or maybe when we fail in his dreams."

She stood in front of David's desk, her hands on her hips, waiting for him to respond. He didn't stand up, instead sat in his desk chair, positioning himself behind his desk like it was a protective shield. He looked flustered, with the expression of a schoolboy who has been caught breaking a rule.

"Denise," he said as calmly as he could, "I understand you're upset. And, actually, we're in total agreement. I had no idea Dick was going to fire off that inflammatory memo, and I did tell him you insisted on handling the communication as a condition of taking the job. But," his voice had a defensive edge now, "do you actually think I have any control over Dick? We're in this mess together now. We have a common enemy and both of our futures are on the line. Let's put our heads together and figure out how we can counter this."

But Denise was still angry. She couldn't help it. She had to take out her rage on someone. and shifted into sarcasm.

"Oh, by putting our heads together, do you mean I should bail you out once again? Okay, okay, let me think. I did say I would take the job, as disagreeable as that now sounds. What could we possibly do with this mess Dick created? Maybe be honest? Yeah, honesty, that would be a novel approach around here."

There was a pause. Denise took a deep breath, and began to think and speak more calmly, though there was still an edge to her voice. "David," she said, "as I think about it, if we have any chance of digging ourselves out of this, we need to be transparent. The way forward is for you and I to have an all-hands meeting, explain the mess we are in, and plead and beg for the team to work with us to win. They need to be convinced we are on their side and our backs are against the wall, just like theirs. I guess that's where the common enemy comes in. Us and them, together, face a common enemy, senior executives, and that needs to bring us together instead of tear us apart. I really do not see any other way."

David turned his head and looked out of the window. Denise knew that what she was asking was no small thing; he could lose his job over this. Still, she did not follow his gaze. She kept her eyes fixed on him like laser beams. In the silence, Denise could hear the low hum of the machines from production. The pause began to stretch. *I'm not going to speak first. If he can't make up his mind, I'm just going to resign.*

After what seemed like minutes, David turned his gaze back on Denise.

"OK," he said, "we're both frustrated, or, let's call a spade a spade, we're both angry about Dick's email. But we can't make it unhappen, nor can we control him, so fighting with each other is not going to help. We need to direct our energy to where it is now needed to move forward."

Denise did not speak. She wanted to see where David was going.

David sighed. "You can't bail me out anyway," he said. "The responsibility for what is happening to such an essential part of the plant is with me. If we fail, it's first and foremost me that fails, especially with a new CEO coming in soon. I'm not going to make this a blame game and by the way, we don't need to. We'll make this a success. I know we can, if we work together.

"What we need to do now is focus and act because the three-month clock is already ticking. You want honesty. I want you to lead our troops because I think you are our best hope. In this situation, you are better equipped than I. What I've seen you do, having your team practice scientific thinking while you coach them, is exactly the kind of rapid experimenting to reach forward movement that we need now, though we do need to do it at an accelerated pace. We need to blast through the obstacles as quickly as possible.

"And, listen, from what you've been doing, I've seen a change in your team as well. There's a kind of comradery between you guys, a secret language you use to communicate, which I've never seen before. It's a bit like watching a special forces unit move as a squad. That's what we need now for the motor manufacturing team to succeed. Denise, please, can we work together on this?"

Denise could feel her mood shifting as David spoke. She was warming to the idea of getting in the game with David. There was a reason he had become a senior manager, after all. At the same time, she couldn't help but feel like David was manipulating her. *He just knows how to get me on the hook*, she thought, a little annoyed. But still, the opportunity of leading a 120 person team in such an endeavor drew her in like a magnet. And trying out all that she had learned about Kata under these egregious circumstances was a challenge and, she had to admit, kind of an interesting one at that.

"Your rah, rah cheerleading is certainly persuasive, David," she said at last. "But don't think I didn't notice that you didn't respond to my idea of an all-hands meeting where we tell the whole truth and nothing but the truth. What do you think about that?"

"Of course Denise," David replied, a little dismissively, Denise thought. "We'll have your meeting and we'll be honest. I'm not sure airing all our dirty laundry in front of the troops is the best way to go, but I have been wrong enough times in the past when you turned out to be right. So, we'll go with your approach, and I will go before the troops and confess the sins of senior management, even if it gets me fired."

"OK," she said, "but I'll be watching you closely. If you play a trick on me you'll regret it, badly. And that desk will not protect you," she added, faking a stern look and then cracking a smile. David smiled back.

"Great!" he said, as he instantly brightened up. "I knew I could count on you. Now, I suggest you ask your friend Maggie to help us. Maggie, that's her name, right? The ex-consultant from the gym you told me about."

Denise was surprised David had even thought of Maggie. After all, she had already mentally hired Maggie.

"You mean to bring her in as a consultant, right?" she asked.

"Yup," said David, "you'll need to do a lot of coaching, and we don't want your assembly team to fall behind. From what you've told me, Maggie seems to be an experienced Kata practitioner and coach, and she was an ace consultant, right? You might need someone sharp thinking at your side for this deployment, and my capability in Kata is still limited. Of course, there's no extra budget allocated to this project, the most important one in the company, but let me deal with that. I'll find a way to finance it. We'll pay her full fees. Just keep the hours manageable. Do you think Maggie would be up for it?"

Denise felt cheered by the fact that David had come to this idea on his own that their thinking was, at least in this way, completely aligned.

"I love the idea," she said. "I don't know if she'll accept since she got out of the consulting business long ago, but I'll ask her. We'll probably want more of her time than she is willing to give so limiting hours will not be an issue."

"Good," David replied. "Ask her as soon as possible. And let's set up an all hands with the motors team for this afternoon shift changeover, as you suggested. I'll join you and together we will explain the situation and announce your new assignment, OK?"

"OK," Denise replied, still a bit astonished by David's positive response to her fit of anger, "I'll arrange it. You speak first."

David nodded. "Great, see you then."

Denise turned around and left his office, slowly closing the door behind her. Her mind was spinning. *Was that really David in there? How could he switch on a dime from maudlin to happy cheerleader? Did I make the right decision?* Half of her wanted to run away, while the other half was thrilled by the challenge. And she really had an opportunity to save a lot of jobs here. What did she have to lose? No matter what happened she would learn a lot.

TUESDAY, MARCH 7 – 7:30 AM, A BREATH OF FRESH AIR

Denise noticed that she was still wearing her jacket because she had marched directly to David's office from the parking lot, so she decided to take a walk outside. *I need some fresh air to clear my mind.* She sat down on the bench directly outside the building. It was still early morning, but it was March and so finally the sun was starting to rise earlier each day. Thank goodness spring was just around the corner. You could almost see the buds forming on the trees, though morning frost was still the norm. This was upstate New York after all.

Better call Maggie, Denise thought. She pulled out her phone and dialed.

"Good morning," said Maggie.

Denise felt her confidence grow just from hearing Maggie's voice.

"What gives me the privilege of getting a call from you this early?" asked Maggie.

Denise explained what had happened over the last 12 hours, and Maggie listened quietly until Denise ended with her request.

"To make a long story less long," Denise said, "let me come to the bottom line, and I am hoping you will consider it. It would be awesome if you could come in and help me to develop more coaches on my team. We need to scale this thing, pronto. Of course, you should charge your full consulting rate, and add a little extra. Let's stick it to them!" Denise exclaimed with gusto.

For a few seconds, there was silence on the other end of the line, and Denise began to feel nervous. Then Maggie laughed, a warm chuckle.

"Well, you know," Maggie said, "when I left consulting, I promised myself I would never go back. But I guess this is an opportunity I can't turn down, working with you, helping save a plant and the livelihoods of so many people, and learning more about Kata. The Goldberg plant is just around the corner from the gym, and I could easily come in for a few hours several times a week. This does really sound like a fun project, especially the working with you part."

Maggie has a strange definition of fun, Denise thought.

"You know, this is really wild timing actually," Maggie continued. "Right now I'm participating in one of Tilo Schwarz's Kata-Dojo online master classes where we've all been asked to set up our own dojo. Remember how we talked about how Tilo has set up a kind of learning laboratory for practicing coaching? In Japanese karate, the place you practice is called a *dojo*, a kind of practical classroom. Practicing off the shop floor in a controlled environment allows the coach to try out techniques, and repeat them until they get it right.

The coaching dojo is ideal for developing new coaches as well as scaling effective coaching across an organization, and, as you say, I guess that is just what we need to do in your case. So, I might as well combine my assignment from Tilo with your project. I am not sure saving a plant in a crisis in three months is what he had in mind for homework, but why not?" Maggie laughed.

"I'm so glad, I mean relieved, you are willing to help," Denise managed to squeeze in, before Maggie continued, already in coaching mode.

"So, what's your target condition for this week?" Maggie asked.

"Well," Denise replied, "by the end of this week, I want to have my team set up and everybody on the same page. That is, we all have to have a common understanding of the challenges we face. And then, of course, we need to grasp the current condition. It was luxurious when I could coach Joe and Mark individually, but this is a big group and we need to go through this as one big team."

"So where are you now?" Maggie asked.

"Right at the start, I've just reconfirmed my decision with David that I'm all in."

"So, what are the obstacles?"

"Well," Denise paused, thinking for a second. "There is getting the whole department on board, which means recovering from Dick's destructive memo. But assembling and engaging my core team is number one. I don't have a proper team setup. There is no one having experience with Improvement Kata stuff, the story board and all that. And well, I don't really have a clear picture of the overall challenge. I mean, it's clear generally that we want to make the motor-parts cost competitive, delivering good quality products. But what exactly does that mean in numbers? I need to get my head around that.

"And, then, of course, the current condition is unclear, too. What are the drivers of high cost and what causes the bad quality? I need to get all these addressed this week."

"Which one are you addressing today?" asked Maggie.

"First I need to get the larger motor team on board," Denise said. "I'll start climbing out of the hole Dick put me in with David this afternoon at the all hands meeting."

"Wait a second," Maggie interrupted her. "Who exactly do you need to be on your core team?"

Well, Denise thought, *good question, as usual*. She's using the old stand on red on me – and it's working.

"I need the key leaders in the motor department, of course," Denise replied. "And everyone working in production needs to be informed about what we are trying to achieve.

"Actually, we probably need a second meeting to do that because the night shift won't be there to attend this afternoon for today's all hands."

"Don't get ahead of yourself," said Maggie. "Who do you need on your core project team, those you will coach to make all this happen?"

Ah, repeat and add, she does it so smoothly, Denise thought and pondered about Maggie's question. "OK," she said at last, "with all the quality issues we apparently have, we will need to have Sarah Burlow, head of quality management on board as well. I'll talk to her." Denise paused to think further.

"And who else would you like to have on your team to support you?" Maggie asked, filling the silence.

It was then that Denise realized that she had addressed the question about who needed to be on her team from a purely technical perspective.

"Well," she said, "ideally, I guess I'd really like to have Mark and Joe join me. They're my fellow Kata practitioners. We speak the same language and have the same mindset about how to deal with crazy stuff. So, I guess, it would be really great to have them by my side. This hasn't been announced yet, but Joe is due to get a promotion. He's going to work for Sarah in quality. He starts in the new role on April 1st. So, actually, it would be perfect to involve him in the quality-related issues with motors right from the start.

I still have to figure out who will replace him in assembly – shoot, there is so much to do. And maybe I should promote Mark to manager of assembly, or at least acting manager while I am tied up with motors. But then I would have to find two team leads for assembly."

Denise paused to catch her breath. She realized her thoughts were racing, and her mouth was struggling to keep up.

"I know what you are thinking, Maggie, don't ask" Denise said, laughing. "I suppose let's put the project team together first. I should think about how to solve the vacancies in assembly later."

Denise paused again to return her thoughts to the matter at hand: who else she might need on her new project team?

"Ok, so back to who I need on motors, I should probably have a good engineer on board, one who has a deep technical understanding of the pumps and the manufacturing equipment. I suspect we will need to really get into the weeds on this one. And sales," she added. "That will be important too. I'd really like to have Jason on the team. We need some allies in sales to stop this craziness of constantly shifting customer orders."

"And it doesn't hurt that you like him," Maggie added, laughing. "Has he taken you out for dinner yet?"

"Oh, shoot," Denise nearly jumped up. "I forgot I invited him over to my place for dinner tonight. I need to buy some stuff on the way home."

"Is that a date?" Maggie asked, still laughing.

"No, no, it's not," Denise answered defensively. "We want to discuss what we've learned from practicing Toyota Kata in his sales team and how we can spread it further throughout sales. But I really don't know what to wear. Any suggestions?"

"If you're wondering about what to wear, it's a date," Maggie stated matter-of-factly. She sighed. "Denise, come on, I'm speaking as your friend now. Don't run away from the fact that you like Jason. Don't try to avoid it by making this a business meeting. It's a date. So don't talk business. Just relax and enjoy yourself. And, you know what, that's not just Maggie your friend speaking. That's strong advice from your high-priced consultant concerned about your mental health."

"Ha, ok. But I still don't know what to wear."

"Oh, come on. Don't make this stiff and formal. You're past that with Jason. Just wear something sporty, comfortable. Be yourself. You're the prize. He needs to win you over, not the other way around," Maggie replied.

"Now, you can think some more about who should be on your team," Maggie continued. "I've checked my calendar and I can come in for the first time this Friday afternoon. I have to wrap up a few things before then, but from then on I can meet you and the team once or twice a week. So let's meet Friday, and we'll see what you have by then. Let's take it from there, ok? Enjoy your evening with Jason," Maggie added coyly, then ended the call.

Denise put her phone back in her jacket pocket, then looked down at her fingernails. *I need to get a manicure,* she thought. *I have to get an appointment. But with what's going on right now, that's not gonna happen anytime soon, I guess.* She sighed, stood up from the bench, entered the building, and made her way to the assembly department. She was not looking forward to sharing her news with her team. *Those jerks in the C-suite!* she thought. *Always making my life difficult.*

20

Denise Becomes a Motivational Speaker

TUESDAY, MARCH 7 – 7:45 AM, NEWS TRAVELS FAST

WHEN DENISE ENTERED the assembly area, she saw Joe, who was leading the morning shift, talking to one of the operators in line three. Joe waved and gave her a big smile. After he finished his conversation, he came over.

"Hey boss, congratulations on your new job," he said, looking sly. "I guess that's what they call a promotion around here."

News is spreading fast in the plant, as always, Denise thought. *The employees who were born and bred in Guilderville, like Joe, are all connected. As an outsider, you never really get to be a part of the whisper network, but it's nice that they have each other's backs.*

"Thanks," said Denise. "I see as usual you're already informed, so I don't need to bother with the details. David and I are setting up an all hands with the motor fabrication team at shift changeover today to begin to clean up the mess Dick created. I'd really appreciate it if you and Mark would join as well. Strength in numbers."

"Sure," Joe replied, nodding. "I'll text Mark to come in a bit early. I'm sure he'll be eager to hear you explain the news. And I'll bring some towels in case *it* hits the fan." Joe gave her a big encouraging smile.

Denise returned the smile, but she doubted it looked genuine. She appreciated Joe's effort to cheer her up with humor, but the truth was she was feeling extremely nervous. *Is this guy bulletproof?* she wondered. *Doesn't he see what a disaster this could be?*

Then, as though he could read her thoughts, Joe's expression turned serious.

DOI: 10.4324/9780429347023-23

"Denise," he said, "I never properly thanked you."

"For what Joe?"

"For your great coaching, of course," Joe replied. "I do a lot of joking around, but that process has really changed me. I was thinking back to all the grief I gave you when you first brought it up, how I pushed back and almost gave up. I was convinced that the way we did things was the way we did them, and there was nothing to improve."

"Oh, Joe, it's okay," said Denise.

"No, seriously, let me finish. The turning point for me was that quality issue we had where the operators were having trouble inserting the piston straight. I was so proud of myself for figuring that out, and for suggesting that they simply insert the pistons straight. A little instruction and the problem goes away. Boy, was I jumping to the wrong conclusion. After some initial observations, it was clear that it was really hard to do. When I thought about the obstacle differently, as the need to properly align the piston when it was inserted, that led to all sorts of new ideas about how that could be done. Some failed, but the solution we found in the end was so simple. I was so proud that I personally built an assist that holds the piston in place and moves up and down so it could easily be inserted properly. Now, those defects are gone. And that helped us reach our target for changeover time. It was that good old scientific thinking you always talk about ... and a little elbow grease. Now I can't stop thinking that way, and it gives me confidence we can improve many more things around here."

"Joe, you don't know how much that means to me," Denise replied, her voice full of emotion. "I've put a lot of time and effort into learning how to coach, and you have taught me so much. Hearing how you have grown is probably the best thing that has happened to me in this job. So, thank *you* Joe. I want to continue this conversation, but I need to get going and set up the meeting. And I need to take a look into the current condition of cost and quality in the motors department, so I can get at least some understanding of the damage, I mean opportunities."

"Don't mention it, boss. Oh, and you might want to talk to President Jack Van de Berg from the workers' union before the all hands. I have a feeling that might save you some trouble," he added, winking.

Good point, Denise thought and nodded. "I'll be sure to do that," she said. "Thanks for pointing that out. You're my guy."

TUESDAY, MARCH 7 – 2:00 PM, THE BIG MEETING

At 2:00 pm, two shifts of the motor fabrication team gathered in the goods-entry area where the inbound trucks full of materials were unloaded, right next to the motors department. As it was shift changeover time, no trucks were currently arriving, so the area was mostly empty with just a few pallets and large boxes standing around waiting to be picked up by the logistics team.

There must be close to 100 people, Denise guessed. *I wonder if some of the night shift team came in just to hear what's going on.* People were standing together tightly packed, and a constant murmuring filled the air. They seemed concerned, and a bit angry.

So much for Dick's managers-only email. The news has obviously spread, just like I knew it would.

David took hold of a microphone and stepped up to speak, and everyone went quiet. His voice calm, he explained the situation and the three-month challenge that had been set. He spoke about his decision to get Denise involved, emphasizing why they all needed Denise's leadership and how fortunate they all were that she agreed to the expanded role. He also made it clear that for both he and Denise this was personal and that they were committed to keeping motor production inhouse.

Denise was impressed. *David is usually a good speaker, but this is a tough thing to communicate, and Dick's email hasn't made it any easier. People are afraid, and the goal of cutting costs by 30% is obviously daunting.*

David pointed to past success stories, mentioning people who had contributed to these efforts by name and giving them a nod as he spoke. But the fire wouldn't spark. The crowd was still restless, and the murmuring continued.

At least he's made it clear that he'll go all in to make this work, Denise thought. *That's probably as far as we can get right now.*

"We all owe a debt of gratitude to Denise Shelsky," David was saying. "She has the full backing of the management team and I have the utmost confidence in her. I'm sure that if we all pull in the same direction, we'll come out of this stronger than before. I just want to say that this, uhh, decision by senior management was as big a surprise to Denise as it was to all of you. And her first requirement when she took the job was she wanted to talk to you herself before any memos were fired off by others. But unfortunately the memo is out, and so Denise's first response was we need to talk to you all and be completely transparent. And, I want you to know that she said she would take the job only to help save your jobs."

With that David was done. Nobody clapped. The room was all silence and staring. David invited Denise up to the microphone.

As Denise stepped forward, she grabbed the mic and got the thrill sound of feedback. She thought that only happened in movies. She looked a bit nervous as all eyes shifted toward her. She was glad Joe and Mark were standing just a few feet behind her.

"You've got this," Mark had whispered.

Now, Denise could see Sarah Burlow, head of quality management, standing in the back of the room, toward the left, and giving her an encouraging nod. Denise had spoken to her this morning and asked for her support and participation in the project team. Sarah had wholeheartedly agreed. Denise also saw Ray Diaz from the purchasing team who led the project screening for alternative motor suppliers nestled in the crowd. She had also spoken with him, and, like Sarah, he had been very supportive. Purchasing wouldn't let them fake any improvement numbers, but they would be fully transparent on data about competitive cost and quality.

Jack Van de Berg from the workers' union and his deputies were also there. At least Jack wasn't scowling too much. *Glad I talked to him before this*, Denise thought. He had been furious at first. And, of course, he had been hard charging; he had to be. That was his task as an elected representative. But he was also smart and practical. So, when Denise had shown him the numbers, he understood they were in trouble – deep trouble. Jack had made it clear that he would watch her every move for fairness.

"My people are not going to pay for management mistakes," he had said several times.

Denise took a deep breath and began.

"Hi, I'm Denise, the new kid, and I am very glad you're all here. This is further proof of the Guilderville plant spirit I've witnessed since my first day on the job. It's a spirit of engagement and pride. Pride in workmanship. And it's fully earned. The ingenuity and effort you put into your work surpass anything I've seen at other companies.

"Look, I'm angry as hell and I'm sure you are too," she said. Denise paused, and there was some murmuring from the crowd, her words still echoing throughout the large space. She pulled out a printout of Dick's email and started reading verbatim. "Major quality problems, cost overruns, and customer backlogs in motors are an existential threat to the business. Thus far, the targets we have set have not led to any measurable improvements. To deal with this crisis, we decided to seriously examine the option of outsourcing motor production to a competent source with a competitive cost basis."

"Ahh … this is so wrong," Denise said, looking up, "and I know we're better than that. Now, don't get me wrong, from the numbers David has shared, it's clear we have a problem. But it's not the people, it's the processes. And it's poor management, starting at the very top. And that makes me confident we can do much better. Some of you might think, 'it's not our fault,' and I kind of feel that way, too. But you know what? It doesn't matter whose fault it is. Look around," Denise paused and waved her hand toward the motor production area.

"Boxes stacked up to the ceiling. And then, look at all the scrap boxes," Denise pointed to a long line of large red boxes at the far end of the wall. "Overflowing every day. Is this an environment you love working in?" she asked, then paused. Nobody said anything, but they did look like they were listening intently.

"When you go home every day, do you feel proud of your place of work?" Denise asked and paused again. She could see some were starting to shake their heads no.

"So then do you want to keep on working like this?" she continued.

More people started shaking their heads.

Denise went on. "And do you want to wait for others to come around to clean up your processes?"

"Damn it, no," shouted someone from the back. It was Sam Wheeler, one of the team leaders from the motor manufacturing team. He was a sturdy athletic guy, one of the tallest in the plant. Denise noticed that even Sam seemed surprised that he had spoken out loud and that everyone was now looking at him.

Denise flashed him a bright smile.

"Exactly Sam," she said. "'Damn it, no!' We're gonna do it ourselves because we live with these processes every day and they belong to us. Nobody else is going to mess with our processes."

Denise saw several others nod.

"And we're going to prove all these critics wrong," she continued. "To be honest I never signed up for this. And this memo," she said waving it in the air, "seems to suggest that we might fail and that they are ready and willing to pull the rug right out from under us, without a second thought. But listen, I don't for a second believe they really understand the problems or understand what we are capable of. They are happy to sit in their ivory tower and investigate alternatives. No offense Ray. I realize you were simply following orders and providing options. And we're happy to have purchasing on our team. We will need you.

"We do not have any ivory tower to sit in. We are smack in the middle of reality. Over the next three days my project team will work to understand exactly what currently stifles our processes. We will be coming around to tap into your deep knowledge of the situation. And likewise, you can ask me about what's going on at any time. I am committed to giving you the unvarnished truth.

"Now, as David pointed out we can't promise a job guarantee, but what I can promise is that there will be full transparency on where we are and what needs to be done. We will hold monthly all hands like this to keep you updated. And, no one that joins in getting things done will be left behind if I have anything to say about it. I will be fighting for you every day.

"By the way," Denise said and she waved the memo around again, "I never agreed to lead the team to shift production overseas. I would resign first, but I'm confident that I won't have to. I'll do it all and more to make this a success, and I am counting on each of you to do the same."

There was no cheering, but when Joe and Mark started to clap, most at least half-heartedly joined in.

With that, the meeting was over. People started to file back to their workplaces. Those at the end of their shift either stood together in groups or made their way to the locker rooms. A few looked up at her and gave a friendly nod. David gave her a big thumbs-up, as he left the floor.

Denise saw Jason at the far end and was very happy to see he had joined the meeting. He gave her two thumbs-up. *Gosh, I'm really looking forward to our dinner,* Denise thought, feeling desperate for a good end to the day.

Denise walked back to her office in assembly with Mark and Joe. Mark gave her a friendly clap on the shoulder.

"Well done boss," he said. "You really put your heart into it. I didn't know you were the motivational speaker type."

"I didn't know either, and I would rather never do it again," Denise said quietly, starting to feel exhausted as her adrenaline level dropped. "But I still need to repeat this with David for the nightshift."

She spent the rest of the day preparing for her first meeting with the project team the following morning. The core team she finally assembled consisted of the four team leaders from the motor department—Sam Wheeler, Doug Laundry, Betty Preston, and Drew Bolton—Luther Ropes from logistics, Ray Diaz from purchasing, Derek Menlo from scheduling, and Sarah Burlow head of quality management. And then there were some ex-officio members not expected to participate in everything like Phil Lowe who was an engineering expert on the manufacturing processes and Jennifer Billington who was an all-around expert on motors and machining and, of course, Jason. And she was so thankful Joe would be part of the effort in his role in Sarah's group, though not officially in the core group.

Denise had asked her core members to empty their calendars for the next two days so they could grasp the current condition. She wanted to do it as a team workshop, all hands on deck.

At 5:30 pm, she looked at her watch, then leaped out of her chair. *Oh no, I need to get going. Jason is coming at 7, and I still need to get the chickpeas and tahini for the hummus. And I need some cilantro too. And I desperately need a shower after this day, even if I can't get my nails done and wear a drop-dead gorgeous outfit*, she thought, hastily making her way to the parking lot.

In the end she just made it. She bought all the stuff she needed, had a shower, put on fresh jeans and her favorite polo, prepared the food, and had just finished setting the table, when Jason knocked on the door.

21

Preparing for Launch Day

WEDNESDAY, MARCH 8 – 6:05 AM, STARTING ON A HIGH NOTE

DENISE WAS DRIVING to work early as usual. *This is going to be a long day*, she thought. Nevertheless, she was happy. The evening with Jason last night had been perfect. As Maggie suggested, that is demanded, they did not talk work. Their conversation had been profound, even philosophical, and Denise realized how much they complemented each other in their ways of thinking – different, but together. They had enjoyed some good wine with dinner, the bottle she kept for special occasions. Unfortunately, they had to cut the evening short so she could go back to the plant for the all hands with the nightshift.

When Jason got up to leave, Denise followed him to the hallway and helped him into his blue Canadian Goose-down coat. Jason slid his arm into the second sleeve, swung around, and hugged Denise. Then they kissed. Denise couldn't remember who had started it. But it was a nice long kiss, their first. Finally, Jason pulled back.

"Good night, I'll see you tomorrow," he had whispered and then left. Denise had quietly closed the door of her apartment behind him. *It was a date after all. Who knew? Maggie, I guess.*

She was up half the night with the all hands, but driving in her car now she felt like she was on top of the world. Everything felt lighter this morning. Even the massive challenge she now had to conquer with the motor manufacturing team seemed manageable. She was excited and eager to get going.

The next two days would be filled with grasping the current condition of the process of manufacturing motor components to be later assembled. Diving into the thick of it sure beat memos and verbal sparring. She had set up these next few days as a full-time, hands-on workshop with her new

DOI: 10.4324/9780429347023-24

team. Thinking about Rother's book and what she knew about Toyota Kata, she wasn't sure if that approach involved intensive, several-day workshops like this. But Denise wanted everyone on the team to see things on the shop floor firsthand and discuss what they saw. The only way she could see of getting them together for enough time to really dissect what was happening was to block off days to do this and nothing else. And besides, this needed to be Kata on steroids.

She had led more workshops than she could count as a consultant, but this was different. In those days, they did a quick analysis of the current state, brainstormed a bunch of improvement ideas, and then went to work implementing as much as they could. What was left over went on a homework list. It was not very scientific – *We did not know what individual impact any of the changes had, we did not learn anything from one experiment that would inform another, and we left the people at the frontline confused about what they were supposed to do with all these new procedures they did not understand.*

This workshop was all about planning and getting them set up so they could go to work. It was a quick launch of Kata and they needed an intensive dose of reality. Or not just a dose, but to fully immerse themselves into what was going on. *That's how we'll find the leaders we need to make a difference fast. We don't have time for lectures, or sharing superficial impressions in a conference room. We need to get to the meat right away,* Denise thought.

Then her thoughts shifted to her assembly team and especially to Mark and Joe. They would also have to step up their game. *Mark needs to run the department now, with David's support. I won't have time to do my old job in assembly, and Joe will be busy in quality, supporting me. I think I can get David to go to all the boring management meetings and play some of the politics for them, but Mark will have to lead the daily management work.*

Then Denise thought about Joe's upcoming promotion to a group leader in quality management reporting to Sarah. *Joe may be right where we need him. We really have some serious quality issues.* Denise remembered checking the warranty data yesterday. So many motor defects slipped through to the customer, way too many. *We have to stop that, and I'm glad I'll have Joe by my side to tackle it. Maybe we should get him to start digging in right away.* She made a mental note to talk to Sarah.

That'll create a hole in my assembly team, though. Hmm. Oh, how about Josh? He got the hang of Toyota Kata quicker than anyone else and has become a very practical scientific thinker. I think he's ready to take on more responsibility. He could fill Joe's place as team leader.

And Mark can have a shot at the department manager role, or at least a group leader position. He has the experience, is good with people, and while he was skeptical at first, he's now all-in on working toward his next target condition and running quick experiments. He'll probably try to back out because he's afraid of stepping on the battlefield of upper management politics. But David and I, mostly David, can dodge the bullets from above and outside.

I need to somehow squeeze in talking with David, Mark, Sarah, Joe, and Josh about all this today. And I need to talk to Sarah about Joe starting on my team immediately. Denise used the voice command on her phone to dial Sarah.

She spoke with Sarah who could not have been more supportive. Somehow talking to women often seemed easier than to men; there was less ego involved for the most part. Sarah had agreed to assign Joe full-time to Denise's team immediately, and Denise would speak to him later today.

With Mark hopefully becoming department manager and Josh moving to team leader, that still left one team leader slot empty in assembly. A light bulb switched on in Denise's mind. *Perhaps I could move someone from the motor department to assembly. We need to reduce costs quickly and that first and foremost includes the cost of personnel.* Denise remembered checking the numbers yesterday. They looked grueling. *And whoever I move can learn a lot from Mark and Josh about Kata—more cross-fertilization.*

Denise's thoughts were bouncing all over the place, and she thought about all the positions they would lose in motors as they became more productive. But when they improved manufacturing and uncorked the bottlenecks, more motors would flow, and there would be even more work in assembly. She guesstimated that at that point assembly would need as many as five or six new team members, personnel she could move over from motors. Even that wouldn't be nearly enough to save all the jobs she wanted to save.

I'll talk with David. That's what he needs to bring to the party. We have to create new work outside the motor team so we can retain good people. If the new products don't make up for that, maybe we could insource rather than rely on suppliers. That would be ironic. Just the opposite of what Dick has in mind. Nice!

WEDNESDAY, MARCH 8 – 6:45 AM, PREPARING FOR THE BEST WORKSHOP EVER

The first thing Denise did when she arrived at her desk was open her laptop and print some spreadsheets she had put together. She had gathered all the data she could get about motor manufacturing and condensed it into several reports and charts. She had also set up a meeting with David for 7:00 am today. She wanted to clarify and agree on the challenge with him before she met with the workshop team at 8:30 am to kick off the current state analysis.

While the printer was warming up, Denise poured herself a coffee from the machine just outside her cubicle. Sipping on the somehow always stale brew with a grimace, Denise ran through her mental list of topics she wanted to discuss with David. Besides the challenge, she also wanted to discuss his role in leading assembly with Mark.

The printer finished churning out pages, so Denise grabbed the pile, threw her still partially filled paper cup into the trash next to the printer, and made her way to David's office. When she arrived, David was standing at a whiteboard at one side of the office. He was wearing jeans and a white shirt. He hadn't put on his clunky safety boots yet and was wearing yet another pair of shiny brown, Italian shoes. *He must have quite a collection of shoes, and most of them are really classy ... and expensive.*

"Good morning Denise, good to see you," David said, looking over his shoulder while he finished what he was writing on the whiteboard. He seemed refreshed and ready for action. *How can he be like this with all the pressure and political maneuvering?* Denise wondered. *Probably, he's become hardened to it. I doubt I could ever be.*

"Hi David, good to see you too," Denise replied. "Can we talk about the challenge for the motor manufacturing project? And afterward, I'd also like to discuss the team setup and some changes I need to make regarding my assembly team."

"Sure, let's go," David replied, turning fully toward her.

"OK," Denise fired. "So, what's the challenge?"

"Well, as you know Dick wants us to reduce the cost of the motors by 30% in three months," David replied, continuing to smile.

Denise took a deep breath. "I did hear that," she began, "but as I told you when we first talked about the project on Monday, that's more like cutting internal costs by 60% because a huge part of manufacturing cost for our motors is material. I checked the details yesterday and actually, it's 54% material, to be precise. And reducing internal costs by 60% within three months is simply impossible, it would be unlikely even if we had three years. I've gone over the numbers and with the high depreciation cost of the new fancy equipment, and the fact that we get practically nothing for inventory reduction, we would have to eliminate almost all manual labor. It would be interesting to see the components move to the right machines and build themselves, like Fantasia where the magic spell makes the mops, brooms, and sponges clean up on their own."

David looked at her intently. "Hey," he said, "that's not like you giving up before we've even started, and I have the feeling you're getting ahead of yourself. I have some ideas about how we can work this out, but why don't we look at the data you've brought first? Let's grasp the current condition before we jump to conclusions. Isn't that what you always say?" David added with a teasing smile.

He's right, Denise thought. *We should practice Improvement Kata at all levels. Good catch David.*

"You're right," she said. "Let's do it."

Denise hung her reports onto another whiteboard. They worked through her analysis step by step, with David asking questions and probing the conclusions Denise had drawn.

After a while, three main drivers of cost emerged. One clearly was labor costs, heightened by low productivity. The second one was rework- and scrap-related costs. *I bet these two also influence each other*, Denise thought. With all the chaos and bad quality, productivity had plummeted.

The third driver was connected with material, which was actually driven by the design of the motor. Not only were the precision parts used for the newer motors very expensive, but the precision required complex automated machines that were constantly breaking down, reducing productivity big time.

Overall they ended up with three main issues for the challenge. Denise started writing on the whiteboard and tried to put it into the familiar sentence structure.

"Wouldn't it be great if we could reduce the cost per motor by 30%? Therefore we have to increase productivity, reduce the cost of bad quality, and reduce the cost of materials."

Then, they went through the figures again to attach numbers to each of the three aspects of the challenge.

"These are still all percentages, though," Denise said when they were done with their calculations.

"Yes," David said, nodding, "We should have absolute numbers here. I'll get Randolph from accounting to join your team. He'll help you with that. It'll be good to have him on, anyway. He'll add legitimacy to the numbers. No one will question their accuracy."

Overall, the improvement they needed had to come about evenly from each of the three aspects: about ⅓ from improving productivity, about ⅓ from improving quality, and about another ⅓ from engineering design to reduce material cost.

"That still is a 30% increase in labor productivity and that means we definitely have to reduce headcount," Denise said, verbalizing her internal monologue. "And I don't want to lay off people. That's going to create fear and will not help us to get the improvement we need, not to mention the union reaction."

David looked at her sternly. "Denise," he said, "you know the cost for the motors will only decrease if we get the headcount down. We have several options we can move people to within the plant. Assembly needs more staff, and so does electronics. However, there will be a number of people we will have to let go. Otherwise, we won't succeed in keeping motors inhouse, and they will all lose their jobs. Just like you said to the team yesterday, nobody joining the improvement effort will be left behind. But I doubt that will be 100%, and we can't let those who don't engage affect everyone else. That's part of our job as managers as well. Besides, I have a suspicion that as we start to make a lot of change some people will be happy to leave, perhaps with a severance sweetener."

Denise looked down silently, gathering herself. *Breathe deeply* she told herself. David waited patiently. Denise pursed her lips. Then she nodded.

"I see your point," she said, "but I think we can do better than just ushering the extra headcount out the door. I am doing more than my share keeping assembly going, and leading the charge to save motors. I need something from you. Take on the challenge of finding work for the displaced people. I do not know what the answer is, insourcing work, finding new business, outplacement. I do know I need you to commit to working on this."

David hesitated, looking thoughtful.

"Look, Denise," he said, his voice full of empathy, "I care deeply about these people too. You realize there is a limit to what I can do to bring additional business inhouse in three months. But I will commit to investigating it thoroughly. I will get together with purchasing and human resources first thing tomorrow to get started. I will even try your Kata approach to work toward a challenge."

Denise was taken aback, in a good way.

"Thanks David," she said. "I mean it. That will really help me focus on our challenge.

"I guess the quality-related costs are where we can show the quickest impact," she continued. "And there are certainly labor productivity opportunities. On the other hand, I do not see how engineering can redesign the motors and specify new materials through purchasing in three months. Without that we are screwed," she said, feeling her blood pressure rising.

"I agree," David replied, "but not that we are screwed. I agree that your first focus should be on quality issues. Improving that will free us from the nasty customer complaints and of course reduce the bleeding on the cost side. In the meantime, I'm still not giving up on a redesign by engineering that would cut costs. Now, if in three months we've got quality under control and the related cost down, productivity up by 30%, even if the headcount is not reduced but used for increasing output, we will prove what we and the team can accomplish. Then if we have a sound plan, to reduce the material and design-related costs, I think I can talk executive staff into accepting it. And, between you and me, with Alexander Aspen coming in as CEO on May 1, I am pretty confident things are going to change around here quite a bit, for the better. I never said that by the way," he added with a sly smile. "That I'm playing a bit of a waiting game here – or at least hoping to run out the clock on Dick's absolute power."

"OK, So, we are in agreement on the challenge. Want to talk about the team setup?" David said, efficiently moving on to the next topic.

"Sure," Denise replied. She walked David through her thinking about the roles in her assembly team, with Joe moving to Sarah's team and Josh stepping up as his successor. "And then I thought Mark should have a shot at managing the department. I think he is capable, but he will need your help in running interference in some of the management meetings. Then we will need another team leader…."

David interrupted her. "I think you're putting too much focus on your old team," he said. "They are experienced guys, and they know how to run assembly. Why don't you keep Joe in his role for another three months? He can move to Sarah's team then. Right now I need you to focus on motors. You've coached Mark and Joe a lot and now they can show what they're worth."

Denise tensed. *That's the old David back. Why can't he see that developing people is an ongoing process? It never ends. And we need to give people room to grow. If I hold back Joe now he'll look for new challenges elsewhere, likely outside the plant.*

Suddenly she remembered what Maggie had told her in their call the day before. "Make sure David supports you properly. You need to feel free to fully focus on the new project." Denise felt inspired. She gathered all her courage.

"David," she said firmly, "you're right. I need to focus fully on this project. It's just too important for the plant. But there are things I need from you, things that are frankly non-negotiable."

David gave her a surprised look, clearly taken aback by her directness and the change in the tenor of the conversation.

"Okay," he said slowly. "I did say I would give you full support and I meant it. What do you need?"

"I need the new David, not the old David. I need the David that is forward-looking and values developing our people, in case we actually get through this.

"So, first, quality is number one and I need Joe to lead that. I promised him the promotion to quality and we worked it all out with Sarah. He deserves it and I need his Kata expertise on the motors project.

"Second, I need Mark to take over my assembly team. He'll be hesitant, but we can start by making it an acting position due to my new role. I need to trust that assembly is well-managed, and for my people to continue to grow. I also have some ideas for back-filling on the team leader roles in assembly, including a transfer from the motor department."

Denise took a deep breath. "One more thing," she said. "You are 100% correct that I need to fully focus on this project, so in his new role, Mark will report to you. You can then run interference in attending all the management meetings. This will also give you an opportunity to practice your coaching. Didn't you tell me you wanted to do more of that?"

Denise paused. She could feel her heart beating faster. She braced herself for David's reaction. She had never been this direct, even domineering, with a boss before.

Then David started laughing. "Denise, Denise," he said. "What a move. I didn't expect that from you. You really have grown in your leadership. This is an unconventional way to force your boss into getting his hands dirty. But I believe there is a difference between aggressiveness and assertiveness. And you are asserting yourself for the good of this company and our people. How can I criticize that? In fact, I'm proud of you. I agree to all your, uhh, demands. But just to be sure, don't you want to keep the assembly seat open for yourself so you can return if the project doesn't fully succeed?"

"No," Denise stated bluntly. "I don't need to, and I don't want to. This will be a success. Or, I'm gone anyway, hopefully with your recommendation. But I expect to succeed and move up beyond managing assembly."

"OK, OK," David said, still smiling. "I just wanted to be sure. Anything else?"

Denise thought for a second, then shook her head.

"No," she said. "I better get going. I need to talk to the assembly team, and then we kick off grasping the current condition with the project team at 8:30."

"Sure, keep me updated. I'll talk with Mark as soon as you give me the green light."

Denise walked out of David's office and made her way back to assembly. *Well, I spoke my mind and didn't get fired. I have to admit David's a trooper.*

Meanwhile, Denise had a workshop to prepare for, perhaps the most important one of her career. She had a rough plan for the two days. She needed to parse what was happening in motors, boil it down to a few high-impact focus areas, get teams assigned to each of these, and then agree on a specific, measurable three-month challenge for each which would add up to the overall challenge she needed to accomplish to save the plant. And yet, before that work could even begin, she had to talk to Joe.

WEDNESDAY, MARCH 8 – 7:45 AM, GETTING A TRUSTED ALLY ON BOARD

"Joe, I need you as an ally on the quality side," Denise said.

She had asked Joe to join her for another terrible coffee, and then, cups in hand, they had moved into her office to talk in semi-private. *Good thing he has not tried the great coffee in the executive castle*, she thought.

"I spoke with David and with Sarah, and your promotion is a go," Denise continued. "Also, Sarah agreed to assign you full-time to my motors team. She will give us full support and join our team meetings as well, of course. That way you'll move into your new role quickly, and I can continue coaching you."

Denise thought Joe would be delighted by the news, but to her surprise, he was shaking his head and seemed conflicted about something.

"What's on your mind?" she asked.

"Well, it feels like the right move, and I've always wanted more responsibility. But now that it's here it also feels like a loss. I'm leaving my teammates in assembly behind. I had planned the next three weeks as a kind of phaseout, now it feels more like a parachute jump. Woosh, I'm gone."

Denise nodded.

"I understand, Joe," she said. "But the thing is, no matter how much time you spend transitioning, the end result is always the same. You're gone, and your team keeps going." She paused, looked him straight in the eye, and smiled. "They understand this project is critical to all their futures. They've run the show without you when you were, say, out on vacation, right? So, don't worry, they'll be fine."

"You're probably right," said Joe, nodding slowly. "I should move on. It's just been such a long time. It feels like I've been with the assembly team forever – we're like family. But I'm not gonna get sentimental. I'll do it. And I am glad I can continue to learn from you."

"Great," Denise replied with a warm smile. "I knew I could count on you. Our first priority for getting cost down is to improve first-time quality. It will take all the problem-solving skills you can muster."

Joe frowned again. "There's one more thing that concerns me," he said. "How about my coaching skills? We planned for me to do some coaching over the next few weeks here in assembly with you acting as my second coach. That would have prepared me for my new role where I would like to coach my new team just like you coached Mark and me. What now?"

Denise thought for a second. "Well," she replied at last, "I guess we'll find a way to get you up and running. We are going into fresh powder, to use a skiing saying. Nobody in motors knows anything about Kata. There should be plenty of opportunities. In fact, Sarah is really interested in Toyota Kata and asked me if I could coach her. You could join those coaching sessions as an observer and likewise Sarah could observe when I coach you. After a while we could switch to you two coaching each other with me acting as your second coach, just like I did with Jason and Mary in sales," she said.

"No way!" Joe exclaimed. "Having her watch you coach me is tough enough. You want me to coach my new boss – never!"

Denise started laughing.

"I guess it's a little outside of the norms around here to teach your boss something. But, in this case, you have a lot to offer her. And Sarah is one of the good ones. She wants to learn this, and she'll appreciate your experience with Kata."

Joe still looked concerned, but his face was beginning to brighten.

"Hmm, I just got a promotion and now you want me to coach my boss. But one step at a time, I guess. I just won't think about it now. I've got enough to worry about. Though I guess I did have to train you when you came here all green out of consulting," he added with a little gleam in his eye.

There was the old Joe humor Denise had come to rely on. She smiled encouragingly.

"Great," Denise said. "I'll tell Sarah and she'll get in touch with you about getting started in her team. We'll take next Monday as the official start day. Oh, and don't forget to join the project team kick-off meeting at 8:30 this morning."

Joe nodded. Then he turned around and left.

He still seems unsure, the opposite of a go-getter angling for promotion, Denise thought. *I'm so used to advising and teaching people who are on a fast track to promotion from my consulting days that it just seems normal to me. But Joe was raised in this traditional hierarchy... I need to work on putting myself in the place of others and showing real empathy. That's the only way to get the best out of people.*

22

At Last: Grasping Current Condition

WEDNESDAY, MARCH 8 – 8:10 AM, FINALLY, OFF TO THE WORKSHOP

DENISE LOOKED ON her watch, 8:10, just 20 minutes to go. She needed to get ready for the project team kickoff. And she needed to talk to Mark about his new role. That would have to wait until her lunch break. *Good thing I stashed some low-carb protein bars in my desk drawer,* she thought.

She texted Mark asking him to meet with her at noon. Then she grabbed the documents she had prepared for the workshop, pulled some markers out of one of her drawers, and made her way to the newly assigned project room that she had reserved indefinitely. *It's surprisingly large, Denise noticed. That will be good because this is going to be a working room, not a sitting room. We need to make things visual,* she thought. *The storyboards will help with that. And it's good for the suits to be able to look over all the information in the conference room and feel as close to the factory floor as they ever seem to want to get.*

The meeting room was empty. There were still 10 minutes to go. Denise turned on the lights and started to set up everything for the first meeting. There was an old yellowed rectangular table in the middle that would block free movement around the room. That would have to go, but for now she would make due. *Why do meeting rooms always smell so stale?* She positioned two flip charts at the front of the room and used sticky tape to hang up the graphs and spreadsheets she had brought on the wall at the front. Then she turned on the projector and hooked up her laptop.

By that point, group members were beginning to arrive one by one, looking a bit hesitant as they entered. Denise welcomed each one. When everyone had arrived, she opened the meeting with a brief warm-up exercise so that everyone shared a little about their background and

DOI: 10.4324/9780429347023-25

favorite activity outside work. Then she asked each participant to share the reason they were committed to helping to keep motors inhouse.

Denise felt a bit overwhelmed by her team members' emotional stories about why the company was important to them. They talked about all the hard-working competent people who were in machining – saving their jobs was a common rallying cry. Two spoke teary eyed of their families and the generations who had lived in Guilderville, and how shutting down motors could mean they would have to move.

The only real downer was when Randolph from accounting spoke up. "I want to make sure we have the correct numbers so we can make good decisions about the future here," he said, then noticed the glares from every corner of the room. "But, of course I'm happy if they point our way," he added meekly.

"Randolph, I'm glad to have you on the team," Denise replied. "We need solid numbers to know what to work on and, of course, to prove our success. You're a vital member of the team," she said with a big smile.

Denise then summarized the meeting she had had with David.

"The marching orders are clear. The challenge from top management has been issued. I have written it up here on the board as David phrased it. It includes three main drivers he and I discussed based on some preliminary data." Denise then turned to read from the board. "Wouldn't it be great," she said, "if we could reduce the cost per motor by 30%? Therefore we have to increase productivity, reduce the cost of bad quality, and reduce the cost of materials.

"I am sure we will do some refining of the areas of focus. But that comes later, after we deep dive into understanding what is going on in motors today."

Denise went on to explain how they were going to grasp the current condition by walking the shop floor. Before they left the conference room, she showed them a simple version of value-stream mapping. She realized that few people in the room had experience with the method so kept the explanation to just two symbols.

She explained as she drew on the white board. "Let's keep it simple. As we walk the floor make a square for each process step and write in it the name of the process, like machine xx. Below that you can write in any relevant data, like machine cycle time, uptime, percent defects. And between processes draw a triangle and write in the amount of inventory, for example, 30 pieces. You then connect the dots with arrows between steps so it looks like a process flow. That's it. Any questions about this?

"Ah, that's like the block diagram we made for steps in our office processes," Jason, who now felt like a Kata pro, chimed in.

"Reminds me of the flowcharts we do for software," Jennifer Billington from engineering added.

Denise was pleased several people could relate the mapping to something they had experienced. "OK, everyone grab a clipboard, a scratchpad, and a pencil and let's go," she said.

The group left the conference room and set out in formation like a flock of geese.

Denise had preselected two types of motors they could use to follow through production step by step. They began with the first, following its production backward from shipping to assembly, or upstream as Denise liked to call it. Starting with the finished product was what Rother recommended in his book about mapping value streams. This way you could see the finished products and then see how they built up each of its parts.

As they walked from the finished motors backward, Denise always asked two questions to direct their survey. "How do parts get here?" and "Where do they come from?" After a while, Sarah Burlow picked up the questions and sometimes took over. Denise could see how engaged Sarah was, and her natural leadership abilities shone through. *Great*, she thought, *we'll need all the leadership we can get to get us out of this mess.*

They kept going, and each team member actively wrote in their notepads.

Then, suddenly, Sam Wheeler called out, "Hold up. My drawing is completely crazy; it's a mess. I need to start over." Sam was the tall team leader who had spoken up during the all-hands meeting on Tuesday.

"I've been working here for over 13 years now. We run all these processes every day. Believe me, I know this department like the back of my hand. But this," he shook his head, "this is just crazy.

"Look, I've filled the fourth page now, and we're only halfway through." He paused, holding his clipboard up for everyone to see, and flipped through the pages with his scribbles.

Sam had gone beyond the boxes and triangles and was sketching each movement of material and people, taking detailed notes.

"I didn't know our processes were such a mess. The material flow looks like a big pile of spaghetti. I guess I need to redraw this to make any sense of it."

Sam was right. It was true that many of the machines, especially the new ones, were as good as it gets from a technology standpoint, and they had been expensive, but while in some cases the machines worked as hoped and eliminated handling, in other cases the machines were so unstable that people stood by them pulling parts out and reinserting them to adjust to equipment breakdowns. And the manual handling processes between machines were bizarre. Parts came out of the machines in an almost random order, leaving employees rushing to sort them into groups for delivery to the next process.

Betty Preston, another team leader in motor manufacturing, turned to address Sam. She was an energetic slender woman with short, curly brown hair. She was wearing a hoody and her signature baseball cap on backwards. She sometimes leaned toward sarcasm, but not this time.

"Hold on, Sam, I think your messy drawing is kind of the point. It's so good for us to get this big-picture perspective. I think the reason we normally don't see all this craziness is that we're usually going from one process to another fighting fires. And the chaos starts to feel normal. What I see here is a great opportunity to do a lot better," she said. "I would be nervous if everything was going smoothly and somehow we had to squeeze 30% out of these processes."

"Absolutely," Denise chimed in. "Thanks for that insight Betty. Sam, don't worry if your sketch is messy. It reflects reality, and you are doing a great job. We can discuss the diagrams later, and if needed draw a clean version. For now, let's continue our quest."

With that, on they went.

After they finished sketching the value stream for the first motor type, Denise could see they needed a break. They went to the area where people usually took their shift breaks. Everyone got their favorite junk food from the vending machines and grabbed a coffee or a soda. While she snacked, Denise noticed the four team leaders for motors and Joe standing at one of the round tables. They were obviously engaged in a heated discussion sharing their new found awareness of how messed up the processes were.

"Bowl of spaghetti," Denise could hear Sam saying again.

"My jaw dropped as I saw the chaos we live with every day," added Betty.

Derek Menlo from scheduling was standing with them as well.

"Now I know why the lead times we have in the scheduling system never work out," Denise was happy to hear him respond.

Joe added a positive note, "that is why we are here, to clean up this mess. And I believe we are up to the challenge."

At a table on his own Randolph from accounting had his laptop open and was hacking away on his keyboard. *He's probably looking for data to underpin what we can see in reality,* Denise thought.

She walked over to where Sarah, Jason, Luther Ropes, and Jennifer Billington were indulged in a discussion as well.

"This is incredible," Luther, head of plant logistics, blurted out. He was of medium height and a bit stocky.

Luther is a typical logistics guy, Denise thought. *I've never seen him without his rugged blazer and his baseball cap. That's probably because in logistics they go in and out of the building so often. And he loves to ride a forklift whenever he can, like a cowboy on his stead. Impressive that the head of logistics gets his hands dirty.*

"All these parts go through strange patterns between the machines," Luther continued. "No wonder people on my team are not happy when they get assigned to the motors logistics route. It's easy to mess things up, and there seems no good reason for why we carry stuff back and forth all the time. If I had to explain this to my family I would be down right embarrassed."

"You're right," Sarah said, piping in. She also had her laptop open. "I've just pulled up the spreadsheet that shows what parts are processed on which machine. Look at this." She flipped around her laptop so everyone could see the screen. Anyone could clearly see that there were so many different paths for the wide array of motors that nearly every machine depended on all of the other machines in some way, an incredibly inefficient system. "No wonder the diagram looks like spaghetti and the material handlers are going every which way. There is no rhyme or reason to the flow," she added.

"Well, there certainly are technical reasons for the current process," Jennifer the engineer who helped design most of newer motors exclaimed, sounding a bit defensive. "But, from an engineering perspective, my aha moment here is that we mostly focus on designing the individual pieces of a product and, at best, optimize a bit for individual process steps. We never look at the big-picture flow and I doubt anyone in engineering has ever mapped that with the real process flow. I must admit there may be opportunities in the design of the system."

This is going in a good direction, thought Denise, keeping quiet, allowing for the conversation to take its natural flow.

Jason interrupted her thoughts and asked, "I wonder why we have so many different motor variations?", bringing up what Denise knew was his pet peeve. "Many of them are already very old. I need to check the numbers, but I wonder if our customers really want the old models. A lot of the complexity we see is because of so many different motor designs – different parts to be handled, many changeovers of the equipment, and many opportunities for errors."

"But Jason, remember our last annual portfolio review, and how sales insisted on keeping many of the old products," replied Sarah. "'That's what our customers want,' they said. 'Customers come to us because of our wide array of pumps!' That's what I remember hearing over and over. So, as a manager in sales, what do you say to that?"

"Look, as you know, I'm still pretty new to the company, and, of course, I have to listen to the experienced sales staff. I agree sales typically block attempts to cancel older products, but," he paused for a second, then continued, "I do not think our sales team has any idea what this does to our processes, and at the end to our cost. I want to go back and challenge some of these products. We will need that to achieve our challenge."

Denise clapped her hands to get everyone's attention.

"Great discussions all," she said. "I love hearing all that you are learning about the current process and ideas about how we might reduce complexity and cost. Now, let's see what more we can learn by mapping a second motor type."

With that, everyone headed back to production with clipboards and paper in hand.

As they mapped the value stream for the second motor type, some new patterns emerged. Again they started at the end of the process, and this time they noticed a huge pile of scrapped and reworked parts.

"Hey, what's this?" Sarah asked. "Didn't we agree that every scrapped part should be reported to my team for control measures immediately?"

The team leaders seemed to take this personally. Doug looked at his feet, while Sam looked just plain frustrated.

Finally, team leader Betty spoke up.

"Well, you know, Sarah," she said, "I agree we have way too many scrapped parts every day. Your team complained that we were filling the measurement room with boxes and they couldn't go about their work. So, we agreed that we would collect parts here for them to pick up once or twice a week by the box. They cleverly created some marked spaces in front of the measurement room where they store boxes in the sequence they will check the parts, like first in, first out. I thought that was a new best practice to organize things."

"Oh gosh," Sarah said, exhaling. "I didn't realize producing junk was a daily occurrence. And if we inspect bad parts a week after they are produced, how can we expect to find out what's causing all this? This is a disaster."

Okay, I have kept my mouth shut to let this play out, but I may have to step in, thought Denise. *At this point we can't get into passing around blame. Our task is to document what we see.*

But just as Denise was ready to take over, Joe jumped in.

"I think we might be making assumptions, or at least drawing conclusions too early," he said. "My understanding of what we are trying to do here is to grasp the current condition and take a fresh look as a team. Is that right Denise?"

Denise felt instant relief. *I'm so happy to have Joe on the team.*

"Absolutely Joe," Denise replied. "Thanks for being the voice of reason and getting us back on track. As Joe said, our purpose here is to map the value stream and collect information that reflects the process as it is today. We're like detectives gathering the facts for later analysis ... without prematurely drawing conclusions."

The team took Denise's cue and went back to mapping the value stream. There was plenty of information to collect, and the map became increasingly more detailed ... and complex. They soon discovered that the scrap and rework at the end of line was just the tip of the iceberg. There were quality issues throughout the processes, and by the end everyone felt that they were starting to understand why these led to so many defects at the end of the line, and why they were in such serious trouble.

WEDNESDAY, MARCH 8 – NOON, TO LUNCH AND MEETING WITH MARK

After mapping the second value stream everyone was hungry and they practically ran over each other to get to lunch. Denise looked on longingly thinking, *getting their blood sugar up will relax some tensions. I certainly could use that now too.* She headed to her office to meet with Mark munching on her protein bar as she walked.

When she arrived, Mark had already taken a seat in her office.

"Hi Denise, how's it going with the motors team?" he asked.

"Interesting," Denise replied. "It's a totally different world, and the team has been running without proper support for a very long time. I feel like we can and have to do something for them. But it's not going to be easy."

Denise realized as she was speaking that she now felt comfortable venting to Mark. In the space of a few months, her relationships with Mark and Joe had changed completely – thanks in large part to how they were learning together through Kata.

Mark nodded in agreement.

"Sounds about right," he said. "So, you wanted to speak with me. What's up?"

Denise explained to Mark her plan to designate him as the informal assembly department manager so she could focus on the motor prefab project. She emphasized how much she, and the whole plant needed his help and what a great opportunity this was for him. She laid it on thick.

"This will give you a chance to try out this new role for the next three months. It's a no-risk move. If you do well and like it, you can then move up to become the official department manager," Denise said, keeping her tone upbeat.

Mark didn't seem immediately enthusiastic, but he did look like he was considering it.

"So, I'd be doing this to help you out," he said at last. "And I assume 'informal' means I don't have to take on all the responsibilities of the role, like going to plant management meetings and playing politics? You know I hate that stuff."

"Exactly," she said. "I have talked with David, and he will take responsibility for those meetings and politics and shield you from them. In fact, you will report directly to him. Deal?"

"Wait," Mark said, jumping up. "You should have told me that. That changes the whole thing. I thought I was still going to report to you."

"Sit down Mark, let's talk about this," she said. "David's not a bad boss to have. What exactly is your concern about him? You can tell me."

Mark looked at her like he was deciding how transparent to be, but then he sat down, his expression open.

"To be honest, Denise," he said, "David seems more like a politician than a real manager. He plays with the big muckety-mucks. I do not think he really understands assembly, and he can't keep me going on Kata. I would have to teach him."

"I can understand why you say that Mark," Denise responded sympathetically. "David has been very busy with meetings and politics. On the other hand, he has gone to quite a few coaching sessions, and given me some great feedback. He's a quick learner. And teaching him some new tricks might not be so bad."

Mark listened intently. Some part of him was obviously flattered by Denise's offer.

"You know Denise," he said, "the most important thing you said was that you need my help. You certainly have done plenty for me. I would not be in this position without your coaching me. So sure, I'll do it. I'll take one for the team," he added with a sly grin. "And, if David will listen, I think I can teach him a thing or two about the real world."

Denise smiled back "David will listen," she said. "I think getting to work on real problems will be a breath of fresh air for him. Endless debate and politicking can't be fun for him either. So welcome aboard the senior management team."

Denise held out her hand to Mark, who, despite his obviously mixed feelings, shook it heartily.

WEDNESDAY, MARCH 8 – 1:15 PM, RECONNOITERING TO REFLECT

Back in the conference room, the group was busily posting the information they had collected on the walls. Denise walked by the posted papers, examining them one by one and felt pleased with all the great data on display, even if it all pointed to waste every which way. *Well, lot's of low-hanging fruit*, she thought. *We need everything we can get.*

"Okay everyone," said Denise, bringing the group to order. "You sure have been busy. You've pulled together great information about the current condition. I think we have plenty to dig into here. Our first step is to reflect on what we learned and create some type of order out of the massive data dump. Then we'll work to identify focus areas where there are cost-saving and quality-improvement opportunities and prioritize them. I would like to leave here today with initial assignments. Does that sound good?"

The group murmured agreement as they looked at all the sheets hanging on the walls. They obviously felt overwhelmed by the massive amount of data, which seemed to indicate problems everywhere. Where to start?

For the next few hours, they worked diligently on sorting and visualizing the data they had gathered. Denise split them into two groups. Each group sketched a large version of the current state value stream for one of the motor types they had observed. Denise could see how the motors team was totally stunned by what they saw. They knew every detail of their process from day-to-day work but had never stepped back and considered the overall picture.

"This is unbelievable," Betty exclaimed to Denise, while the other motor department team leaders nodded in agreement. "I just cannot believe how often I have walked through this department without really seeing all this waste and dysfunction. You said the book Mike Rother coauthored is called *Learning to See*, right? Good name. This has really opened my eyes."

After each team had presented their maps of the current state value stream, they identified key points that drove cost and quality issues.

"Look," said Sam, "we can clearly identify three points in our process that kill our productivity Denise. I have to admit that I was skeptical about all this paperwork when we started, but now I can see that the map perfectly highlights what we experience every day. Its crystal clear where the ugliest parts of our process lie."

"Exactly," Betty said, jumping in. "This is what we spend most of our time reacting to each day, but focusing on symptoms, not causes. Now, we can see it clearly. Look, we have problems with the same machines on both value streams."

At that point, Drew, so far the quietest of the team leaders, chimed in, his voice skeptical.

"Yeah," he said, "do you really believe we can do much about it? You guys both know how tight space is at these machines, and also how we need to be careful when inserting parts. We don't want to get bad quality just because we urge people to work faster."

Ah, threshold of knowledge, Denise thought. *This is where I should start coaching them.* In the past, she would have tensed up at Drew's negativity and tried to counter with a solution. But now Denise realized how thinking scientifically helped her to relax. *Practicing Kata has really allowed me to become comfortable with not knowing and not having the answers.*

"Drew, I agree that these are tough problems, and I agree that solving them will not be easy," Denise said. "You've all done a great job of identifying these opportunities. We'll just go step by step and see what can be done. The approach we are going to learn is designed to help us prioritize and overcome obstacles one by one."

Joe chimed in, "that is how we did it in assembly. We did not have a clue when we first started out how we could eliminate the backlog. I for one was as skeptical as they come. But through Kata we chipped away and won the battle."

Denise could see that team members were engaged and listened, but many seemed confused and uncomfortable. After all, Kata was all new to them. *I think there was a quick hands-on Kata exercise Maggie mentioned to get people familiar with the concepts. I need to talk to her about that.*

After a mid-afternoon break, the group continued evaluating the data. Both groups had drawn on their maps big red circles around the loop where partially machined parts for their newest motor left their factory to go to a supplier for coating. They saw that it took three to four days to come back, and when it did there were often quality issues. This supposed cost-saving measure added extra cost in logistics and rework, and it was often a bottleneck.

"Now I understand what caused my productivity to plummet over the last year," Luther Ropes, head of plant logistics, said. "This loop creates a mess in logistics."

"And it is a constant source of bad parts," added Sarah. "Often the coating is damaged on the second run-through. We can see that from my team's quality data analysis."

"But the coating needs to be done before we do the final machining," said Jennifer Billington from engineering, again with a defensive edge in her voice. "Otherwise, our motors will never work. For the new engines, we're running a level of precision at the edge of physics."

Denise felt sympathetic and decided to intervene.

"Thanks Jennifer for explaining the importance of coating before final processing, at least in the current design. I expect that the collective minds of this group can solve the quality issues when we get up to experimenting. At this point, it's great that we have highlighted this key issue."

Last but not least, the large quantity of motor types, especially the older ones, was an issue they put on their list. Jason wanted to investigate that from the sales side. Denise felt confident he would get some traction to reduce the number of motor types by at least a modest level.

They listed all these key areas on a flipchart. Denise was happy to see they clustered into the same three areas that she had identified with David. She stepped back and thought, *this is a good starting point, and we need to get to defining a challenge for each of these key areas and first target conditions. But it is already past quitting time. That will have to wait for tomorrow.*

She gathered the team.

"It's been a long day and we've come very far," she said. "I know we haven't solved anything yet but getting a clear understanding of what we need to work on, having a clear focus, that's a big part of success. We're all tired so let's call it a day. We'll meet tomorrow morning at 8:30 sharp and carve out specific assignments so we can get started. Thank you all for the great work today."

The team filed out of the room, chattering and looking both exhilarated and exhausted. Those who worked the second shift and had had to change their sleep pattern for the sake of today looked especially tired.

When everyone was gone, Denise grabbed one of the chairs from a corner of the room and sat down. *Phew, what a day. A good one, but I'm as exhausted as the rest of the group.* Overall, though, she felt very happy with how far they had gotten and how engaged her team was.

One last thing before she called it a day. She phoned David to discuss Mark's new role.

"Hi Denise, what's up?" David was still in his office.

"Hi David, I've talked to Mark. He's in, and you're good to go to take over assembly."

"OK," replied David. Maybe we can meet and walk over now to talk with him together."

Denise sighed. "Can you please do that? I need the relief from assembly matters we talked about. I am completely tied up getting the motors team going. And, oh, please also announce Mark's new role so it is official and he can get started."

"Certainly," David replied, "I'll do that tomorrow." The message was loud and clear that that was something he needed to do alone.

Denise briefly summarized the day's activities, and David suggested she deserved a night off.

I sure do, Denise thought. She had arranged to meet Jason tonight. A local band they both liked was playing at a bar nearby, and Jason had asked if she would go out with him—definitely a date. She checked the time on her laptop. 5:45 pm. *Home, shower, dress up, get to the bar. I will be a little late. I'll text Jason.*

With that Denise left work behind, anxious to meet up with Jason and finally unwind.

23

Workshop Day 2: Stepping Back to Clarify Direction

THURSDAY, MARCH 9 – 6:00 AM, SUNRISE, ROUSING AFTER A DELIGHTFUL NIGHT ON THE TOWN

When the alarm on her cell phone buzzed, Denise felt like it had been just minutes since she had fallen asleep. She managed to drag herself out of bed feeling woozy after a memorable night out.

Long workdays plus a long night out midweek don't go well together, Denise thought, sighing. *But last night was great. I wouldn't have wanted to miss it.*

This was the good life she'd imagined: a stable job and maybe soon even a stable boyfriend. After work, she had taken a quick shower and then slipped on her favorite jeans and a white peasant blouse. To add some pizazz, Denise had accessorized with the turquoise and silver necklace she had bought on one of her trips to New Mexico, along with the turquoise earrings she had once bought there from a Navajo artist. *Let's go country style tonight.*

When Denise had arrived at the bar, Jason had already been there together with some of his friends. She had quickly ordered herself a drink, a non-alcoholic Mojito, because she had come by car.

The band hadn't started yet, so they had decided to play pool at one of the tables in the back. It had been her first time, and Jason had introduced her to the game. He had shown her how to hold the cue and guided her in, moving her arm while standing behind her – it had felt decidedly romantic. Although they had lost their game to more experienced players, guys who seemed like they hung out at the bar every night, Jason and Denise made for a good team. They had laughed a lot.

DOI: 10.4324/9780429347023-26

When the band had started playing, they had all moved to the front of the bar. Suddenly, the place had been packed. The band had played well-known country rock songs that were easy to sing along with, at least the chorus, and by the second song the crowd was fully engaged. The atmosphere had been a bit raucous, but so fun.

The band had come back for three encores before the crowd had let them go for the night. When Jason and Denise had finally made their escape, it had been almost midnight. Denise had volunteered to drive a slightly tipsy Jason home.

When they had arrived at his place, Jason had invited her in: "Why don't you come up for a drink or maybe a cappuccino?" he had asked with a hopeful look.

Denise had hesitated, but then she had thought a quick goodbye and kiss in the car would make it seem like they were back in high school.

As they had entered the apartment, Jason had flicked on the lights, and Denise had glanced around the room, curious to see how Jason lived. His place was smaller than hers, with an efficient layout. Jason had decorated it functionally, yet also tastefully. It was clean and neat – not a given for guys her age. *He even has some plants, and they seemed ... alive.*

Denise had gone for an espresso rather than the whiskey on the rocks Jason had chosen for himself. He had quite a selection of single malt whiskeys, Denise noticed, a little surprised. Jason had made her an espresso on his obviously expensive Italian-brand espresso machine which took up prominent space on the counter between the small open kitchen and the living room.

"Hey, it's super late now. Why don't you just stay?" Jason had offered after they had been chatting for about a half hour.

But Denise had looked at her watch and shook her head no.

"I'd love to, but I need to be at work early tomorrow to prepare for our second workshop day, and I certainly can't go dressed in turquoise and country." Seeing that Jason was obviously disappointed, she had added, "why don't we plan something for the weekend. Maybe a hike and stay at my place or at some hotel in the mountains?"

"Sounds like a plan," Jason had said, hugging her.

"Great," Denise had replied, "See you tomorrow with the team."

They had a long kiss, and Denise left. When she had finally sunk into her bed, it had been close to 1:30 am.

Okay Denise. Head out of the clouds. You have to get to work, she told herself.
She quickly ate her usual bowl of Cheerios™ with a little granola stirred in
and headed out the door.

On the highway, Denise blended with the traffic, her mind wandering
to the plan for workshop day 2. She wanted the team to build a storyboard
for each of the three areas of focus they had identified yesterday. Of course,
her ultimate goal was to establish a first target condition for each of the
focus areas so she could start coaching the team.

Denise remembered when Maggie had first explained how critical it is to
have a clear direction and focus. *And there was a third thing she mentioned,*
Denise thought, *wasn't that pace? I still never fully understood that. Note to
self, ask Maggie about it when we next talk.*

Maybe I should give Maggie a quick call, Denise thought, *it's super early,
but she is an early riser.* Denise set her phone on speaker to call Maggie,
just as the sun was rising from behind the nearby hills.

"Good morning Denise, you're up early, what's up?" said Maggie.

"Hi Maggie, sorry for disturbing you this early."

"Ah, no worries, I'm just having my morning tea, enjoying the sunrise
from my porch. So, what's on your mind, my dear?"

"Today I have the second workshop day with my team, and we need to
establish target conditions for each of the focus topics we identified in the
value streams yesterday. I'm running through how to structure it in my
mind, and I thought I would check in with you. To me it seems that we
have to go through the first two steps of the Improvement Kata again but
now for each of the focus topics. And then I've been wondering about that
pace thing you mentioned a while back. It seems we have direction and
focus now, but what about pace?"

"Wait a sec," Maggi interrupted her, "that's a lot of questions. Let's back
up. What's your target condition for the team today?"

Denise thought for a moment and then replied, "That we have a target
condition established for each focus topic."

"OK, great. So what's your current condition? What is it you already
have?"

"We have a lot of data about the current condition, but it's mainly broad
statistics about the value stream, and probably not specific enough to set
target conditions for each focus topic," Denise replied.

"So, what exactly is it you don't know about the focus topics?" Maggie
continued.

"It's the detailed current condition on each of them. It seems we do not know enough to set target conditions, if that makes sense."

Denise paused, but Maggie remained silent. So Denise jumped back in. "Ah," she said, "I see it now. We need to revisit the overall three-month challenge and develop more specific challenges for each of our focus topics. Then the teams can go deeper into the current condition to find out where we are in relation to their specific challenges. It's kind of like having a hierarchy of challenges, a top level and then that is broken down into a set of more specific ones, and it can keep going. But how do we get a second-level challenge for each topic? Maggie, are you still there?"

"I'm still here. I like how you're thinking. Now, thinking back, how did you define a challenge with your old team in assembly?"

Ah, she's just dodged my attempt at getting her to give me answers and just smoothly continued coaching me, Denise realized. *She's too damn good.*

Denise thought about Maggie's question for a moment.

"Well," Denise said at last, "usually we made it a sentence and used the 'wouldn't it be great if' start Mike Rother suggests. Oh, and then we developed the habit of always having a second level described by a second sentence connected with 'therefore'. So, I guess we can do the same now. All the focus topics need to be guided by the same overall challenge concerning what we need to achieve for motors to stay alive. And then we could add 'therefore' on this focus topic we need to achieve such and such. That would give each team a more specific focus to then go back and deep dive into the current condition."

"Again, good thinking," Maggie replied. "So, what further obstacles prevent you from reaching your goal with the team today?"

Denise chewed this over in her mind while taking a right turn onto the road that led toward the plant.

"I think my main obstacle is that the team doesn't know anything about the four steps of the Improvement Kata. I guess I should start with some basic introduction. Maybe I should put together a few slides."

Maggie immediately jumped in. "Denise, what is the real obstacle to your goal today?"

Ah, she's right. I was jumping to the next step and falling back into my old habits as a consultant – preparing some explanatory slides, she thought for a moment.

"I guess it's not so much that the team lacks experience with Kata in general, but rather they don't know what they should do today and how.

So, basically it's them understanding how to define a challenge, grasp the current condition, and establish a first target condition. I shouldn't do too much teaching then but rather give them some simple instructions on those points only as they need them."

"And then coach them," Maggie added.

Denise immediately responded, "But I do feel like I need to give them some direction, and then I can coach them based on that."

"So, what directions were helpful for you and your team when you started?" Maggie asked.

"Well, we still use the recipes I have in my notebook for grasping the current condition and establishing a next target condition. And then of course we use the target condition form with the simple T shape.

"Good, good," Maggie jumped in. "You just mentioned several Starter Kata as Mike Rother calls them – recipes for getting started. The target condition form, your two recipes for grasping the current condition and establishing a next target condition, and then, of course, the storyboard to put it all together."

"I think I'll print one card for the current condition recipe and another for the target condition for everyone in the team," said Denise "That way, they'll have them at hand today and can work through them step by step."

"That's a great idea," Maggie replied. "One caveat, though. The recipes may not work as well as you think. Every situation is different so you will need to actively coach. You will see what I mean."

"Uh, yeah, sure," Denise replied, not fully convinced that the recipes would be difficult to follow. "If we can shift to another topic, I'm still confused about the third aspect of target deployment you mentioned a long time ago – pace. I have a feeling it will be particularly important to achieve our challenge, given the intense timeline here."

"Great insight, Denise," said Maggie, "and I agree pace will become critical moving forward to get the results you need. What time frame do you have in mind for the target conditions you want the team to establish today?"

Denise thought for a second before answering. "Normally I would say one to two weeks, but in light of how challenging our three focus topics are, I think one month might be more realistic. That way we'll have three target conditions to our three-month challenge."

"I see what you are doing," Maggie said, interrupting her, "to adapt to the huge goal you have to achieve in three months, you're assuming that taking a few long leaps is more effective than a larger number of small steps. That's a common misconception. But one month is far too long. Your next target conditions should still be for one week. By doing that you ensure focus and priority. Remember? You want your team to be 100% clear on what to work on each day.

"As for pace, let me introduce you to something new that has worked well for me. What you need is a target bridging the three-month challenge and the one-week target conditions. I suggest adding one-month goals. I call this the 3-1-1 approach. That is, a three-month challenge, one-month goal, and one-week target condition. You will be setting the three-month challenge for each of the three focus topics. Next you break down each of these sub-challenges to a smaller scope of one month. That gives you three control points for each topic within the three-month time frame. You can easily use your 'therefore' structure to connect the two. For each focus topic, let the team formulate their challenge along these lines: 'Our overall three-month project challenge is this. Therefore, we must achieve such and such for our focus topic within the next four weeks.'

"Then you ask each team to establish a new target condition at the beginning of each week. That not only creates high focus but also establishes what is a priority. And, above all, 3-1-1 establishes a distinct pace of work for working toward targets on each level. I like to think of it as a pacemaker, like for the heart. It creates a pace of improvement on each level."

"Ok, I get," Denise said, "that's what a good target deployment process should look like – direction, focus, and pace."

"Yup. Wow, we've gone through a lot in your drive to work. Anything else on your mind, Denise?" Maggie replied, sounding a little hurried. "I need to get going."

"I know, I'm sorry, but I do have one more thing. My team needs some sort of introduction to the Improvement Kata and Coaching Kata. Didn't you once mention a fun and short activity to introduce Kata? I think you told me about a puzzle exercise."

"Ah, right, yes, that's a good idea," Maggie replied. "That's the Kata to Grow exercise Mike developed for teachers in schools, but it also works well in business. Today you are fully booked. So I'll come in early tomorrow morning. I'd like to see the storyboards. Then I'll run a hands-on introduction to Kata with your team using the puzzle. It can be done in an hour, but we should encourage a lot of discussion throughout, so maybe we should schedule two hours. If you want to be real ambitious, tomorrow afternoon we can also try out the Kata Coaching Dojo I mentioned a couple days ago. You will need to select a few people, maybe three or four, who have the most potential to be coaches and get them to the session after lunch. I will bring everything we need. Good luck today. You've got this."

With that, Maggie hung up.

THURSDAY, MARCH 9 – 7:00 AM, CAN DAY 2 GO AS SMOOTHLY AS DAY 1?

Five minutes later, Denise parked her car at the plant and went to her office. Once there, she immediately began preparing everything she had discussed with Maggie. She typed the two recipes from her notebook into a Word document and printed them on cards she could hand out to the team.

She also printed the forms for three empty storyboards one for each focus topic. She mocked up an example storyboard with some generic documents to illustrate what a storyboard should look like. She took all the printouts to the conference room and posted them and the example storyboard on a wall. She also wrote out all the focus topics on a flip chart. Just as she finished her preparations, people began to file into the room, stopping to look at the documents posted on the walls before they took their seats. They mostly seemed upbeat.

When everyone had arrived, Denise welcomed them to day two and explained the storyboard pointing to the example one she had mocked-up. Then, she asked them to build a storyboard for each focus topic in teams of three and four. Suddenly, the room was abuzz with chatter, faces were alert, and everyone seemed to be really engaged in the activity. Of course with Joe's Kata experience, and Sarah's general smarts and organization, they were able to get theirs put together very quickly, and Joe started walking around and helping others.

Denise then reminded them of the three-month project challenge: "Wouldn't it be great if we could reduce the cost per motor by 30% and keep production inhouse? Therefore, we have to increase productivity, reduce the cost of bad quality, and reduce the cost of materials." They spent the next hour going through data to figure out how much they had to increase productivity, reduce the cost of bad quality, and reduce the cost of materials to reach their goal.

At that point, Randolph from accounting began mumbling.

"The numbers don't work out," he said. He was hunched over a piece of paper and was fiddling with his calculator. "I just can't get the numbers to work out."

"What's up Randolph?" asked Denise. "What numbers don't work out?"

Randolph was still fiddling with his calculator. Without looking up, he said, "I don't think we can get the full 30% cost reduction in three months. Also, we have existing contracts with our suppliers that bind us for more then three months. I have worked the numbers over and over, and I don't see any way we can make it," he paused, raising his eyes to meet hers. "I'm sorry Denise."

Denise walked over and looked at the paper with all Randolph's calculations. He quickly walked her through them, his voice disappointed.

"You know what Randolph?" she said, when he had finished his explanation. "I think you're right. It just does not seem possible. Some of the important changes can't be completely implemented in three months, particularly those involving materials and suppliers. I'm not sure what to do," she paused. "OK, folks, let's take a five-minute break, and I'm going to call David."

Denise walked out of the room to call David from the hallway, nervously drumming her fingers on a random printer stationed in the hall as she waited for him to answer. To her surprise, he answered on the second ring. As calmly as she could, she explained the numbers Randolph had projected to David. She apologized profusely, but admitted, based on what she'd seen, 30% in three months was simply not realistic. To her surprise, David agreed.

"Denise, I believe you, and I suggested that Randolph join your team because he is a wizard with numbers," he said. "Remember I said I thought if we got most of productivity and quality under control in 3 months and had a plan for materials to get the rest we could sell that? I am going to stick my neck out here and say you should come up with a stretch, but realistic three-month challenge. Our new CEO will be in place by May and I believe he will appreciate great progress and recognize that building our own motor components is part of our core competence. So, get with your team and come up with a realistic three-month challenge. We can then have a plan for the additional savings after the three months."

Denise thanked David as profusely as she had apologized. She returned to the room as the group was reconvening and chatting among themselves.

"Folks, Randolph did a brilliant job of crunching the numbers and discovered our overall challenge is out of reach within three months," Denise explained. "So I called David and good news," she said. "He agreed with Randolph's projections and said we should come up with a stretch, but realistic challenge for three months. He is convinced that he can get us through this if we make great progress. I trust him. So, let's revisit the challenge. Think about the 30% as a six-month challenge, and we are going after the first leg."

Randolph looked over his paper, tapped on his calculator, and agreed that with six months to accomplish their goal, the numbers worked. Pleased, Denise asked the team to discuss what a realistic three-month challenge would look like. At first, they thought they would simply slice the existing challenge in half. While it seemed feasible to get a 15% cost reduction, they decided they needed to discuss each of the factors that contributed to productivity, bad quality, and material cost to really figure it out.

"I think we have to get further than just halfway in the next three months for productivity and quality," Sarah said. "Maybe, two thirds, because the last third will be a lot harder to achieve."

"I like your thinking Sarah," said Denise, looking impressed. "Team, what do you think?"

Doug, one of the team leaders, spoke up.

"I think that sounds plausible. It's challenging but having a steeper ascent in the beginning in theory makes sense," he said.

"You're right," Joe chimed in. "That gives us some room to maneuver for the second leg. We can't turn back time if we don't get enough done on the first leg." Then he quietly sang "If I could turn back time…," making a percussion sound at the end.

He's a rocker at heart, Denise thought, smiling. *I must go see his band play one of these evenings. Maybe with Jason.*

"All right," Denise said, turning to a flip chart and flipping to a fresh page. "Let's write that down. I heard that we will go for ⅔ which is a 20% cost reduction target. So, let's try that for a start." She started writing.

Wouldn't it be great if we could reduce the cost per motor by 20% and keep production inhouse. Therefore we have to...

· *Increase productivity to x*
· *Reduce the cost of bad quality to y*

Denise checked the calendar and added "…by June 8th," which was the date in exactly three months' time. June 8th also turned out to be a Friday, which made for a nice deadline.

Denise turned toward their trusty accountant and asked, "Randolph, can you work your magic and help us with absolute figures? I wrote in x and y as placeholders."

"I'll figure that out in the next hour," Randolph replied immediately. He seemed happy to contribute to a team in a positive way; it was clear he didn't want to only play the role of naysayer.

Denise had left one bullet free on the flip chart for the third factor – cost of material.

"I've looked into the numbers with David on the cost of material, and here's what we found," she said. "Several of the purchased parts for our new motors are high precision. That makes them very expensive. In addition, there are some complex automated machines in our plant that add big time to our production cost. The equipment is expensive, and maintenance is sky high."

"We can't water down our specifications," Jennifer Billington from engineering said, immediately putting her foot down.

She still hasn't bought into this project, realized Denise, *and only engineering can help us develop products that can be produced in a way that is efficient without sacrificing quality. I wonder how I can convince her that what she says are obstacles can in fact be overcome?*

At that point Ray Diaz from purchasing jumped in. He was energetic and cheerful, and always wore a suit. Today he wore a light gray suit that had a shiny touch and perfectly matched his dark black hair. *Purchasing is exactly the spot for him to be. I bet he's a tough negotiator*, Denise thought.

Ray turned to Jennifer. "Jen, you really think there's nothing we can do from an engineering perspective to keep motors inhouse?"

He looked at her and waited.

Jennifer frowned. "Well, no, I did not say that," she curtly replied, "but the requirements for the motors are extremely high. We can't just lower technical specifications."

Ray gave Jennifer a big smile. "Great," he said. It sounds like there may be a few things we can at least consider? Like, say, reviewing dimensions to see if they need quite the level of precision we think?" He paused.

Jennifer nodded tentatively.

"Jennifer, you and I know how it is," Ray continued. "During the design phase the timeline is always tight, and we purchasers always push you engineers to give us drawings and specifications as early as possible, so we can start looking for suppliers and negotiating. And we also both know that this usually leads to specs erring a bit on the tighter side than is really needed, in retrospect, I mean. Is that completely wrong?"

"No, that's right," Jennifer admitted hesitantly. "At least, sometimes," she added.

Denise could see how Jennifer was struggling not to give in. *Ray is doing a great job, though,* she thought, *he certainly is a superb negotiator.*

Ray smiled again, still fully focused on Jennifer. "We work together all the time and I admire the great job engineering does, particularly under the pressure my team creates for you all. So, I really appreciate your openness to reviewing the specs of the expensive parts Denise has identified one more time to see what we can learn together. Once we know where tight specs are mandatory and where there is room to relax them a little, my team can work with our suppliers to adapt their processes and renegotiate the price. I have two awesome guys on my team with an engineering background. I am sure we'll find some potential for cost reduction. Is that a completely crazy idea?" Ray paused, waiting for Jennifer to answer.

"No," she said, a faint smile on her lips, "let's give it a try."

"Super," Ray responded. "I'm really glad we're on this team together." Then, he turned to Denise, "We won't see much effect from that in the first three months because the parts coming in in the next weeks are already authorized for shipment. But we could have a substantial effect in the second leg." He smiled again.

Denise couldn't help smiling to herself. *What Ray just did was awesome,* she thought. *There are really some good people at Goldberg. It's just great how a transparent challenge and going through this process engages and aligns people.*

"Thanks, Ray, for demonstrating the art of strong arming, I mean negotiating," Denise said with a laugh "I certainly wouldn't want to be a supplier going up against you. And, yup, I'll put it all down." She started writing on the flip chart again.

Wouldn't it be great if we could reduce the cost per motor by 20% and keep production inhouse. Therefore we have to...

- *Increase productivity to x*
- *Reduce the cost of bad quality to y*
- *Reduce the cost of material to z*
    ...by June 8th.

That was a great exercise, she thought, *looking at three months has helped us to define our focus topics much more precisely.*

They then sorted the list into what they were going to address over the first three months and a few topics that they would address in the second half. They also added who would be responsible for each topic – Denise wanted one person in charge, each paired with at least one support person. They ended up with a list that was satisfactory to all.

Productivity:

Machine group AX-3031 – Betty + Doug
Machine group AX-3045 – Sam + Doug
Logistic process motor prefab – Luther + Derek

Quality:

Damaged parts – Joe + Sarah, Luther, Drew
Motor housings out of tolerance – Sarah + Joe, Jennifer, Derek
Material cost:
Cost of purchased parts – Ray + Jennifer, Luther
Internal cost of machining for housing and lid – Phil + Ray, Jennifer, Derek, Luther

General:

Reduce number of (old) motor types – Jason + Derek
Value-stream double-loop internal/external – Jennifer + Phil, Luther ← second leg

Denise felt good that the assignments were clear, and those assigned seemed willing. She did have one concern about Drew, the fourth team leader, who had a minor supporting role for damaged parts. He had been very quiet and reserved all morning and seemingly had many concerns.

"We need someone to connect us with reality and answer questions about the process," Denise had explained. "Are you OK with that, Drew?"

Drew nodded, and Denise put his name down. Time flew by. It was already just past 10:00 am.

Denise turned to the team.

"Well done," she said. "How about a short break?"

Everybody agreed, and they decided to reconvene at 10:15 am.

24

Establishing Goals to Set Up the 3-1-1

THURSDAY, MARCH 9 – 10:15 AM, A DEEPER DIVE AND DISCOVERY THAT STARTER KATA NEED GOOD COACHING

AFTER THE TEAM returned from their coffee break, Denise assigned each team to develop a one-month goal for their focus topic. "Where do we need to be with your topic one month from now to reach our three-month challenge?"

As everyone began working, they all realized that they had to return to grasping the current condition to drill deeper into their assigned topics. That's when Denise handed out the cards with her Starter Kata for grasping the current condition and gave a quick explanation (see Figure 24.1).

At first, the team seemed happy to get some guidance from the recipe, but then more and more questions arose. *How do I do this? What does this mean in the case of my topic?* Denise had to be everywhere all at once. *Give them the Starter Kata as a guideline and then coach them*, Maggie had said. *Easier said than done*, thought Denise.

"Hey Denise, can you have a look, please? I can't make sense of this step in your recipe," Betty called from one end of the room.

"I'll be with you in a second, Betty," Denise said as she finished up a conversation with Luther from logistics who had asked to discuss the focus of their material logistics current condition analysis. *Phew, I need more coffee, desperately*, Denise thought. *But what a delight to have people coming to me to pull information instead of trying to push Kata onto them.*

"Betty, how can I help you?" Denise said when she finally managed to walk over to Betty.

"Look," Betty said, holding up the card with the Starter Kata in one hand and pointing to a pile of papers in front of her with the other.

DOI: 10.4324/9780429347023-27

Recipe: Grasping the current condition of a process

1. GRAPH OUTCOME DATA

    o How is the process performing over time?

    o Draw a run-chart.

2. LOOK AT CUSTOMER DEMAND / REQUIRED PERFORMANCE

    o What do the customers of the process want or need?

    o How frequently should the process do what it does, to meet customer demand / the required performance?

    o What margin do we need to add/deduct?

3. STUDY HOW THE PROCESS WORKS NOW

    o Draw a block diagram of the current process steps and their sequence. Time the steps.

    o Measure several process cycles and draw a run-chart to make variation visible.

    o Record any observations you have about the current operating pattern.

FIGURE 24.1
Starter Kata for grasping current condition, adapted from Mike Rother, *The Toyota Kata Practice Guide*, McGraw-Hill (New York), 2018.

"I printed a bar chart for step one, 'How is the process performing over time?' This is our daily productivity for motor prefab over the last eight weeks." Betty showed Denise a chart. "In addition, I've split up every day into the three shifts."

When Denise looked closer, she saw that each day consisted of three narrow bars next to one another, each resembling the productivity for one shift.

"So far so good," Betty continued. "But then my assignment is to get data on labor productivity for machine group AX-3031, the machines with the most problems. That is where I am stuck. I can't get data on productivity for an individual machine group. As of now, we don't track how many people work in a machine group or for how long.

"Often they work on my machine group for a full shift, but then there are other days where they switch to another machine group for an hour or more. It varies from day to day depending on the particular parts being machined that day. So, I'm trying to figure out how to measure labor productivity for the specific machines you assigned to me."

"Hmmm," Denise kind of hummed, nodding. "So, what did you do next?"

"After spinning my wheels for a while, I decided to put that step aside and focus on the next step, which is to look at customer demand. Well, our customer, basically, is assembly. That's where my motor-parts go next, as you know. Assembly schedules a different mix of motors that are made up of different parts each day, so my demand varies from day to day. What do I use as the rate of customer demand when it varies all over the place? Since we started working three shifts because of the crazy backlog last year, we usually meet the assembly demand. So, now I'm like, how does looking at customer demand even help me to improve productivity? When you first described these steps for process analysis, they made sense, but as I tried to apply them to his complex process, they seemed to fall apart. To be honest, I'm feeling pretty lost. I need help."

Denise frowned as she poured through the charts Betty had spread across the table in front of them, marveling at how organized Betty was. Her back was starting to hurt from bending over to read them. Actually, she had to admit she was stalling, trying to figure out what to say in response to Betty, or what question to ask to "coach" her. It would be easy if Betty was simply missing the point. But she had legitimate questions, and Denise did not know the answers.

Suddenly, Denise straightened, turned around, and called over to Randolph from accounting. "Hey, Randolph, have you got a minute to help Betty and me over here?"

Randolph was once again sitting at a table alone with his laptop open in front of him.

"Give me a second," he replied without looking up.

He finished what he was typing into what looked like a spreadsheet. Finally, he closed his laptop and walked over to Denise and Betty.

"Look," Denise said, "Betty has printed the productivity for motor prefab over the last eight weeks. But that doesn't help her focus on machine group AX-3031. What measurements do we have on how that machine group is performing individually?"

"None actually," Randolph replied. "We can't measure productivity for an individual machine group because operators have various assignments that are often between machine groups. If we want to know the productivity of an individual machine group, that has to be done manually by observing it during a shift. And then of course it varies from shift to shift."

Betty sighed, "That was also my conclusion," she said, clearly frustrated. "What am I supposed to do now? Should I start following operators around and measuring their productivity when they are at a specific machine? I'm just as confused as before."

"Wait a sec, Betty," replied Denise. "Let's take a different angle. Instead of focusing on trying to measure the amount of labor for a particular type of pump, maybe we can focus on reducing cost per pump for your set of machines in another way. What levers do we have to influence cost?"

Randolph thought for a moment. Then, he replied, "Well, we can reduce cost by using fewer people to produce the same amount of output or ..."

"How's that supposed to work?" said Betty, interrupting Randolph mid-sentence.

"Or," Randolph continued, ignoring her interruption, "if we get more parts per hour from each machine with the same number of people that will in effect improve productivity."

"Parts per hour, that's a good way to measure how the process is performing over time," Denise fired back with enthusiasm, "just like we do in assembly. Pumps per shift, and per hour."

"No it's not," Betty replied, her face hardened. "In assembly, each line makes similar products, but in motors the difference between parts is much greater. Some are super quick to machine; others take double or even four times more time on a machine. On a day when we run parts that have a very long machining time, we get fewer pieces compared to running parts with a super-short machine time. That doesn't mean that running the long cycle-time parts is less productive."

Betty paused, then continued thinking out loud. "So, that means we still don't have a single productivity measure to compare over time. It's not apples to apples. It's more like comparing apples to kumquats." She shook her head with frustration.

Randolph listened silently. "Good point", he frowned, clearly thinking deeply. "Well," he said, "if you think about it, what matters is the runtime we get on a machine and how much personnel we need to get those minutes."

"You're right," Denise said. She started smiling. "With that we can...," she began, but then she stopped mid-sentence, hearing Maggie's voice in her ear. *Don't tell, coach and let them think for themselves.*

"Anyway, Betty, thanks for clearing that up for me. I'm a newbie. I don't know the machines and processes like you do. That is why I am the coach and you are the expert. I'll leave this in your and Randolph's capable hands. I think Sam and Doug need some help." With that, Denise gave Betty and Randolph a clap on the shoulders.

For the next hour Denise circulated from group to group. It was the same problem everywhere. The nice, neat card she had given them to do the current condition analysis fell apart as soon as they tried to apply it to their particular topic. It best fit simple, repeatable manual processes where there was a clear-cut demand pattern like in assembly. Most of the groups first struggled through the process of collecting data, and then they would find that the data didn't answer the questions they were trying to answer. Denise would talk it through with the group, and then the group would find themselves starting all over. It was chaotic, but they were making progress, moving forward more than they were moving backward. *Maggie was right about struggle with the Starter Kata. We have plenty of it! But it sure gets people thinking.*

Denise herself struggled to keep each group going. She felt like she was racing to and fro spinning plates, trying to keep each from crashing down and breaking.

Eventually, Denise returned to the corner where Randolph and Betty were still collaborating.

"I think we're getting someplace now," said Betty, looking up from the sheets of paper they had laid out in front of them. She had a faint smile on her lips and obviously was in a better mood than before.

"Yes, indeed," said Randolph, joining in. "We've found out that we can measure how much time a machine is running each day. Actually there are two ways, even. Whenever a box of parts is completed it gets scanned and booked into the system. So that tells us how much has been produced. Or the other way is…."

Denise realized that Randolph was playing on his turf now: data mining. She could not help smiling. *Awesome, he's hooked*, she thought. She looked on as Randolph went into some detail about the data they could collect and how they could use it, with Betty periodically chiming in excitedly.

Wow, that's a lot of data, Denise thought, looking at their charts. Then she thought back to the Coaching Kata questions and asked, "so, what did you learn from taking that step?"

Randolph paused for a moment. Then he answered, "I calculated how many more minutes of machine runtime we would need to achieve our cost target, that is with the same amount of labor. Then, we took a look at the actual minutes each machine is running."

"Yeah," Betty jumped in. "That was pretty shocking. On average, every machine in my group runs between 35 and 37 min per hour. The rest of the time it is idling for one reason or another."

"That's roughly 60% of the time available to run," said Randolph. "So, I calculated how many minutes we would need to run with the same number of people to meet our demand. As you know right now we are the bottleneck. Mathematically, we would need 45 minutes on each machine per hour, that is, 75% of the time. If we can get to that without adding people we will meet our productivity target."

"That's great," said Denise. "Now, you're really getting your arms around understanding the current condition, and clearly you're already on your way to defining a next target condition. Our goal for today is to get to your one-month challenge, and then break it down into your first one-week target condition. I'd say you're getting close. Great work, both of you!"

Denise continued circulating among the groups. Slowly but surely, each group was making progress toward some meaningful way of understanding the current condition that would allow them to develop a useful first target condition. The groups were progressing at different speeds, and none of them were able to exactly follow the process steps on the Starter Kata card she had handed out, but it was all good, and Denise felt like everyone was learning a ton. She certainly was. She couldn't help but smile, beam even. Then she clapped her hands.

"Hey, team," Denise said, and for the first time it really felt like they were one. "It's 12:30. Let's get some lunch. And let's reconvene at quarter past one. OK?"

There were some head nods and thumbs up as people started filing out of the room toward the canteen. Denise noticed the team leaders walking toward their cubicles. *I guess they're not used to going to the canteen and have brought their own lunches. And probably they check in with their teams and read emails. I should get some pizza for everyone next time and make sure everyone gets an actual break*, Denise thought to herself as she followed the group heading for the canteen.

THURSDAY, MARCH 9 – 12:30 PM, ON TO A PRODUCTIVE AFTERNOON, WHAT A RELIEF

After grabbing a quick lunch at the canteen Denise returned to the production area and noticed one of the team leaders, Drew, standing alone by a vending machine with a can of cherry Coke. It was clear he was not engaged in the workshop. Denise wanted to understand why and try to get him on board in some role.

They made some small talk, and then Denise dived in. "Ok, Drew," she said. "How do you think this is going?"

"Honestly, Denise," he said. "I've seen this so many times before. I get it. You're young, you're excited, you want to change the world. Believe me, I was the same – but many of the changes you are hoping for are not going to happen. There's just too much inertia in the system."

Denise looked at him. "That sounds like you've given up?"

Drew frowned and stared at his hands for a while. Denise waited for him to sort out his thoughts.

"Well, I wouldn't go that far," he said at last.

"I'm glad you're saying that because I need you on this team, Drew."

Drew looked skeptical. "You're just trying to get the negative guy to be a team player Denise."

"No, I'm not. If we want to succeed, we need to do things differently. Very differently. We need new ideas, and we need to test them fast, even the crazy ones. That's going to be close to chaos. So, I need someone to stabilize the ship while all the others go diving. I need your healthy skepticism to keep us in line. Can I count on you?"

Drew looked at her for several long seconds, then he nodded. "OK," he said. "I'll do that. But don't expect me to be super enthusiastic. I am just not a rah-rah guy."

Denise laughed. "Deal. That is why we need you, Drew."

With that, they headed back to the workshop room.

Fortified by food, it seemed like finally all the groups were getting the hang of the Starter Kata for the current condition analysis. They realized that it was more about the underlying pattern the recipe laid out than literally implementing it word for word.

As the afternoon progressed, group after group succeeded in grasping the current condition well enough to start working on establishing a one-month challenge.

Denise enthusiastically handed out and explained the second card she had prepared: a Starter Kata for establishing the next target condition (see Figure 24.2).

Immediately, Denise realized that people were confused. *Maybe this wasn't such a good idea*, she thought.

Recipe: Establishing the next Target Condition

1. REVIEW THE CHALLENGE

2. DEFINE THE DESIRED OUTCOME

   o What is your outcome metric that links with the challenge?
   Add current value and calculate target value.

   o How and how often will you measure it?

3. SKETCH THE DESIRED PATTERN FOR THE PROCESS
   How should the process run? Draw a block diagram of the desired steps and their sequence.

4. SET THE ACHIEVE BY DATE FOR YOUR NEXT TARGET CONDITION
   1 to 4 weeks max. is a good timeframe.

5. DEFINE YOUR FOCUS OF WORK FOR THE NEXT TARGET CONDITION
   What part of the desired process pattern will you establish until the achieve by date?

6. DEFINE HOW YOU WILL MEASURE PROGRESS

   o What is your process metric for measuring progress regarding your work focus?
   Add current value and calculate target value.

   o How and how often will you measure it?

7. ESTABLISH THE FRAMING CONDITIONS.

FIGURE 24.2
Starter Kata for establishing the next target condition, adapted from Mike Rother, *The Toyota Kata Practice Guide*, McGraw-Hill (New York), 2018.

"I don't quite get it," Sarah said, clearly speaking for the team. "You told us we should establish our one-month goal now. But the title of the card suggests it's a recipe for establishing the next target condition. Isn't that what we are supposed to do after we've got our one-month challenge defined? I'm sorry to be asking so many questions, but what is the difference between them, anyway, besides the time frame?"

Denise thought for a moment. *Sarah's right. This is confusing. Rother has a recipe to help define the challenge and one for the target condition, but he does not discuss a monthly goal toward the challenge. I guess I didn't really know myself how to do this so I just pulled out the target condition recipe ... When Maggie proposed the 3-1-1, it all made sense. But now....*

Oh well, I guess we'll just take it step by step and figure out how to make it work. We'll kata it, Denise thought, realizing how much more comfortable she had become experimenting and learning as she went. It was becoming clearer that practicing scientific thinking was as much a personal learning journey as a way to get results.

Denise pulled herself out of her internal monologue. Everyone was staring at her, waiting for a response.

"Sarah, you're right, this is confusing and I should have explained better," she confessed. "The problem is that in the books about Kata there is no recipe for a one-month goal. We came up with the one-month goal to get a pace set for our work because the three-month challenge is so big and far out, and I wanted a shorter-term milestone to aim for. Now, we could use the recipe for a challenge, but I wanted a more defined goal, with more detail.

"What I've learned is that 'target condition' has two useful meanings. First, it describes the next state we want to achieve toward our challenge. And that should be close, a small bite we can chew." She paused as she saw people nodding their heads.

"Secondly I like to think of a target condition as a better format for defining goals in general," Denise continued. "A good target condition has four elements: First, an outcome metric, linking to the challenge and measuring the impact of our efforts. Second, a desired operating pattern. A picture or description of the desired condition for the process. You could think of the two like this: The outcome metric is like the score of a soccer game, the desired operating pattern describes how we strive to play the game to win."

"Score and how we play the game," Sarah summarized. "I get that." She made a note on the card in her hand.

"The third is the process metric," Denise continued. "That's for measuring progress at a chosen focus point." Denise saw Sarah frown along with some others. *I've lost them now,* she thought.

"Let's take the soccer example," Denise said, in the hopes of giving them an example they could relate to. "Our description of how we want to play the game will contain several areas we need to develop. Say we want to get better at controlling the ball after a pass, passing the ball to teammates who are open, and playing defense, for example. Those might be just a few elements of a long list of things we need to do to win. Now of course, we can't work on achieving all of them at once. Otherwise we'd lose focus, the team would be confused, and we'd end up nowhere."

Denise could see that several people including Sarah were nodding.

"OK," she continued, "so we have to pick a focus area to work on first. Let's say we choose to improve controlling the ball after receiving a pass. How do we know we're improving on that?"

"That's easy," Doug jumped in. He was obviously a soccer fan. "We can measure the pass-completion rate."

"Dang." Denise smiled. "That's 100% right, Doug. And that's what the process metric is for. Helping us understand if and how much progress we're making on the aspect of our desired process that we're currently focusing on."

"Ah, now I get it," Sarah said, making another note on her card. Denise saw a few others scribbling on their cards as well.

"I like that you're adapting your cards by adding notes and making them your personal recipes," Denise said. "Keep doing that. We'll use these cards often."

"So what's the fourth thing a target condition needs?" Betty asked.

"Oh, right," Denise said, "an achieve-by date, of course."

Everyone nodded.

"My thinking is that using these four elements might be a good way to set a one-month goal, in addition to the one-week target conditions. Can we give it a try?"

She waited until she saw enough people nodding their heads.

"Good," Denise went on. "What I want you to do now is establish a one-month goal for each of the focus topics. We'll use the target condition format, the four elements I just described, to define your one-month goals. To do so, go through the recipe you have on the card I've given you and fill out the T-shaped form on your storyboard, which we'll use again for the target condition."

As the groups went back to work, Denise made the rounds and helped them with the four elements, three really, since the one-month achieve-by date was fixed.

This is working OK now, but it was a mistake to think they could apply the Starter Kata without a coach. It's really not as straightforward as it seems. I have to remember what it was like for me when I first started learning it, Denise thought as she circulated through the room. *Once again, Maggie was right. She said something like, "have them practice the Starter Kata and coach them while they do." Well, here we are.*

The afternoon went by in a blaze. At 4:30 pm, every team had at least a draft version of a one-month goal documented on their target condition forms at the top left of their storyboards.

"OK, everyone." Denise clapped her hands. "I see you all got your one-month goals more or less defined. Now, we need to establish our next week's target condition. What is it you need to achieve by Friday next week in the direction of your one-month goal?"

Right away confusion set in again. Denise could immediately see and hear it. People were looking at their boards, seemingly not knowing what to do. Then, they started discussing. Quietly at first, but the noise level in the room rose higher and higher as more and more people expressed their exasperation. *Don't panic. Have them practice and coach them while they do*, thought Denise. She walked from team to team to find out what each was struggling with.

"Denise, I don't get this," Luther said when Denise arrived at the logistics group. He pointed to the target condition form on their storyboard.

"Our challenge is to reduce the number of people we need to move parts to where they are needed for motors from four to three people per shift. That's our contribution to reduce the overall cost. Therefore, our outcome metric for the one-month challenge is the number of motor logistics team members per shift. Within the next four weeks, we want to reduce that number from 4 to 3.5. Of course, we need another measure since there's no such thing as half a person.

"Anyways," Luther continued. He was on a roll now. "What we've decided to do is reduce it to three people right away, with one person on standby. The process metric we've chosen is how many minutes the standby has to support the other three on each run we do on the logistics route we've sketched."

"Or how many minutes the standby is helping the person loading the carts we use to deliver materials," Derek added.

To get to a target condition you told us we need a good understanding of the current condition. We have observed material handlers and they are all over the place and every person does the same job differently. There is no stable current condition to measure. So, we decided we need to create standard routes for them to run and time those to get the current condition measures.

"That's right," Luther said. "Now, you've asked us what we want to achieve next week. But we haven't designed and run the routes yet, so we don't yet understand the current state in detail. So how can we know where we will be by the end of next week? We first need to run some tests and get more data."

"I agree guys," Denise replied, trying to be encouraging. "In fact, you are a step ahead of me. You seem to be on the right path so keep at it. By the way, there is nothing wrong with having a target condition that says you will have the new routes designed and tested."

Denise found herself having similar conversations with the other groups. At one point, Betty asked, "where do I write down next week's target condition on the board? Do I need another T template for that? And is it just taking the one-month goal and dividing it by 4?"

Denise found herself struggling to give good answers. She was feeling a bit sorry for herself, thinking. *Why do I have to have all the answers guys? I am just learning along with you.*

After a while, Jason noticed Denise struggling and pulled her aside.

"Hey, Denise," he said, "The team is progressing, but there was so much confusion at the beginning, I think they're exhausted."

"I can see that," Denise said, acknowledging his concern, "but my target condition was for them to have completed their target conditions by the end of today."

Jason's face softened. He clearly saw how stressed Denise was.

"Maybe just call it a day," he suggested gently. "Tomorrow is another day," he added softly, with a smile.

"I guess you're right," Denise replied. "Sorry for pushing back," she added, squeezing his arm.

Denise whistled. The room quieted down instantly.

"I have come to a major decision on how we should complete the next step of setting a target condition," she said.

The group gasped.

Denise paused for a moment, then smiled. "We should all go home and save it for tomorrow. It will keep," she said.

The room echoed with relieved laughter.

"You all have worked so hard and done such a great job in such a short time. I have walked around and many of you have legitimate questions, like how can we set a good target condition without a deeper dive into the current condition? And, do we just divide the one-month challenge by 4? We can take this up tomorrow. To be honest I think you all are further along in developing your target conditions than you realize. And, in some cases, a deeper dive into the current condition makes a lot of sense. But the important thing is to go home and relax and celebrate all the great work we have done."

The group spontaneously burst into applause.

"But first," she said after a pause, "we have just a few small scheduling issues to address."

A number of people sighed. The group was clearly ready to go home.

"These two days have been fabulous. We'll pick up tomorrow. From then on, we'll meet every Monday to check our progress, address interdependencies across groups, and make decisions that can't be made by the individual teams. And, of course, we will set our next target conditions for the week."

After a brief discussion of schedules everyone put the recurring meeting in their calendars. Next, Denise went around the room team by team to schedule daily coaching sessions. Denise soon realized that people didn't understand what the coaching sessions were about; they were reluctant to take time out of their busy days to plan for them. Joe tried to help, piping in to explain how great it was to have Denise as a coach. But the team just wasn't buying it. Eventually, Denise realized everyone was too tired, and it was time to quit.

"OK, you know what, let's call it a day. We'll discuss scheduling coaching sessions tomorrow," she said. "In fact, our new consultant, Maggie, has a great way to illustrate what we mean by coaching and she can also help us better understand target conditions. Let's meet tomorrow at 10:00 am for two hours. Maggie will lead a fun, little exercise to help explain what Toyota Kata is all about. It'll be like playing a game. Actually, it will be playing a game." *I seriously hope this exercise Maggie has been talking about is fun. I guess I'll just have to trust her.*

"So, all right, team. Great work! This is going in my books as a successful launch for this challenging process. See you tomorrow," Denise added.

As everyone filed out, Denise automatically began to reflect on the day, and even beat herself up a bit.

We got stuck on trying to define next week's target conditions. I did not accomplish my target condition for today. On the other hand, the group figured out that we probably need to do more current condition analysis first – so they actually are practicing Improvement Kata. Sometimes you have to go back a step, over my thumb.

Even so, Denise had to admit she still felt some anxiety. She had the distinct feeling she was in over her head. *Maggie*, she thought, *I need your help!*

QR CODE 24.1

Insights the team gained practicing the Starter Kata.

25

Prepping for Fun with Puzzles

FRIDAY, MARCH 10 – 6:35 AM, ON THE WAY TO DO ACTUAL WORK WITH MAGGIE

DENISE DROVE HER car out of the underground parking lot in her building just as the sun was about to rise. *Another early start*, she thought, *I wonder what a good night's sleep would feel like?* Denise could feel the toll the accumulated stress and lack of sleep were taking on her body. But never mind. Today, she wanted to get some work done before Maggie came in.

I need to prepare the room for the exercises Maggie wants to run with the team. She said she wants to split the team up into groups of four, and each group needs a separate table. And she will bring a puzzle for each group to practice the Improvement Kata, a 15-piece children's puzzle of all things. I wonder how that'll work. Hopefully the team won't think we're crazy and just turn around and leave. I bet they would be embarrassed if their kids found out they were playing with puzzles at work. "Mommy, what did you do today?" "Oh, a puzzle."

Denise took a sip of freshly brewed coffee from her thermos. Ping! Her phone obnoxiously signaled an incoming message. As usual, she had it clamped into the holder on her dashboard so she could read the first line displayed on the home screen. It was from Jason: "Ready for the weekend? Where should we go? Have you…."

Darn, I totally forgot about our hiking plans for the weekend. Denise felt a sudden adrenaline rush. *I suggested staying at my house or an overnight trip, a stay at a Bed and Breakfast. A trip would be far better. I should have booked something*, Denise thought. *Now they'll be all full. I need to call Jason.*

Denise was a little embarrassed to realize she already had Jason on speed dial. He picked up after the second ring.

DOI: 10.4324/9780429347023-28

"Hey there, good morning," he said, a flirtatious lilt in his voice. "You're up early. So, where are we going?"

I have to come up with something quick, thought Denise. *Where can we go?*

"How about the Clover Crest trail? We can do a two-day hike and stay overnight at the Pinewood B&B," Denise paused and took a breath. "But I haven't had time to book it, so it might be full already. I'm so sorry."

"Ah, so you forgot about our weekend plans," mocked Jason.

"No, I didn't," Denise replied defensively. "Well," she sighed, "maybe I did. It's just been a lot the past few days! I feel like I am constantly digging myself out of a hole ... I *am* sorry."

There was a pause at the other end of the line. *Is he mad at me? Will he still want to go?*

Jason started laughing. "Sorry, sorry," he said. "I was just teasing you. I kind of guessed you might be really busy. So, listen, I found this little hotel near Lake Orchid, and they can accommodate us. It won't be a multi-day hike, but there are nice day hikes in the mountains all around there, and there's also a thermal hot spa nearby. It's a fabulous hideaway and only a two-hour drive. So, we can make it tonight after we finish work. What do you think?"

"Oh, Jason, that sounds awesome," Denise replied feeling enormously relieved. "I'd love to do that. Sounds exactly like what I need after this week. Can you book it?"

"As we speak. And I'll get my stuff packed and bring it to work. We'll go to your place after work and get yours. I'm guessing you haven't packed anything yet?"

"Oh, stop teasing me. You know I haven't."

Jason started laughing again. "Alright, I need to get going, too. See you later."

"Yes, see you at work," Denise said, as they both hung up. Denise realized she had gone from feeling exhausted to feeling energized. *I'm so much looking forward to the weekend with Jason.*

She turned on the radio to a Stevie Wonder song and took another sip of coffee. The sun lit up the sky. It was going to be another nice, almost-spring day, not that she would see it from inside the factory. As Stevie crooned, Denise couldn't help it, she sang along. Denise arrived at the plant shortly after 7:00 am. She parked her car and walked over to the building that housed her office.

As Denise crossed over from the serene farmland to the factory, she heard the humming of the machines. The morning shift had started at

6:00 am. She could smell the distinct odor of the cooling agent that was used in the machines. *Yup, that's production*, Denise thought. The smell, the sound, and the warm temperature rising from the machines always gave her a familiar feeling.

Somehow it feels natural to me to work in production, and I especially like working with production people. They're straightforward, no politics, no nonsense, they just tell you what they think.

Denise walked over to her old assembly team. As she made her way between the assembly lines to her office, she greeted several of the morning shift team members working in the lines. *Everything appears to be running smoothly. So far, so good*, she thought.

"Hey, Denise, how are you?" It was Mark. He seemed to be doing well running the department.

"Good, good," Denise replied. "And how about yourself? Got everything under control?"

"Sure, all up and running," Mark replied. "Or, at least on the surface. I guess you don't want to know about the dirty details now that you're not our boss anymore. And you sure have enough on your plate." Mark gave her a sly smile.

Denise smiled. "How's it going with David? Did he talk with you yet?"

"I don't know," Mark said. "I mean, yes, of course he's talked with me. He talked with me early yesterday morning. And then he was back a second time yesterday afternoon, just before I left. He told me to run the department like we've done in the past. He's not aiming to step in and change anything, at least not now. 'You know your processes best,' he kept saying. To me, that sounds like he's not really interested in the details.

"Something about the whole thing just doesn't seem right. I mean, he said he would take over the department while you were on the motors project. I think he should be more hands on, like actually running the department, not just leaving me alone."

Denise frowned. She could see old behavior patterns bubbling up, patterns she thought Mark had overcome long ago. *I'm not going to let Mark fall back into waiting for orders just like he used to do before I got here.*

"David is the *acting* department manager," she said. "He agreed to take the role until you're ready to take over. That was one of my demands when they wanted me to take this new job. His main responsibility is to attend management meetings and run interference with top management … and keep you out of trouble." Denise chuckled. "This is a completely new role for David, just like it is for you. Or, actually, there are way more unknowns for David. You're still running the same lines with the same people. How do you think David feels, especially being the plant manager?"

Mark nodded his head. "You're right," he said, smiling. "It's just that everything is so new. There's so many decisions I need to make now. How do I know I'm doing things right? You used to coach me. David is not a coach like you are."

"I know," Denise said, her voice full of empathy. "But give David a chance. Please work with him. What do you think?"

Mark thought for a second, then replied positively grinning now, that old teasing look on his face. "You're saying I should put on my big boy pants. Okay, Denise. You're right that Joe and I were essentially running the department anyway. I should know what I'm doing by now."

Denise felt relieved. Another crisis averted.

"Mark, I am so proud of you and you are allowing me to focus my attention on saving the motors department. Thanks so much." She looked at her watch. "Maggie will be here soon. I need to get going. Let's talk again next week."

FRIDAY, MARCH 10 – 7:15 AM, FINALLY A CHANCE TO PLAY WITH PUZZLES, BUT FIRST...

As Denise walked into her office, she glanced at her watch and was startled by the time. *7:15 already. Just 45 minutes until Maggie arrives. I need to get through my emails. Oh, and I need to set up the room for the puzzle exercise Maggie will run. I'll ask Joe if he can help me.*

Denise grabbed her phone and dialed Joe's number. He picked up on the first ring.

"Morning, Denise. Recovered from yesterday?" Joe said in a friendly tone.

"Just barely," she replied, only half-joking. "I'm still a little overwhelmed by how quickly we need to get results. I believe in practicing Kata, but most of our team has no clue about that yet. And yesterday I felt like I was from Mars when I mentioned coaching. I just hope the exercise Maggie runs today makes a difference."

"Ah, right. Maggie's coming in today. Cool. I'm really looking forward to meeting her. From what you said she is a magician. So, why'd you call me?"

"Oh, yeah, can you give me a hand setting up the room for the exercise with the team today?"

"Sure. I'm already here actually. Was just working on my storyboard. I wanted to add some more data about the current condition."

"Great. Thank you," Denise replied. "Meet you there in a minute."

Denise hung up and searched for Maggie's email about how to set up the room. She printed it out and made her way to the conference room. In the conference room, Denise and Joe looked over the email together. "I guess we need four tables with five people per table. We're expecting around 20 people. I invited some extra people to come, colleagues who've expressed interest in what we're doing," said Denise.

They went to work.

Once they had the tables arranged, Denise said, "Joe, I need to go. Maggie's arriving soon. Could you please make sure we have enough flip chart paper? And oh, Maggie wanted each group to have a pencil, eraser, and red marker. And she sent me some handouts to be printed out too. Might you be able to organize that?"

"No problem," Joe replied.

"Thanks Joe. I'll forward Maggie's email to you. See you at 10."

With that, Denise made her way back to her office to get through some of her daily tasks that had been piling up.

At 7:55, Denise's phone rang. It was Maggie.

"Morning, Denise. Can you let me in? I'm at the entrance."

"Good morning, Maggie. Of course, I'll come get you."

Denise jumped up and made her way to the other side of the building.

At the entrance, Denise greeted Maggie and handed her the keycard badge she had gotten yesterday.

They made their way back through production to the project room.

When Maggie saw where they were headed, she said, "Denise, could you give me a quick tour through production please, along the value stream for making the motor parts. It will help if I get a first glance at the current condition?"

Ah, she's right. Denise thought. *Get a fresh look, first hand, and with her own eyes.*

"Sure, let's do that," Denise replied.

They did a quick tour of the value stream and Maggie listened intently to Denise's explanations. She asked only a few clarifying questions here and there, penciled several notes into her tiny notebook, but gave no comments.

After about 15 minutes, they finished the tour and made their way to the project room.

"So, what do you think?" Denise asked.

"I like it," Maggie replied. "You have a great playing field here for practicing Kata with your team."

Once they were in the project room, Denise showed Maggie what they had done in the workshop, starting with the challenge they had formulated for the project.

"Wait a sec," Maggie said. "Before you take me through the details, what is your target condition for the team for this week?"

Ah right, there goes Maggie, coaching me, Denise thought.

"My target condition for this week is to have the challenge for the project defined, have the one-month challenges in place for each focus topic, and also have a target condition for next week established, again for each focus topic. And that's actually what I wanted to discuss with you. We struggled a bit with the one-week target conditions yesterday so I put them on hold," answered Denise.

"Wait, hold on one sec," Maggie said. "What is your actual condition now?"

"Well, we got the challenge defined," said Denise, "and the one-month goals are established quite well for, I'd say, most of the topics. We used the target condition recipe for the one-month goals. But we haven't got the one-week target conditions yet. That's where we stopped last night. The team was exhausted, and I was too. They were struggling to understand what a one-week target condition would look like compared to the one-month goals, but we got past that. Then they realized they needed a better understanding of the current condition, which was great, but we ended without next target conditions."

Maggie nodded. "OK then," she said. "let's go and have a look at what you have."

They walked over to the flip chart with the overall challenge statement they had come up with. Denise explained how they arrived at 20% in three months, instead of the original 30% and said they were keeping their fingers crossed they would be approved to keep going and get the additional 10% in the second three months. And she explained that they still needed real numbers.

Wouldn't it be great if we could reduce the cost per motor by 20% and keep production inhouse.

Therefore we have to...

- *Increase productivity to x*
- *Reduce the cost of bad quality to y*
- *Reduce the cost of material to z*

...by June 8th.

They then went through each storyboard, and Maggie made some comments here and there and gave some advice when Denise noted that the team had struggled. They paused to discuss the two quality focus topics Sarah and Joe were working on which had given them a bit of trouble the day before.

"Look over here," Denise said, pointing at the board for one of the quality topics. "We tried to follow my recipe for establishing the next target condition. But we struggled to come up with a desired pattern for the process. See." Denise moved her finger to the target condition. "There is no desired process pattern."

"What about the current condition?" Maggie asked. "How is the process running now? What are the steps and sequences?"

Denise paused. "Oh right, that information is missing too."

"OK," Maggie asked, "at what step in the process are these quality defects detected?" Maggie pointed to one of the red circles showing where a defect occurred on the part.

"That happens after the last process step on one of the machines. The operator does a self-check on every tenth part or so."

"Good," Maggie pulled one of the flip charts closer and turned to a new page. She sketched a box in the middle of the page. "Let's say that's the step where the detection happens." "Now, what are the steps that happen before this point?" she asked, pointing to the box she had drawn. "Upstream that is," she added, her finger moving to the left side of the flip chart.

"Ah, now I get it," Denise said. "Before that is logistics." She paused. "And then at some point all the way back are the steps that happen at our supplier."

"Right." Maggie nodded while she drew several empty boxes to the left which formed a block diagram, like the Starter Kata recommended. They then discussed steps after the inspection all the way to shipping to the customer.

"And each of the steps could have an effect on quality," Denise said, nodding. "And, of course, the process is different for each of the parts. It might even be a bit different for different quality aspects of the same part. So, we need to sketch multiple process patterns to grasp the current condition. Not just one."

"Ta da," Maggie said. "You got it. Now what obstacles are preventing you from reaching your personal target condition for this week?" Maggie asked.

"As I said," Denise replied, "the team still has not developed their target conditions. I was pleased that they understood enough to want to go back to the current condition. But I still think they're going to struggle with the desired process pattern. Now that you showed me this my hunch is that getting them to work on block diagrams of the current and future processes like you just demonstrated will help a lot."

"Great," Maggie said, "you've got it," as she looked down at her watch. "When did you plan for the Kata puzzle exercise I'm supposed to run with the team?"

"At 10."

"You know what, let's get to that room now and check it out. We're almost out of time. Let's discuss your obstacles with the one-week target conditions after the puzzle exercises and include the team. Then we don't need to do it twice. Would that work for you?"

"Sure," Denise replied, noticing how late it was already. "Let's go," she added, and they started walking toward the room.

26

Kata to Grow Exercise

FRIDAY, MARCH 10 – 9:50 AM, BACK TO SCHOOL FOR PUZZLE TIME

DENISE WAS RELIEVED to see Joe had laid out the project room exactly as Maggie had described in her email. Maggie had brought several 15-piece children's puzzles depicting a farmyard. At the center of each puzzle were three cows and a cat. The farm scene in the background was full of bright, contrasting colors, making the puzzle relatively easy. Maggie went round and placed one puzzle on each table. Also on each table, Joe had set out a form to record how many seconds it took to build the puzzle for each round. Standing beside each table was a Kata storyboard on a flip chart stand. On the walls there were blown-up versions of the Improvement Kata four-step model and some rules for the game.

"This looks great, Joe," Denise said. "You're awesome."

It's so good to have a Kata geek at my side. I guess that's what you would call a coalition of first movers, Denise thought.

Maggie looked around the room approvingly and hooked up her laptop to the projector at the front of the room.

"Denise," said Maggie, "please observe how I run this exercise so you can run it yourself next time."

"I guess I better take notes then, Denise replied. Maybe I can create a script for running the exercise."

Soon team members piled into the room, coffees in hand, and grabbed some of the muffins Denise had laid out. Denise noticed that they seemed particularly chatty this morning. She was happy to see her team members getting along with one another, but anxious to begin. Most of all, she felt the relief of having someone else take the lead instead of always being center stage.

DOI: 10.4324/9780429347023-29

"Alright, everyone," Denise said, after the room had quieted down, "as you know, we have a very special guest instructor. Actually, she's our senior advisor on Kata and working with me as my coach on this project. So, I'm delighted to introduce Maggie, my mentor, friend, and personal trainer. Maggie worked at the same consulting company as I did in a previous life. Then our lives took different paths. Maggie opened a gym where she runs a fleet of personal trainers and also became an avid practitioner of Toyota Kata.

"It kind of makes sense since the term 'kata' comes from the martial arts where students practice in a gym guided by a coach. Maggie has used the Improvement and Coaching Kata to develop all her associates to think scientifically about how to best provide service to their customers, continually improving every day. With that I will turn it over to Maggie."

"Thank you, Denise," Maggie said, stepping forward. "That was certainly a buildup, probably more than I deserve. Basically, I just like helping people achieve a higher level of fitness and feel better about themselves. I have been trying to do my job well. I discovered Kata after I left consulting and started to live my dream, as Denise said, running a gym. As I got more into Kata, I've read many books and attended various seminars by Mike Rother, the father of Kata, and Tilo Schwarz, who taught me a great deal about coaching.

"You probably know a bit about Kata already, and I know you've worked through some of the planning steps for your motors challenge. Kata has two meanings. It's a form and also a way of doing. Each kata provides something like an exercise for practicing specific skills, much like any coach would assign to their players – a drill, really. Over time and through practice, a kata can turn into a way to do something and even a way of life.

"In this case, we are practicing the meta-skill of scientific thinking so that it becomes our natural, default way of working toward our goals. With a kata we take a complex skill and break it down into smaller manageable pieces and practice each, one by one, until we perform it according to a standard pattern and eventually transform the pattern to make it our own.

"The Improvement Kata was developed by Mike Rother based on his time spent observing a number of the best Toyota-Production-System master trainers in the world. They had their own unique approaches to developing people, but Mike discerned a common pattern that is shown in this cartoon-like diagram." Maggie pointed to one of the blown-up Improvement Kata figures on the wall that Denise had originally used to teach Mark and Joe (see Figure 26.1).

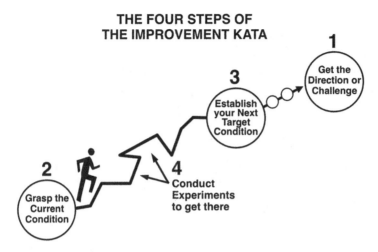

FIGURE 26.1

The Improvement Kata Model, Mike Rother, *The Toyota Kata Practice Guide*, McGraw-Hill (New York), 2018.

"The starting point is the direction which Mike called the challenge. Every Toyota master coaching an improver would issue a challenge, concrete, measurable, and usually about three to six months out. The challenge would be audacious and maybe even seemed impossible at first. You may be feeling that way about your current challenge.

"Next the coach asked them to understand the current condition. Statistics were not enough. They had to go and see and observe firsthand. This led to what you have started to work on as the current condition analysis. Then, still planning, they would ask them to identify a first focus area and define what they wanted to accomplish, which Mike called the target condition. Finally, came the fun part that I am sure you are all looking forward to – action. That is running experiments.

"We are going to practice all these steps with the technically complex task of assembling the 15-piece puzzle in front of you. You can show off to your kids at home later, brag about how fast you can do it, though we probably won't get as good as they are," she said with a big grin.

The group smiled back tentatively, everyone looking a little uncertain about where this was going.

Maggie surveyed the room. "But that's enough talk for now," she said. "Let's get started. The first task is simply to assemble the puzzle as a team. Empty the puzzle pieces on the table. Then assemble the puzzle. You don't have to record your time or anything. Just dive in like a child would and take, say, the next two minutes to assemble the puzzle. Ready, set, go!"

The groups were still a bit hesitant. Team members looked at each other. But then, at each table, someone started handling the pieces and others joined in. Soon, the room was noisy as everyone was intensely focused on the game. Within a few minutes they all had a finished puzzle.

Maggie jumped back in, "Great job! You all have a future in puzzle assembly. Now, over the next 60 minutes, we will do this puzzle several times and record the times. Your objective is to reduce the puzzling time from round to round. But, there's a catch, we want to practice the Improvement Kata working toward our goal. So, what do we need to do first?"

"Decide on who's the boss for our team," Team leader Sam shouted jokingly.

"Define who does what," Betty threw in.

"Set a work standard," Phil from production engineering proposed, obviously feeling proud of himself.

"OK, OK, I understand you want to jump ahead to action," Maggie said. "You're already proposing solutions. But, based on the Improvement Kata model, what do we need to do first?" Maggie pointed to the big poster on the wall.

"Understand the direction," Jason said.

"Exactly," replied Maggie, smiling. She advanced a slide on her laptop. "Your challenge is to build this puzzle in 15 seconds. How do you feel about that?"

Immediately people began murmuring and looking at each other in disbelief.

"Impossible!" shouted someone.

"That's definitely a challenge," came from another corner of the room.

"How do you know?" Maggie asked after a while, projecting her voice over the noise.

"Because that means one second for each piece," someone threw out.

"So is that easy or hard?" Maggie asked in return.

"Super hard," came the immediate response – Sam again.

Then Joe spoke up. "Actually," he said, "we don't know. We haven't grasped the current condition yet. So we don't know where we are and how far away 15 seconds is."

"Exactly," Maggie said. "See?" She pointed to one of the posters again. "Step two of the Improvement Kata – grasp the current condition. Just like with your motors challenge. Don't panic, let's grasp the current condition first.

"Let's do that now and build the puzzle again, this time following a few rules. She pointed toward the rules on the wall. The most important thing is to start with the puzzle pieces randomly sorted, stacked upside down on the table. No peeking. We will all start building at the same time. You'll know when to start because I'll announce it. So, we're going build the puzzle twice more, timing the rounds and following these rules. Record the times on the sheet in front of you. There is no need for planning in these baseline runs. Just do what comes naturally. I need each team to pick a person to be a timekeeper. That person will also be responsible in general for recording information. We'll refer to him or her as the recorder."

"Please get ready following these steps:

1. Pick a recorder.
2. Turn the pieces upside down randomly and build a pile on the table. There is no need for planning.

Go to it?"

The groups got started, again a bit hesitant at first, but then they all picked a recorder and set the pieces up as asked. Soon, they all began talking about how to build the puzzle. Who would do what? Should two people build, or three? Some thought it was a good idea to start with the outer edges. Others suggested they start with the animals at the puzzle's center.

"Three, two, one start!" Maggie shouted above the din.

They all built the puzzle, each group struggling a bit as people's hands bumped into one another, trying to grab the same pieces. After the puzzle was built, the noise level in the room rose, as team members chattered to each other about how they would approach the puzzle next time.

Maggie tried to call the group to attention, but they were having none of it, intensely focused on their puzzle discussions. Finally, she took out a silver whistle, the kind many hadn't seen since gym class, and blew it, creating a loud, shrill noise. Everyone stopped. Some put their hands over their ears.

"Please, I need you to follow the rules! Remember, planning is not necessary at this point. We simply want to build the puzzle the best we can and time it. There will be multiple opportunities to experiment with your ideas in five experimenting rounds. This is just a baseline to figure out our current condition. Remember, we are on step 2 of the Improvement Kata. Now, we are going to do the same thing again. Please set up your pieces in the center of the table."

The groups obeyed.

"Three, two, one start!" called out Maggie.

Again, the groups built the puzzle, and then, immediately after they were done, the volume rose as people discussed what they had done and how they could improve.

Maggie blew her whistle and took control of the chaos.

"Congratulations! You have now completed the two baseline rounds. Think about these as the way motors is running now, before any improvements. Lots of opportunities. How long did it take to build the puzzle on average?"

"90 seconds," someone called out.

"75 seconds," shouted another proudly.

"We took 130 seconds," someone said meekly.

"Okay, don't feel bad," Maggie said in a gentle voice.

Maggie went around the room checking whether the recorder for each group had recorded the times on the form for the current state. They had. She then asked them to add bullet point descriptions of the current condition.

People wrote things like "disorganized," "no process," "hands in each other's way," and "no standardized process."

When everyone had put their pencil down, Maggie again called the group to order.

"Now, we will start the improvement process following the Improvement Kata. As you know, our challenge is to build the puzzle in 15 seconds."

Again, the murmuring began.

"Can't be done," someone said.

Another shouted "good luck with that!"

"Okay, okay, calm down," Maggie said in a reassuring voice. "The good news is that we do not have to achieve that today." She pointed to the poster with the Improvement Kata again. "All we need at the moment is to set one next target condition on the way to the challenge, our only target condition for the day. Where do you want to be, as a team, 60 minutes from now? We'll likely have time for five experiments before then. Think of this as week 1 of a several-month process. You can run one experiment per day, like the five days of the workweek. You can determine whatever you think is reasonable to achieve by the end of week 1 as your first target condition on the way to reaching your challenge. Think about your three-month machining challenge of reducing cost by 20%. Would anyone expect to achieve that in week 1?"

Everyone shook their heads. Someone shouted out, "no way!"

Maggie reminded them of the card Denise had handed out with the Starter Kata on how to establish a good next target condition and that it should include the target time as an outcome and descriptions of the process they were trying to achieve.

"So, what's your target condition for today?" Maggie asked.

Everyone set to work coming up with times. One group wanted to go for the 15-second challenge right away, but Maggie discouraged them. It was clear that most groups were struggling with the "condition" part, and Denise came around to help them. They ultimately wrote things like "clear division of labor" and "follow a defined pattern for the sequence of what to build."

Once that was done, Maggie explained that they would now move on to the experimentation phase, step 4 on the Improvement Kata diagram.

To do so, Maggie asked them to discuss and plan their first experiment and write down the idea they wanted to test, as well as the time they expected the puzzle would take on the experimenting record on their storyboards. The chatter immediately started up again, as group members debated different solutions.

On a few occasions, Maggie had to rein the group in, asking them to focus on testing one idea at a time, a single factor, and to record their ideas AND expectations in the experimenting record on the storyboard.

After a few minutes of struggle, each group was able to fill out the relevant part of their storyboard and then run the experiment and record the results. Maggie pushed them to write down their reflections on what they learned from the experiment and plan their second experiment.

"And don't forget to record your expectation for the second experiment!" Maggie called.

When the groups were done, they seemed eager to begin experimenting, but Maggie told them to hold on; they weren't ready yet.

"Now," she said, "Let's practice Coaching Kata."

Maggie asked Denise to lead the first coaching session with one of the groups and handed her one of the cards with the Coaching Kata questions. Denise went through the questions with the group, also asking some deepening questions. Everyone else watched curiously.

Maggie then asked for a volunteer to lead another coaching session with another group, repeating this pattern until every group had been coached. The novices struggled with asking the questions, often creating their own versions, getting lost, and adding leading questions like "don't you think we should build the outside of the puzzle first?"

Maggie recommended they simply ask the questions as written and repeat a question if the answer did not correspond to the question.

After each group was done being coached, they ran their experiments. After that, the groups were able to coach themselves through the subsequent rounds of experiments, with different members rotating through the role of coach and reading the questions from the card.

The energy level in the room was high. The tables buzzed with discussions about various ways to improve how to build the puzzle. Applause would erupt from one corner of the room when a group improved, and dejected looks reigned when times got worse. Maggie blew her whistle on a few more occasions, then reminded the groups to only change one thing at a time and not to jump to assumptions, but, in no time, it seemed, the five rounds were up.

Each group had reached or surpassed their target conditions, and all felt self-satisfied with their progress. Denise couldn't believe how into it everyone looked. Even the original skeptics were smiling, and the atmosphere was completely positive. It felt more like a party than a day at work.

Maggie then led them through a discussion of what they learned about Kata and recorded their answers on a flip chart. They all agreed the Improvement Kata pattern and especially the coaching helped them approach the puzzle building more scientifically. They appreciated the iterative learning process step by step. They said having a coach asking the Coaching Kata questions helped keep them focused on one factor at a time and discuss what they learned before defining the next experiment.

They were surprised by some of the differences between what they expected and what happened, especially when their times got worse, but they said that ultimately they found those occasions to be the most eye-opening.

"It's just incredible how often we jumped to conclusions, thinking we had got it right when we actually had no clue," Betty said.

Various people also admitted that they had gotten carried away by their competitive spirits, focusing on trying to get a winning time and therefore tending to neglect the need to follow a scientific approach.

"I think I forgot I was here to learn about Kata, not just play with a puzzle," said one person with a smile. "I guess the kids in us came out."

As the discussion came to a close, Maggie jumped in.

"First," she said, "let me congratulate you on a job well done building puzzles for five-year olds." She paused as the group laughed, then continued, "and getting great insights about Kata. None of us are experts, including me, but it was a great start. We're all learners here. It's clear you saw benefits to the scientific thinking process we practiced. The distraction of wanting to talk about building the puzzle rather than focus on a scientific approach is not unusual. In fact I have seen that in every group I have run the exercise with.

"That is to be expected. Taking action right away, what has been called 'fast thinking,' is natural for us humans*. 'Slow thinking,' reasoned, deliberate thinking when we are trying something new, is actually painful. It makes our brain shout, 'stop doing that and just play the game. We need to conserve our energy for surviving the day.' That is why it is so important to have a coach, and of course for the coach to give us corrective feedback. Mostly, this coaching should take the form of questions rather than observations and answers. As leaders, your goal should be to eventually start practicing your coaching skills."

With that, Maggie nodded at Denise, and Denise took over.

"I asked Maggie to lead this exercise because we are going to be using the Improvement Kata and the Coaching Kata to reach the very difficult challenges we need to achieve to save motors from being outsourced," Denise said. "I do not think our goals for the motor department are easier than the 15-second puzzle challenge. But if we follow the scientific approach, and do something every day, even run experiments that fail along the way, I am confident together we can achieve the challenge. We can win this, but only if we work together."

Denise then asked them to get into their focus-topic groups and get back to work on their first target condition.

After everyone had reshuffled, Maggie jumped in.

"Before you go back to your storyboards, let me give you some tips on establishing your target condition for next week," Maggie said. "I had a look at your work from the last two days this morning, and I have to

---

* Daniel Kahneman, *Thinking Fast and Slow*, Farrar, Straus and Giroux, 2011.

say you did well grasping the current condition for your focus topics and establishing your one-month goals.

"Denise explained to me that you struggled some yesterday with establishing your one-week target conditions. The target condition is difficult for everyone, especially if you want to do a good job. The target condition really should not be the same as dividing the one-month targets by four.

"I hope the puzzle exercise made it clear how important it is to have a short-term next target condition. It's what gives ultimate focus to our improvement work while the one-month goal connects us to the longer-term challenge."

Maggie paused looking around, as several people nodded.

"In general," she continued, "your next week's target condition should follow the same format you used for your one-month goal and which you can find on the Starter Kata card Denise handed out.

"It is relatively easy to come up with a numerical outcome target, but it requires deeper thought to identify the condition we want to see at the end of the next week. While this might seem like a lot of work, it's actually very helpful. Look at the block diagrams many of you did for the desired state in your one-month goals. Some of you may want to go back and detail that further as it provides the foundation for the weekly target condition. Then describe what you would like the process to look like in the future, again using a block diagram."

Maggie paused again, as the groups moved closer to their storyboards.

"So, how many of the steps in the current state of your process do you need to work on to reach your one-month goal?" Maggie asked.

She waited for each group to answer. Most said two or three.

"Right," Maggie continued, "so how many of those should you work on at a time?"

"One, I guess," said Randolph. "Clear focus, right?" he added.

"Absolutely." Maggie gave him a big smile. Then she asked "so, which step are you going to work on next week? Working on it doesn't mean that you experiment with a new idea each day. You may need to start with a deeper dive into the current condition of that one step. That level of understanding of the current condition and detailed focus is certainly necessary to achieve the challenge."

"Now, once you have chosen your focus, describe the condition you'd like to achieve by the end of next week. Then document that using an empty T-template just like you did for your monthly goal.

"Next, we want to set a goal for the outcome metric, and one for the process metric. Can anyone tell me the difference?"

Betty chimed in, "Denise used a soccer example. The outcome metric is like the score of a soccer game, where one process metric could be the percent of passes that are completed successfully."

"Great example Betty, I love it," said Maggie. "Yes, the outcome is what you want to achieve, and the process metric is about how you will achieve it. You pick a process metric based on what you are focusing on this week."

"But what if we don't have a process yet?" Luther from logistics spoke up. "For us, next week we plan to test our idea of a new logistic route and grasp and measure current conditions. So what do we do?"

"Wonderful point!" Maggie responded enthusiastically. "I love where you're going with that. It sounds like currently there is no semblance of a standard process and material handlers are walking every which way. So, to begin to observe, you have to build a draft process through trial and error. You can say that you are still grasping the current condition or you can look at it as running experiments in a kind of conceptual phase. Ask yourself, 'what do we want to know by the end of next week? What are the questions we want to have answered about the current state as well as about defining your desired state for the process?' Then take your T-template and write down these questions on the right side. Your next week's target condition is to have these questions answered."

"Sure, that works", Luther replied, nodding vigorously in agreement. "And once we have those questions answered, we can come up with a target condition for the next week like the other groups. I see where you're going."

"Exactly," said Maggie. "And now, if there are no more questions, get to it!"

Everyone got to work establishing their next week's target conditions with a much clearer focus than the day before. Maggie and Denise circulated, working with the teams. The puzzle exercise seemed to have helped because all of the groups produced thoughtful target conditions. After they were done, they enthusiastically shared their target conditions with the group, and the mood was very upbeat.

On that note, Denise decided to close the session.

"Thank you Maggie for all you taught us today and for getting us back on track with your excellent coaching," she said.

Maggie got a standing ovation from the group and looked a bit embarrassed by the attention.

Afterward Maggie and Denise stayed behind to debrief.

"So, Denise, what did you think of the puzzle exercise?" Maggie asked.

"At first I thought you were pulling my leg," Denise admitted. "How could a game for kindergarteners teach us about Kata? But I did want the team to do something fun that would raise their energy level. This whole do-or-die motors challenge has made for a morose mood on a good day." Denise paused. "And then, when we actually did the game, I was like, *this is awesome*. It's a wonderful way to learn about Kata. People were engaged and having fun, but they could also really visualize each step we wanted them to follow. And they were able to understand the role of the coach which before seemed just strange to them. Seriously, in the end, I just loved it. It will definitely be a part of my tool kit going forward."

Maggie was beaming. "That is just wonderful to hear," she said. "I suspected as much, but it is so gratifying that it worked out the way I expected. I feel like the teams must have felt when they met or exceeded their predictions for the puzzle." She paused.

"Now, the important thing is to immediately build on that awareness and enthusiasm. We are fortunate we are in a position to do that with a very critical challenge that is by no means a game. In some cases, when I lead this exercise people go home all ginned up but then do nothing and the puzzle game becomes a fading memory."

"Well, that certainly won't happen here," Denise replied. "We're facing an existential threat and a lot of hard work, which definitely will not be all fun and games. But it was nice to start on a positive note. I could also really feel some team-building happening. And I think it helped strengthen my role as the new leader on the block, and your role Maggie as a trusted advisor.

"It was interesting that they struggled to focus on the Improvement Kata pattern and wanted to just focus on winning the game. It seemed like they wanted to default to their natural disposition of jumping to conclusions. Without your coaching, they would have made a whole bunch of changes at once and wouldn't have known which had what effect. It was clear that the scientific thinking pattern did not come naturally to them, but of course that's why we are practicing Kata to begin with."

Maggie nodded her head. "That is such an important insight, Denise," she said. "As you progress with Kata, it becomes increasingly clear how powerful it is to realign our neural pathways and form the habit of thinking scientifically. You don't notice the habit forming on a daily basis, but once

Scan with your mobile to visit
the Kata to Grow website.

QR CODE 26.1
Visit the Kata to Grow website to find out more about how to run the exercise yourself.

you've been doing it for weeks, it's hard to remember when your default wasn't to think scientifically. It becomes obvious when other people are jumping to conclusions based on their biases. I don't have the solutions to achieve the huge challenge we are facing in machining, but I firmly believe this is the right way to get us there.

"And on that note, we still have another fun activity to do today – the first trial of the coaching dojo. I'm especially excited about this since I've never tried it on my own before. This will be my maiden voyage." (Learn more about the puzzle exercise at QRcode 26.1.)

27

Welcome to the Kata Coaching Dojo, A Flight simulator for Coaches

FRIDAY, MARCH 10 – 12:30 PM, DENISE GETS COACHED AGAIN

"I'M SO EXCITED to try out the dojo," said Denise. Maggie had really gotten her hopes up when she had spoken about the dojo as an "accelerator" for developing coaches. Denise needed all the acceleration she could get. "I think it is a good idea to start with a few of our highest potential people for learning Kata Coaching. But first, let's grab some lunch?" Denise added, suddenly realizing how hungry she was.

"No time for that right now," Maggie replied. "Before we get into the dojo you need some help on the basic management of your project. We had a great launch, but now comes the real work, and you need to do some planning. Let's start with the basics. What is your target condition for next week?" Maggie emphasized the word "your" making it clear that she meant Denise's target condition rather than those of the improvers Denise was coaching.

Denise was a bit taken aback by the question. The last thing she expected was to be coached by Maggie as they were getting ready for the dojo. *Aren't we past the point where I'm a student? Haven't I proven myself to Maggie by this point?*

She took a few moments to recompose herself and think. Then, she replied, as casually as she could, "I guess it's not a formal target condition with a metric but what I want is to get everybody going on their topics." She paused. Then she added, "oh, and of course I want each focus-topic group to achieve their next week's target condition by Friday. Want me to write that down?" she asked, a bit sarcastically.

DOI: 10.4324/9780429347023-30

"No!" Maggie replied with a stern look and, to Denise's surprise, picked right back up with her questioning. "How will you measure the outcome of your next target condition?"

Denise thought for a second. Then she said, "I guess I'll measure how many of our weekly target conditions we achieve. Ideally that should be six. So, that's our outcome metric, right?"

Maggie nodded, but the look on her face was still a bit stern. "Please write that down," Maggie said and handed Denise a pencil. Then, Maggie grabbed one of the empty T-templates from one of the tables and taped it to the wall. "Denise," she said, "please add the challenge at the top, too."

Denise looked puzzled. "You mean I really need to define a proper target condition for myself? I'm the project manager and my focus is on getting results through my improvers. They have processes to improve. That is why they have storyboards and I don't."

Maggie looked frustrated. It was the first time Denise had ever seen Maggie look anything other than totally composed and in control.

"I understand that you think that," said Maggie, "and, frankly, that's a concern. But let's just continue on, and I think this will all become clearer. Please fill in the challenge and your outcome metric for your next target condition."

Denise didn't understand where Maggie was going but decided to play along. *I guess she knows what she's doing*, Denise thought, as she copied the challenge statement from one of the other storyboards in the room. That was the same for her as well.

Then, Denise added her outcome metric: "Number of weekly target conditions achieved."

Once she was done writing, Maggie asked, "so, to achieve the target condition, what's your desired pattern of work?"

Denise gave Maggie a puzzled look. "What do you mean? There is no process. I'm the project manager. So, how can I have a desired pattern of work?"

Maggie sighed. She was obviously disappointed with her star student. "OK," she said, "let's dig deeper into this then. How many coaching sessions do you plan to do every day?"

Denise looked at the list of focus topics again. "Ok, I have to coach the teams that work on the issues relating to motor fabrication specifically, so that's two. Plus Luther from logistics. That makes three. And then, I guess, I'll coach Ray on the cost of purchased parts and Phil on the cost of machining. And I expect Jason wants me to coach him on reducing the number of motor types. In total, that makes six. Quite a lot of coaching."

"And how long do you expect each session to be?"

"Around 15 minutes. At least that is what they should take ideally," Denise replied. "At the start, we'll probably need more time as people need to get used to Kata, and I'll have to explain things here and there."

"OK," Maggie said, "So, how long will you need in total for all of these coaching sessions every day?"

"I guess two hours is what I can expect, more or less."

Maggie kept pushing. "And when will you do these coaching cycles?"

Denise suddenly realized that Maggie's question was not an easy one to answer. She had tried to schedule the coaching cycles, but the managers seemed uninterested, but that was before the puzzle exercise. She made a mental note to get them scheduled.

"Good question. The focus-topic leaders are pretty flexible in their schedules. The coaching cycles with the team leaders from motors need to be aligned with their shifts," Denise said at last.

"Actually, if I schedule the sessions at the end of the shift, the second-shift leaders can come in early and be part of the coaching. That may not be best for the salaried folk, but it is critical that I get the team leaders in. That makes sense to me now. I guess I do not know exactly how it will work," she added.

"That is okay that you do not know. At this point it is just a plan. Please sketch that as a block diagram," Maggie requested, still acting a bit more like a drill sergeant than a friend or coach.

Ah, she's walking me through the target condition recipe, Denise realized, starting to warm up to the whole exercise. *I get it. The recipe works for management processes too.*

Denise sketched a block diagram of the desired pattern for her future work days.

Once she was done, Maggie asked, "so how about your week? Could you sketch that as well?"

"Ah, you're right," Denise said, realizing immediately where Maggie was going. "That's a second pattern of work I need to establish. The weekly cycle." Denise thought for a second. Then she said, "I guess the main difference is on Fridays we need to have an all-hands meeting for the project team to establish our next week's target conditions for each focus topic." She sketched the week.

When Denise looked up from her drawing, she saw Maggie frowning. "What is it now?" Denise asked.

"I suggest you also add a daily all hands to allow the different working groups to communicate and synchronize their efforts."

"Hold on," said Denise. "That's too much. I have a one-on-one with each team every day. Why would I need an additional all hands?"

"Because there's a difference between stand-alone, one-on-one coaching cycles and coaching the team as a whole, a kind of birds' eye project-level coaching if you will," Maggie explained. In a complex project like this, the different sub-topics have interdependencies. If teams only meet separately, you are responsible for communicating between the teams – a lot of work for you and inefficient. A daily all hands is a quick way to make decisions together and keep everyone focused. It does not need to be a long meeting."

"I hear you," Denise replied reluctantly. "But I feel like that's a solution for a problem I don't have yet. Why not start with only having Friday meetings? I can always add daily meetings if they become necessary."

Maggie shrugged, looking disappointed. "Up to you," she said. "Now, what else do we need to establish the 3-1-1?"

Denise thought it over. After a short pause, she said, "ah, right. We need to have a bit of a longer meeting on the Friday at the end of each month to establish our next monthly goals." She paused again. "And then, of course, we will need a next target-deployment workshop after we've reached our three-month challenge. And then, there is a three-month presentation to the executives that we need to prepare for and give." She sketched the monthly pattern as well.

"So, what's your next target condition?" asked Maggie

Denise looked at the three patterns that she had been drawing on sheets of paper and arranged them in a row on the table.

"I guess it is to have my six coaching cycles every day," she said.

"Good," Maggie replied. "I'll coach you on that. Let's add in your plan a coaching session just between you and me each morning."

Denise nodded hesitantly. *I'm glad Maggie is on board, but that's a lot. We'll see how it all works out. I desperately need some food now. It's almost 2 o'clock, and we haven't had any lunch yet.*

"Let's see if we can still get something to eat from the canteen," Denise suggested. "My immediate target condition is to have some food in me," Denise smiled.

"OK," Maggie agreed, and they made their way toward the canteen.

When they arrived, people were emptying out of the canteen, and all that was left were some bags of potato chips and other junky snack foods. Everything that was available violated Denise's healthy eating target condition for the week, but she went for it anyway. She was starving, and the impromptu coaching session with Maggie had taken a lot out of her.

FRIDAY, MARCH 10 – 2:00 PM, FINALLY, DOJO FUN

After their meager lunch of snacks, Maggie and Denise met with the group they had selected to participate in the first Kata Coaching Dojo. They felt it was premature to involve the novice leaders in the machine fabrication department. Instead, to get their feet wet experimenting with the Dojo, they had chosen the relatively experienced Joe, Mark, and Jason. David and Sarah, both being curious about Kata, had joined the group as well. The five were already assembled in the conference room when Maggie and Denise arrived.

"In most fields, professionals have a place where they can practice," said Maggie, opening the session. "Athletes go to the gym, and pilots regularly practice in a flight simulator, just to give two examples. So, where do managers go to practice their coaching skills?"

After a few moments, it became clear that Maggie's question wasn't rhetorical.

Mark broke the silence. "I hadn't thought about it that way, Maggie," he said. "I guess the answer is that we don't have a place. Maybe nobody thinks we're professionals worthy of developing. Or, maybe, we think we're pros already," he added, smiling.

Maggie smiled back, and continued. "Exactly, Mark," she said. "And that is precisely what the Kata Coaching Dojo is for: providing a safe space for coaches to hone their skills at much higher frequency than would occur in everyday work. I learned about this concept in a workshop led by Tilo Schwarz who invented the Kata Coaching Dojo. He shared his research on how people learn in fields that invest more in coaching, like developing musicians and training athletes.

"Tilo pointed out that in sports there is a clear distinction between playing the game and practice. Games are usually played at night or on the weekends, and they are all about executing whatever skills the team has already developed to that point. You cannot predict what will actually happen out on the field on game day, what the opposing team will do, and how successfully or unsuccessfully the team will use their skills. After the game, the coaches reflect on what happened during the game, like a current condition analysis. Their findings influence what the coaches ask of their players during the weekdays, which are devoted to practice deliberately, preparing for their next game.

"The week's training includes specific exercises addressing weak points that were revealed during the game, daily repetition of specific drills to hone skills, and preparing for the next opponent. During the game, the team performs, and during the weekdays, that is when the team is learning new skills and fine-tuning old ones. That is when they practice.

"That insight was what got Tilo started in developing the Kata Coaching Dojo. It provides a sports-like approach where coaches can repeatedly practice a series of specially designed training exercises and role-play in a safe environment. The coaches practice with a pre-set storyboard based on a fictional case. In the dojo you do not create the storyboard or play with the process. That has already been prepared. This allows coaches to focus on different coaching scenarios with the content fixed.

"Normally, in the real world, you might do something like set a target condition for a specific case and then you wouldn't reset the target condition until one or more weeks later. So, the possibility of repeating certain coaching strategies – like a drill – and opportunities for feedback and improvement are limited. With the dojo you can repeatedly practice coaching the same situation and make adjustments based on what happens.

"Over time, Tilo developed 20 fundamental exercises that help coaches speed up their initial learning process. Each exercise is focused on a specific small skill, which he calls micro-skills. The way it works is this: someone role-plays the 'improver' and answers the coach's questions in specific ways, often intended to throw the student-coach for a loop.

"As an example, the coach might ask about the one obstacle to address, phase 3 of the Coaching Kata, but the person simulating the improver answers with various solutions. At first the coach struggles, telling the improver what to do or say, or asking even vaguer questions. Then Tilo explains and demonstrates a micro-skill for that situation and then the student-coach tries it.

"For example, one micro-skill that Denise has used here in your company is called 'repeat and add.' When the improver gives an imprecise answer, you as coach can first repeat the question and then add what you want the improver to clarify or re-think. We will get into the details later, but that's just one example of a micro-skill we will practice. Tilo has written all about the micro-skills in the *Kata Dojo Handbook*."

Maggie turned to a tote bag she had stashed under a table and pulled out a stack of handbooks. She handed one to each participant and one to Denise too.

"After attending Tilo's workshop at the Kata Conference, I signed up for his seven-week online Kata Dojo masterclass. Many participants say it was a transformational experience for them, even experienced coaches. I have to say, I fully agree. Tilo's masterclass fundamentally improved my coaching and completely changed the way I develop coaches."

Maggie walked them through the standard storyboard. The use case was about throwing a paper jet airplane into a bucket. That was the process the simulated improver was working on to reach a specific target condition within the next week. Experiments were already documented on the experimenting record. So all the information was there, as if the improver had everything prepared for a coaching session.

In the beginning Maggie always played the improver, a feisty one at that. They started with phase one of the Coaching Kata, and Denise, as a "veteran," was the first to take the coach's role.

"What's your target condition?" Denise asked confidently. After all, she was an old pro at this.

"To improve the Kata Jet process," said Maggie, clearly an intentionally vague answer.

"Oh come on, Maggie, that's not fair. You're intentionally giving a terrible answer. You know better than that."

Maggie smiled at her. "Glad you picked up on that, Denise. That's exactly the point. You can't assume improvers will always give the answers you hope for. Rather the answer helps you understand what they see and how they think. Then you have to coach. What do you do if you don't get a good answer, in a given coaching situation? Now you need to coach me. We'll start again."

They started over, and Maggie gave the same scripted answer, reading from the *Kata Dojo Handbook*. Denise tried to ask some deepening questions like stating that Maggie's reply was not a real target condition and asking for a good one with outcome and process, but Maggie only gave vague answers about the goal and then launched into possible solutions. Maggie was clearly not going to make this easy. After a while, they stopped and discussed.

Joe volunteered to try his hand at playing coach, and Maggie let him attempt to coach her in the same situation. After a few tries, he had achieved a bit more than Denise, getting Maggie to respond with a specific desired outcome, but he fumbled when he tried to get her to talk about the process condition. Maggie flooded him with lots of unnecessary information.

Then Denise thought of something.

"I think *Repeat and Add* might work here," she said while they were debriefing.

"Sure," Maggie replied. "Give it a try."

They started all over again.

"Maggie, so, what's your target condition?" Denise asked

"To improve the Kata Jet process," Maggie replied.

"What's your target condition regarding your outcome metric?"

"To achieve a hit rate of 40%."

Cool, Denise thought, *it's working.* "And what's your target condition in terms of your process metric?" she asked.

Maggie cooperated reading from the target condition form on the board, "to reduce the variation in flight distance to 80 plus-minus 8 inches."

Bam. Spot on. *Repeat and Add* worked. Denise was beaming, obviously pleased with herself.

The session continued with everyone playing the coach. Each time, Maggie started with vague answers and only gave a good answer when the coach properly used repeat and add. Once they had all gotten the hang of using *Repeat and Add*, Maggie started to alter the situation, making it slightly more difficult.

It's surprising how minor changes in wording and body language throw us off as coaches, thought Denise. *I felt like a wizard at this before I actually tried coaching Maggie. But in practice it was so much harder than in theory. This is really a very powerful training approach.*

Then they tried another of the scripted scenarios from Tilo's book. The coach opened with the same question about the target condition, but now the improver, or really Maggie playing the improver, reacted very emotionally, explaining why she thought it was not possible to reach the target condition.

At first, this seemed even harder to coach, but over time the team also mastered that scenario.

Then Maggie split them up into two groups. She pulled up another storyboard for the Kata Jet process so each group had one. Then she asked them to practice both of the scenarios she had shown them and take turns in the different roles. The person playing the improver would always react as Maggie had done, reading the scripted answers from the *Kata Dojo Handbook*, either giving a vague answer or answering emotionally, and then follow up by answering the questions the coach was asking.

The exercise was surprisingly fun. It was especially delightful to play a recalcitrant "improver." Everyone realized how easy it was to throw off a coach. Maggie reminded them not to make it *too* hard.

"It's about practicing and learning the specific micro-skill, in this case, *Repeat and Add*. We don't want to make our coaches look too bad," she said, smiling. "Increase the difficulty gradually and only after the coach has successfully applied the micro-skill we're practicing to the level of difficulty you have played."

They did a couple of more rounds with Maggie supervising both groups and giving feedback and tips.

They worked for an hour, which seemed to fly by. Then Maggie loudly clapped her hands to call the session to an end.

"OK, that's enough for today. Here's the plan: When I come in to support Denise on Mondays, we'll also spend an hour in the dojo in the afternoon. Just 60 minutes. I plan to gradually run you through all the 20 exercises in Tilo's book. That'll give you a good foundation as coaches and definitely step up your game.

"In addition, I want you to practice yourself in each of your two groups once a week — 30 minutes of practice is enough. This is just like Tilo's online Kata Dojo masterclass, except that I'm running you through it in person. I promise you that as you do your actual coaching with your improvers on real projects, you will find opportunities to apply these micro-skills. Just like athletes who practice during the week and play real games on weekends. I will also spot-check some of your real-life coaching sessions and provide feedback."

There was palpable excitement in the room, as everyone put their heads together to schedule the practice sessions.

"Now, let's step back and think about the dojo from a longer-term perspective," said Maggie. "The Kata Coaching Dojo is not a typical class. Although we'll run through kind of a course in the beginning, the dojo is more like a gym where you go once or twice a week. You wouldn't go to the gym for a two-day training course once a year right? Tilo's vision is for organizations to establish permanent Kata Coaching Dojos that are run internally. Wouldn't it be great if there was a dojo like that here at Goldberg sometime in the future?"

"That would be awesome," Denise said. "That would help us develop coaches at a much faster pace. Lord knows we need them. Ultimately, every leader needs to become a coach.

Maggie continued, "it's a really exciting time to be involved in a dojo because all of these tools are cutting-edge and being developed literally as we speak. Myself and others from Tilo's master class have started to develop dojo scenarios for different situations.

"I've transformed the Kata Jet into a scenario that makes more sense for my gym to develop my coaches. Others have developed a coaching dojo for doctors and nurses. Maybe at some point we will develop a customized version for pumps we build here, and also for sales Jason", Maggie said giving him an encouraging look.

"That would be so cool," said Jason.

"Yeah, that sounds awesome," said Sarah, jumping in. "I'd love to be involved in that."

Everyone nodded in agreement.

"Great," Maggie replied. "That's it for today. I'll see you in the dojo next week." She gave everyone a high five on their way out. Denise stayed behind to debrief (QR Code 27.1).

"So, what did you think?" Maggie asked when everyone was gone, clearly anxious to hear Denise's reaction.

Scan with your mobile to visit
the Kata Dojo website.

QR CODE 27.1
Visit the Kata Dojo website.

"Truly awesome," Denise replied. "What a day. I'm totally exhausted. But the puzzle totally inspired the team and taught them the basics. And now with the coaching dojo, you've given me a way to take our coaching to the next level. And, to be honest, it made me realize how much I personally need to learn to be a great coach. I'm much more confident about the whole project now."

"Wonderful to hear," said Maggie. "That's exactly what I hoped.

"Now putting my coaching hat back on, there's one more thing I want to do with you today. I know you're tired, but hear me out. As we are building visual tools to help you manage your projects, I suggest we set up a project timeline on a wall in this room so you and the team can visualize progress for the various focus topics. Again, the role of visual management is to clearly see the standard, or in this case the plan versus the actual, and then quickly make adjustments as reality hits."

Over the next 30 minutes, they created a paper timeline. Across the top were days of the week. Listed for each focus topic there were spaces for the targets for outcome metrics and process metrics (see Figure 27.1).

"Where did you get the idea for that?" Denise asked at one point.

Maggie responded enthusiastically, "from a book called *Toyota Kata Culture* written by Gerd Aulinger and Mike Rother. Check it out some time. It gives you a vision of what coaching spreading to all management levels could look like at Goldberg in the future."

Denise made a mental note to get that book.

"But now back to your board", Maggie continued. "Here's what you do. After your round of coaching cycles every day, you go through this list of focus topics here and ask yourself, 'are we on track to achieving our weekly target condition?' If so you add a green sticker to the box for the respective day and focus topic. If not, you add a red sticker."

With that, Maggie pulled two packs of green and red dollar-coin-sized round stickers from her duffel bag.

"Next, if you coached the person working on the topic that day, add a green sticker in the second row, if not add a red one.

"Then, ask yourself, did the improver complete the last step? If so, add a green sticker to the third row of the respective topic, if not a red one again.

"By doing so you will start to see patterns emerging over time. Generally speaking, if the improver misses steps, red, you should see the process and outcome measures turn red. Missing coaching sessions is likely to lead to missing steps which will also turn red. Got it?"

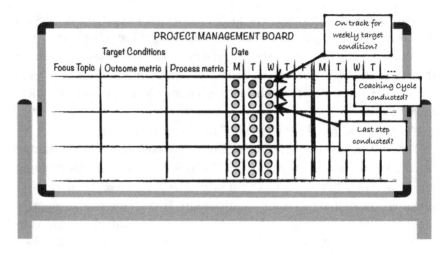

FIGURE 27.1
Project management board.

Denise nodded. Maggie continued, with a sly smile. "If you eventually start the daily meetings, you can ask people about their progress, and then they can actually fill in the stickers for their focus topic themselves and everyone can see the patterns. That will help you to identify where to focus your attention and also where more coaching is needed."

Denise smiled knowingly. "Well played, Maggie. I can tell you are going to lure me into those daily meetings even if I'm resisting them now. We'll see, though. I am still your customer."

"Sure," Maggie replied, "you are the customer and I am simply your humble servant. But this is a make or break project."

"Right." Denise sighed.

Just then, Jason peeked through the door.

"Hey Denise," he said. "We need to get going. Otherwise it'll be dark by the time we get there."

Maggie raised her eyebrows and smiled. "Where's there?" she asked playfully. "Never mind. None of my business. It's almost the weekend – have fun you guys."

Denise blushed. "Of course, got it," she said, turning toward Jason.

"Great. I'll pick you up at yours at 4:30," Jason said and shut the door. Maggie and Denise quickly cleaned up and got ready to leave.

"See you on Monday and enjoy your weekend," Maggie said with a wink as they said goodbye in the parking lot.

"You too," Denise replied. "And seriously, thank you for an awesome day. I'm so glad to have you by my side. I really do not know how I could succeed without you. See you Monday."

Part IV

Upping the Pace
It's a Sprint AND a Marathon to the Finish

28

A Month Down the Road

FRIDAY, APRIL 7 – 8:00 AM, FOUR WEEKS OF LEARNING AND MORE STRUGGLES

THE FOUR WEEKS following the team's launch flew by. Maggie had coached Denise most mornings, mainly by phone, on her successive target conditions, and Denise felt she had improved enormously as a coach. The dojo really helped. Today was their first internal monthly review. Denise watched as the team, one by one, joined her in the meeting room and began to look at the results from the past month. They would review these results and set new monthly targets.

Just in time, Denise thought. She had to present to the senior management team on Tuesday, and, if she were being honest, she was worried about how that would go. Her weekly updates with Dick and David had been no fun – mostly because of Dick. His management mantra hadn't changed. He always wanted more results, faster. He didn't seem to understand, or maybe he didn't want to understand, that improving processes sustainably meant addressing the root cause and not just finding quick fixes to boost the numbers. David helped and tried to fend off Dick. And David took most of the hits for the team during their weekly meetings. But it still was one gut punch after another.

Maggie should be here any minute, Denise thought, tapping her fingers on her desk nervously. Maggie was coming in to join her and the project team for the monthly review as it was their first.

Waiting for Maggie, Denise reflected on what she had learned over the past month. Grasping the current conditions in more depth and, as a result, adding more details to their monthly goals, and weekly target conditions, had mostly filled week 1.

DOI: 10.4324/9780429347023-32

In week 2, they finally got down to addressing their first obstacles. Denise found that that was when coaching became much more challenging. The teams had a tendency to jump to conclusions, proposing a next step prematurely, or a bunch of steps. Denise had to draw on all of her coaching skills to redirect them through questions rather than simply telling them her ideas.

Denise mentioned the challenge to Maggie during one of their daily coaching sessions, and Maggie took it as an opportunity to run her through an exercise in the dojo that simulated the problem precisely: an improver jumping to a premature step.

During their dojo "workout," Denise had learned about a micro-skill called "Go Back." Now, she flipped to the respective page in her notebook:

"If confronted with a premature step, Go Back to Obstacle, Phase 3, to understand cause and effect first."

A helpful coaching question, she had learned, was, "What obstacle are you addressing with this step?" *At its core that's just another version of the "Repeat and Add" micro-skill. Repeat question three and add – "with this step."*

This strategy helped a lot. It got people to step back from the solution and reconsider the obstacle they needed to surmount. After they identified the obstacle, Denise usually followed up with the last question from the Coaching Kata phase 3, "And what exactly is the problem?" That led to a new round of deeper analysis.

Nonetheless, Denise still found that some of her improvers were jumping to conclusions rather than thinking scientifically. In several coaching sessions over the last four weeks, she had worked hard to coach her improvers into seeing how they needed to take smaller steps. One of her coaching sessions with Sam had almost turned sour as they struggled with this issue – the memory of it was still vividly painful (QR Code 28.1).

A knock at the door pulled Denise out of her thoughts. It was Maggie peeking through the glass door. Denise greeted her, and invited her into the meeting room.

Denise did not know what to expect going into the first monthly meeting. It was a milestone event, and all the teams had been hard at work. But she knew from coaching the individual focus topics that there was variation in the results they had achieved. She wanted this meeting to lift spirits,

QR CODE 28.1
Coaching cycle with Sam.

not bring them down. But they also needed to confront the cold reality of where they were and where they needed to go next.

The group assembled, and Denise decided to kick off the meeting with an upbeat message.

"Welcome, team, to our first monthly review," she said. "You've all put in an extraordinary amount of effort, and I can tell you that we are seeing good results in outcomes and in process metrics toward those outcomes. We did a lot of planning and digging into our goals and obstacles and that has all paid off. We are now on a roll. Well done! I am proud of all of you. Now, we want to review where we are and what we've learned, and then plan our next monthly goals."

With that, the first team, Betty and Doug, began presenting their exceptional progress. They were extraordinarily enthusiastic. They explained their process over the past four weeks – their findings and especially all the implemented improvements in great detail. The presentation seemed to go on and on.

Denise was starting to get nervous. The meeting was only scheduled to run two hours. *They might be a little too enthusiastic. I don't want the meeting to run over, but I also don't want to interrupt them and risk making them feel like they aren't valued.*

After a few more minutes, Maggie stepped in. "Guys," she said, "wow, you have done a great job! I love it. You are clearly so into this. I am impressed by the results, but even more impressed by how much you've learned about the processes. Isn't that cool?" She looked at the team, and they started nodding. "I am pretty sure you have even more, right?" The team nodded again. "Ok, that's great, may I suggest you give us a summary of your findings? Am I rushing you? I do not want to be rude."

"No, not at all," Doug replied. Then he waved around the room at the rest of the team. "Otherwise, there won't be time for you folks. That's why we wanted to go first so that we could present as much as possible," he added with a sly grin.

The others laughed politely.

Spirits are high. That's good, Denise thought.

"OK, then," said Maggie. "May I suggest a structure? First, present your monthly goal as you defined it four weeks ago. Then present where you are now in relation to the goal. Make it short. Use the elements of your monthly goal consisting of the outcome metric, the pattern of work, and the process metric you've been tracking for your work focus. What did you intend for these, and where are you now? Does that make sense?"

Everyone agreed. "It sounds like you're suggesting using the Coaching Kata structure for our presentations. Is that right?" Betty asked.

"You got it," Maggie replied. "So then what's next?" she asked Betty.

"What did we learn, I guess," Betty said.

"Exactly," Maggie replied. "Make it a summary, though, and give us your conclusions as I explained earlier. Got it?"

Betty nodded.

"Alright, let's go," said Maggie, smiling and clapping her hands.

After that, the presentations went much faster. The clear structure also made them easier to follow. *Thank goodness these are nothing like the lengthy and unstructured presentations we have to sit through in so many of our other management meetings*, Denise thought.

It was clear from the presentations that they were making progress, particularly on learning, but there were big differences in bottom-line results across projects.

Denise tried to focus on the positives. Betty and Doug had overachieved their monthly goal for machine group AX-3031. They were beaming and in high spirits. Likewise, Sam and his team had improved changeover time for their machines tremendously and were right on target. Luther and Derek from logistics were close. The only minor drawback on the productivity-related topics was that they had not used the improved efficiencies to reduce headcount, as Randolph from accounting pointed out. Still, they had used the higher productivity to increase throughput and reduce the backlog without adding more people. That in itself was an accomplishment and an effective boost in productivity.

One area that still needed a lot of work, though, was quality. And that was a problem. Sarah and Joe had made progress on some pressing quality issues, particularly on damaged parts, but over the last two weeks, progress had stalled. They seemed to be especially stuck on an issue having to do with machining the outside housing of the pump. They still had days where the percentage of parts scrapped was in the double digits. It wasn't that Joe and Sarah hadn't fully understood the issues. It was encouraging that for several of the defects they had nailed the cause, but implementing the solution took time.

Then, there were issues where the cause lay further upstream with the supplier that cast the metal part. Again, these were difficult to analyze for cause, and it was even more challenging to get all the necessary parties, like purchasing and research and development (R&D), involved.

The two teams working on reducing material costs faced similar issues. Ray had identified significant potential for lowering material costs at two of their suppliers. However, he still had to follow their longstanding, cumbersome purchasing process and deal with long-term price-binding contracts with suppliers. Meanwhile, R&D was slow to review design changes because they were focused on new projects. As a result, cost reduction was still far out.

Ray from purchasing was a great presenter, even if he didn't have the best news to share. Their actions all made sense and they were crystal clear on what had to happen next. Denise could barely hide her admiration for Ray. *He's not only a good negotiator, he's also so good at selling stuff. I wonder if Dick will buy this, though. All he wants are results.* She was trying not to think about it, but the management meeting next Tuesday was never far from her mind.

Phil and Ray were still presenting their analysis of the problems related to reducing the internal cost of machining. Everything they said was so smart and spot on. *There's so much potential here*, Denise thought. *If only we could move faster.*

They were proposing to engineering that they redesign the machining process that required different tools and fixtures, which took time to design and build. For some engineers, any questioning by "outsiders" was close to blasphemy. *I'm glad Ray's so good at winning over skeptics*, Denise thought.

Still, Denise was anxious. *I don't want dreams. I want results,* Denise remembered Dick saying at their last weekly check-in. She felt her heart rate rise as she listened to the presentations and realized just how little they had achieved.

We knew from the start the material and equipment savings would be mostly in the second three month. Denise turned to look at the project timeline hanging on the wall. Over half of the topics had red dots in the top row for the last seven to ten days, indicating they hadn't achieved their weekly target conditions.

We need to be faster. We need a different pace.

Soon, the whole team came to a similar conclusion. The next activity involved everyone doing a kind of retrospective on their working process, and many pointed out that they were too slow to make decisions. Addressing obstacles outside their area of responsibility was another big issue. The blame game had begun.

"Denise, no offense, but it takes too long for you to help us," said Derek from scheduling. "I mean, it's not that you're not making an effort."

Denise could see that he was uncomfortable, but she was happy he spoke up. The overall environment was much more open than any other Goldberg meeting Denise had ever attended. She was delighted to see corporate culture shifting before her eyes.

"Derek, don't worry, just say what's on your mind. I want us to give each other honest feedback. The trick is to do it immediately and with kindness. Bottling it up until your frustration grows will do more harm than good. You'll just end up exploding. Seriously, I can take it." She gave Derek an encouraging smile.

"OK," he continued. "It's just that we meet every Monday as a whole team to present our current state and establish our next weekly target condition. Now, if we're stuck and need help, we present that on Monday as well. Then it might take you two or three days to get the necessary people on board or get a decision from higher up. Usually, we don't hear back until Wednesday or Thursday, and then that week is gone."

Everyone nodded.

"I think it's similar when we need to make a decision," Luther said. "We wait till our meeting on Monday to present and get feedback from everyone else. We lose a lot of time that way."

They discussed the issue for a while and finally agreed on having an additional all-group meeting every Wednesday morning. *We are moving in the direction of daily team meetings just like Maggie wanted,* Denise thought wearily. *It can be a little annoying, this habit she has of always being right.*

They used the rest of the meeting to develop the second set of monthly goals for each of the focus topics, just like they had done at the end of the first workshop.

Looking at the management board, the teams saw that they were mostly in the red, but they were still willing to set bold goals for the next monthly meeting. In fact those furthest behind set the most ambitious goals. And, most encouraging, the team was in a good mood. They had learned so much about their processes over the first month, and they saw enough potential in them that they were more optimistic about success. Still, there was a pit in Denise's stomach. She knew that what was happening in the conference room was great, extraordinary even, but convincing management of that would be no picnic. *Dick only sees what is right in front of him, not future potential. The presentation next Tuesday is not going to be fun.*

After everyone filed out of the room, Maggie and Denise went to the canteen to grab some lunch.

"So, what did you learn from running your first monthly workshop?" Maggie asked.

"I like how the team has developed. They have clearly bought into the project and are eager to work on their topics. And they seem so much more comfortable with the overall challenge.

"I like the structure you taught us for presenting last month's results and how it enforces the Coaching Kata model. And the team nailed developing the monthly goals. It took us *days* last time – today we did it in under two hours.

"And, honestly, maybe with a bit more preparation we can even move faster in the next monthly meeting. It should be an uplifting meeting that celebrates our victories, while being clear-eyed about the areas where we need to improve, and most of all it should ensure a clear focus for the next leg. As we progress, I'd love to spread the practice of setting a 3-1-1 across the whole plant. I see now what you mean by calling it setting pace. The 3-1-1 is like a pacemaker for the improvement process. I could see how it could work for any kind of strategy deployment, actually."

While Denise had been speaking, Maggie had been eating. Just before Denise's little speech came to a close, Maggie took a big bite from her veggie wrap. Her mouth full, she gave Denise a thumbs-up across the table.

Denise continued. "Two things worry me. The next monthly goals the teams set are a bit challenging. I mean we need that – but it's a stretch."

"That's why you need to coach them," Maggie replied, her tone even. "Now, it starts. All the low-hanging fruit has been raked in. We're leaving the known zone. Next week, the game really begins. That's what we've been practicing for in the dojo. You can do it." She gave Denise an encouraging nod.

They ate in silence for a while, until Maggie asked, "What else is worrying you?"

"The presentation at the management meeting next Tuesday," Denise replied between bites. She swallowed. "I mean you saw it. Overall we can't show much progress on the outcome level. And there are all those red dots. On the other hand, I feel, or, actually, I know that the teams have learned a ton about their respective processes and there is movement on the process metrics that I am confident will lead to results. It will just take some time."

"How do you know?" Maggie asked.

"Through my daily coaching sessions. Coaching them I have learned what they have learned. If I wasn't coaching, I wouldn't know. That's an aspect of coaching I hadn't thought about previously. It's not just a status check. Coaching gives me deep insight on what the team is learning about the obstacles. No metric could ever give me that insight."

"Give me some hard facts," Maggie pushed.

Denise thought for a moment. Then she said, "There's lots. You know, the project board you helped me set up, shows it all."

Denise took out her cell phone and pulled up a picture she'd taken of the board during the meeting.

"Ok, what patterns do you see on the board?" Maggie asked.

Denise scrolled over the picture. "You can see a lot of green on the bottom row showing the teams are conducting a step every day, and the second row which shows daily coaching cycles are being completed. On two of the focus topics the two rows are all green, and these groups have been reaching their weekly target conditions. These are topics where we have overachieved our monthly goals for the process metric and outcome metric. In other cases, all the days are green and the process metric is improving but the outcome metric doesn't show it yet."

"What does that tell you?" Maggie asked.

"That we're working on the right things and making progress and it is likely we will achieve our desired outcomes."

"And what else?" Maggie asked.

"Well, then there is the third group of topics. The ones, like quality, where there's the most red on the board. That happened especially over the last one and a half weeks. Those are topics we got stuck on and couldn't complete the next steps. Also, it looks like I dropped the ball on some coaching cycles there. And, as a result, we missed the last two weekly target conditions. No progress on process – or outcome metric, then, of course. These are the groups that suggested I needed to up my game to get the help they needed from other groups. That's why we decided to have a second weekly all hands."

"So, what exactly concerns you about the management meeting?" Maggie went on.

"Dick doesn't understand any of this. He does not care about learning or what is happening to the process metrics. All he wants to see is immediate cost reduction – and we can't show that – yet."

"I guess David will have to help Dick make the connection" Maggie replied.

"I'm not sure David fully understands it, or can do anything to convince Dick anyway," Denise said, shaking her head.

"He certainly should by now," Maggie said, frowning. "We've invested quite a bit in educating him." But then Maggie's frown transformed into an impish grin. "To some degree, you just have to roll with it, Denise. You can't change everyone's thinking all at once. And they know if they fire you they are screwed. Anyway, I better get going. I have some coaching sessions scheduled at the gym this afternoon. I don't want to let my team down."

TUESDAY, APRIL 11 – 3:15 PM, THUNDER AND LIGHTNING

With trepidation Denise made her way to the board room to present at the quarterly management meeting. The meeting had begun at 1:00 pm and followed a traditional agenda – dollars, dollars, and dollars. Each person in turn presented on bottom-line results, profits and losses; there was not much opportunity for deeper reflection.

The agenda was always tight, and items usually ran over. Denise's presentation was scheduled for 3:30. She arrived at 3:15 just to be on time.

The minutes ticked by; no one came to get her. At 3:35, she gently knocked and anxiously peeked in. David signaled her to wait outside. A few minutes later, he came out to explain.

"We're way behind the agenda – like always," he said, sighing. "My guess is that you won't be called in before 4. So relax, and I promise all will be okay." David gave his best reassuring smile.

When Denise was finally called in, she began her presentation by going through all the data with examples of findings and successes from the different teams. Dick allowed her a five-minute grace period before he interrupted her mid-sentence.

"All I see here is red," he said. "None of the groups are meeting their targets. They are all messing around with what you call experiments instead of making the real changes necessary to save this plant. You've got to do better than this, Denise."

Right away David jumped in. "Let me take this, Denise," he said. "Dick, I also struggled with the idea behind this approach of taking small steps and moving forward experiment by experiment instead of planning everything out. Remember when we were under pressure to cut down the backlog? Frankly, I thought Denise was wasting a lot of time. But Denise convinced me to at least give her a chance to do this Kata method of hers. She explained they needed to understand problems' real causes to make sustainable change.

"I had her on a short leash and she produced. As you know assembly outperformed the rest of manufacturing. In fact, they reached a level of performance this company has never seen. That is the reason we are putting such an important project in her hands. It seems like she is going slow at first, taking baby steps, but she gets big results. Looking at the various projects, I can see the seeds of big results already. At some point, before the three-month window is up, these seeds will grow into a vine like Jack and the beanstalk and just take off."

Dick had waited, albeit impatiently, as David spoke, but as soon as he opened his mouth, it was clear he still wasn't happy.

"We'd better see some progress on quality soon," Dick said gruffly. "Our sales people are doing an incredible job to calm angry customers but they can't perform their magic much longer."

Sam Watson, the VP of Sales, jumped in, "if production can't do a better job we'll have to recall the new pump." Several people in the room gaped. In its nearly 100-year history, Goldberg never issued a product recall.

"Oh, stop with the nonsense, Sam," said David, losing his temper. "You know exactly why we're in trouble. You, your team, and marketing pushed engineering for the new pump so it could get to market fast. How often did we point out that the technical design still had some flaws that would likely lead to quality issues? Everyone here can recall that no one in sales wanted to hear it." He paused for emphasis. "And, now, we're paying the price. This is not the fault of the people who work in the plant. They do the best they can with the cards we've dealt them." He glanced around the room, a fiery look in his eyes.

Dick raised both his hands, as if to call for peace.

"David, we know the pressure is on for you and your team, and I want to believe you with that Jack and the beanstalk thing. Denise, I sure hope you're good at gardening. Why don't you finish your presentation and tell us how you're gonna grow the vines?"

Denise was just about ready to scratch Dick's eyes out, but she composed herself. She took a few deep breaths, then calmly completed her presentation.

In the end, Dick asked only one follow-up question. "So," he said, "having an all-hands meeting twice a week and doubling down on your coaching, that's what you think will turn the needle?"

He looked around the table for approval, leaned back in his chair at the far end of the room and shot her an expressionless stare.

Denise replied curtly, "I think it will help us move faster. My teams now understand their obstacles and their causes, and are moving the needle on the process metrics, the leading indicators. I am not just guessing and hoping. The outcomes we all desire will follow. They are primed for success."

Denise stared back at Dick. She wasn't sure if her confidence was convincing, but she knew, also, that she was right.

"Well, I'll see you on Friday for the next status update," Dick said. "Hopefully, we'll see some progress then."

Denise closed her laptop, unplugged the HDMI cable from the projector, and made her way out. When she passed behind David he turned and gave her a nod and a thumbs-up, keeping his hand on his lap, so only she could see it.

Walking out of the room, Denise could feel that her back was soaked with sweat. *I'm just glad I'm wearing a blazer.* As she closed the door, she noticed the next project team waiting to present. *Another set of lambs for the slaughter,* she thought.

Denise decided not to go back to the plant. She was too exhausted. *I need a workout to clear my head*, she thought. *I'm way behind on exercise with all this crazy work.*

Denise decided to drive home, get out her mountain bike, and go for a long spin.

I haven't done that in a while. Maybe Jason wants to join me. I'll give him a call and let him know I'm out for a ride.

Thinking about Jason lifted her mood. Last weekend when they had been out for a nice dinner, Denise had decided to take some initiative. They'd only been dating for a month, but Denise thought, *when you know, you know.* She asked Jason if he would consider moving in with her. His place was kind of small, and he stayed at her apartment quite often anyway.

To her surprise and delight, he had immediately taken her up on the offer, and they had started to plan his move. Given his current lease, he had to give four weeks' notice, so they planned for him to move in with her in June, right after the big three-month management meeting..

There are other important things in life besides this project and saving the world for Goldberg, Denise thought, already feeling a bit better.

29

A Fleet of Coaches Is Born

TIME PASSES, PROGRESS ACCELERATES

OVER THE NEXT weeks Denise felt like she was in overdrive. She did more coaching cycles than ever. *As a coach I have to always be impatient,* she thought to herself at one point. *Impatient about finding the next obstacle that is.*

She also realized that the number of coaching cycles she ran was her way to accelerate the pace. *We need to move faster, so I need to coach twice a day — for the topics that are behind that is.*

Removing an obstacle at best takes three experiments. There's one for finding it, one for identifying the cause, and then one for testing a possible solution to remove the cause. That is if everything goes perfectly. Usually it takes more than that. So, with one coaching cycle per topic a day, we can remove about one or two obstacles per week. So, it's definitely the case that if we need more speed, I need to coach more often. I'm starting to feel like a mad scientist. Hmm, mad scientific thinker.

Ensuring small steps, one experiment at a time, rather than combining multiple steps into one experiment helped as well. Small steps for some reason made for faster progress. Was it because people found it easier to get started with just a smaller step on their plate? Was it because it was easier to make time for a small step in your calendar? Or because they learned more from each experiment? Denise didn't know, but it worked.

Betty came up with an interesting approach to accelerating progress in her group. The leader of the first shift would often make observations. That would lead to some ideas for experiments which Betty would share with Denise in their coaching cycle before noon. Based on the coaching

DOI: 10.4324/9780429347023-33

session, Betty and the second-shift leader would conduct the experiment, or sometimes several small, connected experiments. On average, twice the number of experiments per day.

About six weeks into the project, Denise observed something very interesting, or rather, she heard it. It was a noticeable change in language. Betty was kind of coaching the shift leaders. At the beginning of a shift, Betty would give them a "topic for the day," as she called it. Then over the course of the shift they would make some observations or test some ideas around that topic, and Betty would talk to them several times a day, helping them reflect on their findings. Denise even overheard Betty using the Coaching Kata questions several times.

That's astonishing, Denise thought, *Betty has never had any formal Coaching Kata training. She picked this up just from the puzzle exercise and then of course being an improver herself with me coaching her. Maybe I should talk to her and the others about coaching.*

One Friday, Denise got the team together for an hour and shared some background on the Coaching Kata and what she had learned about coaching. The team ate it up. As a result, the coaching approach began to spread throughout the plant. Denise could sometimes even hear it in daily stand-up meetings. They weren't structured coaching cycles of course. And that was not the purpose of these short meetings focused on production. But the team leaders started using some of the questions they had experienced in their own coaching cycles to challenge assumptions. Denise was thrilled. *Practicing Kata is doing its job. Scientific thinking is spilling over into everyday work. I wish people like Dick, and even David, could appreciate this growth.*

Overall, Denise could see how some of the frontline team members took more control of their processes, and, as they did, their confidence and pride grew exponentially. These were a few early adopters, but others were starting to follow. At first, they were hesitant. They were afraid to get things wrong. On one occasion, Denise was coaching Drew, the team leader from motors who had initially been very skeptical of Kata, when he made a suggestion for an experiment testing a small change that involved moving a guide rail for boxes at one of the machines to improve material handling efficiency.

"What is therefore your next step?" asked Denise.

"Well, we would need to move the guide rails," Drew answered.

"Good," said Denise, "so, then go ahead and do it."

"You mean me?" said Drew, a look of shock on his face.

"Yes, you." Denise replied, smiling. "I don't see anyone else here?" She pretended to look around.

"But we have to loosen the screws on the machine side to move the rail. Can I just do that?" Drew asked uncomfortably.

"Sure you can," Denise answered assertively. "You repair your car, and, if I remember correctly, you renovated your entire house."

It's just amazing how previous generations of management have stifled people's creativity and confidence at work, she thought to herself. *The same people doing amazing stuff at their homes don't feel like they can have any control at work. What a disconnect.*

"But what if it goes wrong?" Drew asked, still hesitant.

"Come on, Drew. I've coached you, and you've based your idea on careful observation and came up with a solid hypothesis. Now, things might still turn out different which is great because that's how we learn. There is no such thing as a failed experiment. So now is the time to run the experiment."

"I guess I'll try it, as long as you say it is okay," Drew said, looking at her expectantly.

Denise nodded.

With that, Drew went off and conducted the experiment. When Denise met with him for the next coaching cycle, he was beaming. Not only because the experiment went well and nothing bad happened, but also because he and his team had taken control of their process.

Over the course of the next few weeks, Denise experienced similar situations. It took time for frontline people to feel confident running experiments, but they soon got the hang of it.

Denise discussed these phenomena with Maggie during one of their coaching sessions.

"There's so much talk from up high about empowerment and moving decisions to the front line, but few explain how," Maggie said. "Telling people 'hey, you are empowered, go do it,' won't do the job. People don't know how and they would rather make no decision than a wrong decision. And any failure makes them feel like a failure. To give people freedom and capability to act, they need a clear direction and the ability to work in a scientific way; understanding obstacles, and an understanding that each action is an experiment. This takes practice."

Denise's experiences certainly confirmed Maggie's views. As Denise coached by these simple principles, she saw how they were allowing people to grow, right before her eyes. And as they grew, she grew. She learned alongside her improvers; of course she did. For example, it was thanks to them that she was no longer the bottleneck for support. People did not wait for the Monday all hands to make decisions. They did much more on their own. The higher frequency of bi-weekly all hands helped move things along faster as well. Denise found herself considering daily all-hands meetings. *Okay, point one million to you, Maggie.*

Then they learned that meeting on Monday morning was not a great time for reflecting on last week's target condition and setting the next one. So they moved that meeting to Friday, which seemed to work a lot better. They were finding something like a circadian rhythm for the team. Then the mid-week check on Wednesday helped keep the pace going.

Of course, Dick kept bullying Denise and David in their weekly check-ins, but results were coming in and even he couldn't deny that. Denise even got him to come to the project room and asked the project leads to summarize the storyboards. They were eager to show and tell what they had accomplished to anyone who would listen. She was so proud that they were unintimidated by Dick, though sometimes he seemed more disgruntled about success than failure.

Maybe he is hoping we will fail so he can go ahead with his outsourcing plan, Denise thought, cynically.

Then during one of Denise's shop floor walks with Dick and David, something amazing happened. One of the shift leaders on Betty's team saw them passing by. It was Julia, a rather shy person who hardly ever spoke up when any of the managers were around. This time, before Denise could intervene, Julia nearly jumped them. She practically grabbed Dick and David by their sleeves and dragged them to the line.

"You have to see what we just found out this morning. This is incredibly cool," Julia said. She then enthusiastically explained how they had discovered an easy way to speed up loading one of the machines. David was beaming. Dick did not seem to know what to make of it. Denise held onto that moment anytime she was feeling down. She got goosebumps every time she thought of it.

To top it all off, the second monthly workshop went so much better than the first. Each team had visible and measurable achievements. And they were aces at explaining their progress in Kata terms.

Denise did not have to intervene and could just sit back like a proud mama bear. *Having the Starter Kata recipes and cards has really helped clarify their thinking and way of explaining what they have learned. Following the same pattern enforces their scientific thinking, and they can communicate so much faster. There is even some healthy communication across projects with people challenging each other in a very supportive way. If only this was the culture across the whole company....*

WEDNESDAY, MAY 2 – 4:00 PM, PRESENTING TO THE GHOULS, SUCK IT UP

Denise walked to the boardroom for her second big presentation to the senior team, feeling so much more confident than last time. This month she had real results under her belt. Yet, some part of her was still nervous, like she was walking into the principal's office. She had a little bit of post-traumatic stress disorder from last month's presentation. She tried to shake it off.

After the usual half hour of waiting, pacing in the hall outside the boardroom, she was ushered in to see a new face sitting at the head of the table.

The dapper-looking man with closely cropped gray hair in a blue dark suit and matching patterned tie rose from his chair and made his way around the table to shake Denise's hand.

"Denise," he said. "I'm Alexander Aspen, the new CEO. I've heard a lot of great things about you, and I am looking forward to your presentation."

Of course, thought Denise. She knew that the new CEO, Alexander Aspen was set to start on May 1. *Well, that's a wild card. But now that he's in place Dick is back to just being VP of Operations – he still has power, but not as much. That could be a good thing. And unlike Dick, Alexander seems to have a pleasant demeanor, what you might call manners even. He seems more like a kindly father than a Doberman Pinscher.*

Denise took a deep breath and set up her laptop, steadying herself for her presentation. As she glanced around the table, she noticed that David looked utterly miserable. *These meetings must be torture,* she thought. *Sitting here all afternoon and sometimes well into the evening listening to nonsense corporate speak and flipping through hundreds of slides that have no real substance.*

Denise's presentation proceeded without any drama. Actual results did that for you. Her team was about half-way toward their reduced three-month target for cost reduction, which meant they had half the mountain to climb with only one month left. Dick poked at that a few times, but his assaults were less forceful.

Alexander listened intently. He asked a few deepening questions, and Denise had the impression he really wanted to understand. He even stood up to Dick whenever he got snarky – not in a bullying way, just a gentle forceful one.

When Denise finished, Alexander said, "Denise, I can see that your team has made impressive progress. There's still a way to go, but it seems like there's a chance you're going to make it. Given the importance of this project for the company and especially this plant, I want to get a better understanding of it first-hand. Can you take me on a tour of the plant and show me exactly what you're working on?"

Denise had to keep her jaw from falling open. *A CEO who actually wants to see what is really going on on the shop floor?* she thought. *That sure is a change.* But she kept her face neutral. "Yes," she said, with genuine joy. "I'd be happy to do that."

"Good. My assistant will be in touch to set it up for early next week. Thank you."

Relief overwhelmed Denise as she left the room. She knew she had done well, and she was amazed by Alexander's response. She walked back to her office with a bounce in her step. *Maybe there's hope for the leadership of this company after all.*

As soon as she sat down at her desk, she called Jason.

"I think this calls for a celebration," he said.

They agreed to meet for a nice dinner out. That evening, at a charming Italian restaurant, they laughed, talked, and drank a refreshing Chianti wine. For the first time in months, Denise didn't feel like she had carried work with her into her personal life. It was the best night she'd had since she had moved to Guildersville.

30

If Only You Could Kata Your Love Life

THURSDAY, MAY 4 – 8:00 AM, SOMETHING'S UP WITH DAVID

THE DAY AFTER the presentation, Denise was still walking on air when David asked her to join him for a presentation at sales' annual spring meeting. It was a three-day conference where the East Coast sales representatives learned about new products, went through training, and were pressured by the higher-ups to commit to aggressive sales targets for the second half of the year. This time David, along with Sarah from quality, was asked to present on the latest quality efforts in the plant. The prognosis was that she would face rapid-fire hostile questions, given all the quality issues sales had been fielding for the past few months.

David asked Denise to come along and present her team's achievements on quality. He hoped that would help the plant regain at least some of the sales reps' trust and quiet Sam Watson, VP of Sales, at least a tiny bit.

Denise quickly put together some slides, mostly repurposing them from the management meeting the day before, and walked over to David's office to pick him up. David looked terrible, like he had barely slept.

"David," Denise said gently, "is something up?"

"It's nothing," David replied and waved his hand.

It didn't look like nothing to Denise, but it was clear that, whatever it was, David did not want to talk about it.

When David and Sarah opened the presentation, the environment was clearly hostile. But when Denise took the stage, she was able to show substantial improvements already in the works. Denise then fielded the reps' questions with empathy. The sales reps quickly realized that she took their concerns seriously, and the tension in the room diffused.

DOI: 10.4324/9780429347023-34

Facing an angry customer with a rightful quality complaint is no fun, even though we are making progress. She thought. *Note to self: when there is time, spend a day or two on the road with sales reps. Maybe we should make that the norm for all the managers in the plant.*

David stayed mostly in the background for the rest of the meeting, while Denise and Sarah ran the show. *He really doesn't look good*, Denise thought more than once. *I wonder if it's work, or something else.*

THURSDAY, MAY 4 – EVENING, DINNER IS ON SALES

Sarah, Denise, and David were invited to the evening event with the sales reps. Denise opted to go to the plant first to do her afternoon round of coaching cycles, so she arrived late at the Surf & Turf. When she walked through the door, she found everyone already eating and, of course, drinking. There were large pitchers of beer on picnic-style tables, and the waiters kept bringing new ones. The sales team was in high spirits, literally. It was the last night of the conference. The next day each would go back to his or her sales region with aggressive targets to meet and fire in their belly to sell, sell, sell. From her conversations over the day Denise had realized however that many of the sales reps had no specific plan for what to do differently to achieve their new goals.

Poor guys, they have no set process for improving. We still have a long way to go at Goldberg, Denise thought. *If we want to make sustainable improvements we need to improve our processes first. What should we be striving to do differently so that we can sell more? That should be the question. Just setting aggressive outcome targets doesn't do the job. Why is that so hard to get?*

Denise was disappointed that Jason had opted out of joining her as he had to sort out some issues with his landlord. She looked for Sarah and David. She couldn't spot Sarah but David was sitting at one of the group tables. *It's strange that his wife isn't here. She usually comes to these kinds of events*, Denise thought as she approached him. He had ordered a large burger with sweet potato fries. And a bottle of cabernet sat nearly empty before him. Everyone else at the table was drinking beer. *What sorrow is he drowning in exactly?* David noticed her walking toward him and waved her over. Everyone at the table moved to make room. One of the sales reps brought a chair and soon a waiter came by.

"I'll have a ginger lemonade and the Caesar salad with grilled salmon, dressing on the side," she ordered.

Everyone ate with gusto – it had been a long day. After the meal, almost everyone started to move around and talk to people they knew at other tables.

Denise inched her chair closer to David's.

"I just wanted to say again," she began gingerly, "that you really can tell me what's going on. And you can count on my discretion. You've had my back this whole time. I want to have yours. And don't tell me it's nothing. I know it is something serious. Whatever it is, I don't think you'll find the answer at the bottom of that bottle."

David sighed. "Let's go to the bar. It's quieter there."

David grabbed his bottle of wine, and they walked over to the bar and sat down. There was nobody there besides the bartender who was busy filling up pitchers of beer.

Denise looked at David expectantly. But he just stared straight ahead at the bartender's movements. Finally, Denise spoke, "Is it Dick?" she asked. "Is he up to something again?"

"No, no." David shook his head. "It's my wife, Sandra."

Has she left him? The thought shot through Denise's mind. *I hope not – I know they have kids.*

David didn't turn to look at Denise, but looked down at his hands, clearly emotional. "She went for a standard mammogram," he said, "and it looks like she has breast cancer."

"Oh, no." Denise gasped unintentionally.

David emptied the rest of his wine into his glass and finished it in a few quick gulps.

"You know, we have two young boys," he said. "And then, with all the chaos at Goldberg, I have felt like I've been drowning for months. Sandra has been my stronghold. I can't imagine losing her. And then there's the kids." He paused, and his eyes filled with tears.

"I am so, so sorry David," Denise said, flooded with empathy. "How did Sandra react?"

"She called me crying. It was supposed to be a routine checkup. She wanted me to come home right away, but I couldn't. We had that management meeting. Then, when I finally got home yesterday, she was furious with me. 'This is my life,' she said, 'you couldn't miss a freaking meeting?' But it wasn't about just one meeting. Of course it wasn't. I've been working nonstop recently. She said that too. She said, 'you're never here and now, maybe, our time may be up.'" He paused to catch his breath. "So, she took the boys and went to her parents' place to clear her mind, I guess. She's really close with her mom."

The bartender looked over and pointed at David's empty wine bottle. David nodded to order another. "Another cabernet, please. This time a glass," he said.

"Maybe that's enough, David," Denise said gently. "But what did the doctor say? You know these scans are by no means definitive. And a mass isn't the same thing as cancer."

"He told Sandra that they need to do a biopsy to confirm it."

Denise nearly jumped up. "David, I can't believe the doctor didn't tell you about false positives. I read that less than 10% of positives on mammograms actually turn out to be cancer. Also, Sandra is well below 50, I suppose. I guess it's her first screening, right?"

David nodded, "she just turned 40".

"That makes the result even more unlikely", Denise continued. "Please don't assume the worst. I went through this with my mom. It was in agony waiting for the biopsy results and then it was a false positive. What Sandra needs now is your support, and lots of it."

Denise paused. "Come on," she said and put her arm around David. "Let's get you home. You need to rest. And please, just wait, don't jump to conclusions."

David emptied his glass and nodded. "I appreciate your friendship, Denise. It means a lot. OK, let's go."

On their way out they passed the partying sales reps most of them still there despite the late hour. Vibrant conversation and laughter filled the room and mixed with the loud background music. Denise saw Sarah standing with one group obviously being the center of the conversation and having a great time. At another table they were taking funny group pictures. They wore look alike T-Shirts with some slogan Denise could not read from the distance.

Maybe that's the "party" team from Michigan I've heard about, Denise thought. *They're obviously having a great time. Sales reps sure know how to party. I wonder how many of them will be able to work tomorrow.*

As they walked toward the exit David suddenly slipped and almost fell. Denise just caught him in time. In response, David wrapped his arms around her. She steadied him.

"Woah, there," Denise said, laughing. She was happy to see he cracked a weak smile in response.

Denise walked David to her car and placed him inside. When they arrived at his house, a pretty colonial, it was dark. Sandra had obviously not returned. Denise watched David open the front door with his keys, and poured him a glass of water in his kitchen.

"Drink this," she said. He did, and she poured him another.

"I'm alright," he said, gulping the second glass down. "You get on home."

Finally, back in her own bed, Denise sighed. *What a day*, she thought, relishing in the firm mattress she'd grown to love.

FRIDAY, MAY 5 – 7:00 AM, TROUBLE IN PARADISE

As Denise walked toward her office, her cell phone vibrated. A message from Jason. Her heart leaped. *Just over a month to go till he moves in with me.*

"What's this?" Jason's message read. Then there were two pictures attached. Denise tapped them and waited for the download to finish. When they did, she nearly dropped her phone. The first picture showed her and David sitting at the bar, Denise's arm draped around David's shoulders. The second one was even worse. It was taken the moment after David had nearly fallen down on their way out. It looked like Denise and David were hugging, maybe even kissing, given the angle of David's head.

Who the heck took these pictures, and then had the gall to post them online? Denise nearly yelled. *Whoever you are, I'll find out where you live and make you pay*, she thought. *This is unbelievable, like high school.*

It's not what you think, she typed into her phone and hit send.

Jason responded with just one line: *What should I think?*

I can't deal with this now. I'll talk to him later, after my coaching rounds.

After the coaching sessions, Denise checked the pictures again examining them as if she was a detective. *This is ridiculous*, she thought. *Yes, it looks strange, but David is taller than me, and in the picture where*

I stopped him from falling his head is lower than mine. Pretty clear that he must have slipped.

She began to feel angry with Jason, too. *He's being a real meathead. Why would he assume the worst? Haven't I earned his trust? Maybe living together isn't such a great idea.*

She fired off another text. *Call me after work if you want to know what really happened.*

She put her phone down on her desk and sighed. *This is all a big mess,* she thought. *Not what I need.*

The rest of the day passed in a haze. She waited for Jason to call. *He's being such a moron,* she thought. *He's got to call me. I'm not going to call him first.*

FRIDAY, MAY 5 – 6:00 PM, BREAKUP

That evening Jason called and said hello in a calm but cool voice.

Denise jumped right into explaining what had happened.

"I honestly feel silly explaining all these details to you," she said after describing what David had told her and exactly how she had brought him home. "And I don't really know why I should have to. If you'd been in my situation, you'd have done the same. There's nothing I want or need to apologize for."

Jason muttered something that sounded like "I'm sorry," but Denise still felt angry and betrayed. *Relationships are built on trust,* she thought. *He immediately assumed the worst. Does this guy even really know me?*

"You know, I'm not sure if your moving in is the right thing right now," Denise said at last. "I think I need some time to think about it before taking such a big step, with all that is going on."

Jason tried to push back, but soon seemed to realize that he was in no position to argue. They agreed to put their plans on hold and give each other some time to think about where they wanted to take their relationship.

After they hung up Denise felt completely numb. It hurt. *No matter how much I like Jason, it's clear that we have work to do.* She passed the night tossing and turning in bed.

31

Victories and Setbacks

TUESDAY, MAY 9 – 7:00 AM, AN ENLIGHTENING VISIT FROM THE BIG BOSS

THREE WEEKS TO go until time's up for this first phase of the project, Denise thought, as she anxiously waited as Alexander Aspen approached her on the shop floor.

"Hi Denise, I'm really looking forward to this. It's great to be where the action is," he said, shaking Denise's hand. "I'm excited to learn about all these projects and see what your team has been doing for myself, firsthand."

Denise began by walking him through the value stream. He seemed very interested and asked a lot of questions. It soon became clear that it was not his first time walking the floor of a manufacturing plant. Given that he was a finance guy, Denise was amazed by how quickly he grasped what was going on. He fired off questions – and they were good ones. He seemed almost gleeful, obviously excited to be out of the office and looking at something real.

Denise then took him to the project room and guided him through the project timeline and all the graphs and charts the project group had put together over the past two months.

Alexander was refreshingly honest.

"I'm not sure yet exactly what you mean when you talk about coaching cycles and what you call Kata," he said. "But what I see is that you're working on developing a deliberate system of improvement. And I like it. Your groups are digging into the heart of the problems and knocking them off one by one. The results we see are just an inevitable outcome of the quality of your system. This is really good work, Denise.

DOI: 10.4324/9780429347023-35

"One thing that strikes me as being broadly applicable within the company is setting small targets as a pacemaker for executing strategy. Execution is where so many strategic initiatives get stuck in the weeds. Having a pacemaker is genius. That's lightyears better than execution plans and action lists. It's adaptive and fast."

Wow, he's really getting it, Denise thought, feeling more and more enthusiastic.

Denise had invited the whole team to join them for the second half of the meeting, and one by one they began filtering through the door, each of them looking a little nervous. When everyone had arrived, she asked each focus group to summarize their storyboard using the standard presentation structure they had developed along the five phases of the Coaching Kata. The presenters were tentative at first. Alexander was the new CEO, after all. But he listened patiently, and ultimately, they all did well, their descriptions of their work were clear and crisp. He asked a few questions here and there. They were tough but spot on, and he asked them in a kind way. It struck Denise that he did not provide any feedback on the technical level, nor did he try to give the impression he knew better. His questions were very straightforward, clearly intended to check the logic of each person's reasoning.

He could make good use of the Coaching Kata five-phase model, Denise thought. *Maybe I should show him how it works.*

Suddenly, she felt confident enough to invite Alexander to join her for two of her coaching cycles, the ones she had scheduled following their meeting. She hadn't prepared for him to do so, but it just felt right. *What happens, happens*, she thought. *It will be useful for him to see.*

She conducted the two coaching cycles imagining he wasn't there as best she could. Alexander observed in silence. Afterward, Denise explained the Coaching Kata, while showing him the five-question card and also her picture of the five-phase model.

To her delight, Alexander seemed even more enthusiastic than he had been during the team meeting.

"I've had a lot of experience with business coaching," he said. "I thought I'd seen every method out there, but what I see you doing with the Coaching Kata seems unique. It seems to me that the Coaching Kata is a dual-purpose coaching model. Like every other coaching approach, it aims to help a person or team to reach a goal or solve a problem. But the Coaching Kata, in addition, also helps you develop what you call scientific thinking. If I understand correctly, this meta-skill, or mindset actually, will enable your team to master even bigger challenges in the future.

"And, the thing is, on top of all of that, it actually seems like fun. It's like your team is all learning the same skill together, like taking a ballroom dancing class. I realize these big, challenging targets are stressful, but your team still seems charged up. Honestly, I'm impressed. Congratulations!"

Alexander checked his watch.

"Shoot, wow, I have to hurry to a meeting," he said. "But, Denise, you're doing great work here. You're pioneering an alternative leadership approach we need to spread throughout Goldberg. Keep going! You've convinced me that keeping motors inhouse is crucial. That is why I need you to meet the cost and quality targets, so we can justify keeping motor manufacturing at home. Running a deficit business is never a good strategy."

Denise nodded appreciatively. *I see what he did there, high praise for the process but also reminding me that we still need results.*

After Alexander left, Denise gathered her team together to tell them how proud she was of their excellent and succinct presentations. For the first time in two months, she felt like they could actually win.

TUESDAY, MAY 9 – 1:00 PM, DEVIOUS DICK AT IT AGAIN

After a hearty lunch with Sarah and Joe, Denise was still upbeat about her meeting with Alexander, despite a gnawing feeling in her gut whenever she thought of Jason. When Ray from purchasing asked her to meet him in the project room, she thought nothing of it. But the moment she walked into the room and saw his normally placid face lined with worry, she knew something was up. A few other people were working in the room, team members collaborating in off hours, but Ray stood apart from everyone else, nervously drumming his fingers on the conference table.

"Denise, you won't believe what I just found out," he whispered, as though he was afraid someone might hear them. "What is it?" Denise asked.

"Dick ordered my boss, Pete Cheng, to ask our favored outside motor supplier to build a working prototype for our most popular motor. He's moving ahead under the table."

"What?" Denise shouted.

Several people turned their heads and looked over to the corner where Denise and Ray were standing.

"Let's go outside," Ray said. Denise nodded.

In the hallway, Ray explained the full magnitude of the stunt Dick was pulling. "Between you and me, Pete is an ass-kisser. He never opposes anything Dick tells him to do. So, when Dick asked him to help the supplier build a prototype he just did it.

"What makes it even worse is that the supplier wanted guarantees before going through the effort of building a prototype. So, now we have a contract with them to purchase at least a three-month volume of our biggest-selling motor once the prototype passes our tests."

Denise couldn't believe it. "But why, she asked? That doesn't make any sense. And entire motors?"

"I only found out about it yesterday. When I asked Pete about it this morning, he said Dick came to him and asked him to do that. 'Dick doesn't believe in all this coaching stuff and wants a second option' was all he said."

Denise felt fury rising within her. "That goes against every promise management has made me. I was told we would get a fair chance and that was the only reason I took this stupid job. And our charming CEO Alexander said right to my face that he wanted motor production to stay inhouse. I wonder if he is in on it. I need to talk to David and find out if he knows anything about this."

"I know I am talking out of school, but you needed to know. Good luck," Ray called after her, as Denise practically sprinted toward David's office.

Denise knocked on David's door but didn't wait for him to answer, pushing it open right away. He looked up from his desk, clearly surprised to see her barging in. *Well, at least he looks a lot better today*, Denise thought.

"What's up?" David asked, smiling, but obviously confused.

"It's Dick, that bastard," Denise practically snorted. Then she told David what Ray had just told her.

When she was done, David stayed silent for a moment. Then he looked out of the window like he was in deep thought. Finally, he spoke.

"I am so glad you brought this to my attention Denise. This is unbelievable, but I guess nothing Dick does should surprise us by now," he said, with a sly look on his face. "But I think this time Dick has gone too far. He may have played right into our hands. I'll talk with Alexander. And to answer your question, I am pretty sure he is not in on it and will find this surprising, and enlightening. We meet later today for a review. I'll let you know what I learn first thing tomorrow."

He paused. Denise looked at him and was about to ask about Sandra, but David jumped in.

"Denise, thank you for your help the other night. I'm very sorry. I'm not proud of the state I was in. To answer your unasked question, Sandra went to another doctor for a second opinion, and it looks like she really does not have breast cancer, but they want to confirm it with a biopsy. I looked up the statistics, and you're right that they are wrong about half the time. We're both feeling much more optimistic. I'll let you know how things go. And again, thank you, seriously, for your support."

Which got me in big trouble, Denise thought, wondering if David knew about the pictures. But she was afraid to ask. Still, she was delighted that David and Sandra seemed to have worked it out – and that it sounded like Sandra was going to be okay.

Denise left David's office feeling a bit calmer and more in control of her thoughts. Back at her desk, she picked up her phone and called Jennifer Billington from engineering.

"Hey, Jennifer," Denise said as pleasantly as she could. "Have you happened to hear anything about a supplier building a prototype motor?"

There was a very long pause. Denise waited. "How do you know?" Jennifer whispered. "This morning our boss called me and three of the other senior engineers into his office. You won't believe what he told us. This is just confidential between us, right? I could get fired for talking to you about it."

"Absolutely, between us," Denise said in as reassuring a voice as she could muster.

"Dick involved two of the motor designers without informing our boss. At least that's what our boss said. Can you believe it? I mean shouldn't the head of R&D know if someone on his team gets pulled into some other project, with a supplier no less? Dick asked them to help this supplier with any questions around developing a motor prototype."

Denise tried to remain calm. "So then what did your boss do?" she asked.

"He was furious, of course, but what could he do? We all know Dick does and gets what he wants."

"Jennifer, I really appreciate your trust in sharing this with me. I promise I will not break your confidence."

I just hope David can get this sorted out, Denise thought, sighing audibly.

32

The Grand Finale

THURSDAY, MAY 18 – 4:00 PM, COUNTDOWN, 3 WEEKS TO GO

OVER THE NEXT weeks Denise and the team further intensified their pace. Denise hadn't heard anything more from David about the shenanigans of Dick, but she knew she had to just keep her head down, continue her work, and trust that David would provide cover.

More importantly, she hadn't heard from Jason either – she wasn't quite sure if they were on a break or broken up, but what did it matter? A break was just a preamble to a breakup. He had missed several of the project team meetings, too, emailing his fellow focus topic members to say he was sorry, but "there were urgent matters in sales."

The team now had a quick all hands every morning at 9:00 am, just like Maggie had suggested. That turned out to be a good time as it allowed everyone to sort out issues before diving in for the day. The meetings were short, usually only 15 minutes. All they did was quickly go through the list of focus topics, with each group mostly only speaking for a minute or so. If people were on track for their weekly target conditions, they would just mention the obstacle they were working on or perhaps the experiment they planned to run that day.

The bulk of the meeting was dedicated to roadblocks, areas where someone needed help or for the group to come to a decision. If the holdup was about a decision, Denise encouraged the team member to be as prepared as possible so that he or she could quickly lay out the issue and they could come to an agreement then and there. This practice avoided waiting time and meant no one was stalled for more than 24 hours because of the need to come to some kind of consensus. If someone needed help with an obstacle, they didn't try to solve the problem in the space of the meeting, but quickly agreed on who could help that same day and then moved on.

Denise was surprised to find how helpful daily meetings were. She was so conditioned to the idea that meetings were a time suck – and they were, of course, if they weren't well organized. But the format of these meetings meant that they were always productive and kept everyone on track. *This is a game changer. Why did I push back at Maggie? A need for control? Did I resent her for always being right?* Denise wondered. *I wish I had gotten out of my own way sooner.*

The meetings also helped her see patterns among her team members – different self-defeating behaviors that were prevalent among them – and this made her a significantly better coach. Sometimes people would struggle with an important obstacle three days in a row and still state they were on track for their weekly target condition – hoping for a miracle breakthrough instead of asking for help. Others would bring up issues they could have addressed by themselves, still lacking confidence in their own abilities. *We still have a long way to go*, Denise thought to herself. *But at least I better understand the current condition of my team's skills. I really do kata everything now, I guess.*

Denise now planned her daily coaching cycles based on the insights she gleaned from these morning meetings. She had finally gotten closer to her desired process for coaching, and now had a standing two-hour slot from 10 to noon on her calendar. During those two hours, she walked the shop floor going from storyboard to storyboard and doing coaching cycles. For those that needed additional help, they would arrange to meet for a second time that day. But everyone got at least one coaching cycle every day.

THURSDAY, JUNE 8 – 2:00 PM, TIMES UP!

Three months had passed since Denise had assembled her team for what seemed like an impossible challenge. With Maggie's help, Denise and the team conducted another three-month workshop as well as a planning session for the management presentation. Summarizing everything they had achieved they amazed even themselves. For many focus areas, they had surpassed their expectations. Overall, they had reduced the cost for manufacturing motors inhouse by almost the 20% they had targeted for the first three months.

As expected, they still needed more time on some of the projects to close the gap to the finish line. These had to do with changes that just took longer to implement and areas that were outside of their control. As David had proposed, they would now have to suggest to the management team that they needed another three months to meet all their outcome targets. Still, David felt confident that they could get another three months of work approved. They had overachieved by far what many had expected, and they had a clear plan on what to work on next.

Denise actually enjoyed the three-month workshop. Having done it once before, she saw how three months was a good time frame for setting challenges. They began by reviewing where they were and then moved on to setting the next series of three-month challenges. For the focus topics where they still had work to do they agreed on the three-month challenge for each of them and then broke them down into monthly goals. They even defined next week's target conditions. Denise looked around the room to see happy faces and remarkable engagement. But there was still an elephant in the room: Would the management team buy their proposal?

For the final presentation, Denise asked Ray and Sarah to present with her. She had also asked the four motor manufacturing team leads, as well as Luther from logistics, Randolph from accounting, and Jennifer from R&D to join the meeting. Maggie agreed to come as well.

A group this large was unusual for a management team presentation, but David signed off on it. Everyone knew that this was one of the most important days in Goldberg's hundred-year history and would determine its future for decades to come.

As Denise and the project team members she had selected filed into the room, they found the management team in the middle of a coffee break. Most of the executives were checking their phones, tapping out hurried emails.

Denise heard a ping on her cell phone. It was a cryptic text message from Jason. "This is your show, Denise. I don't want to get in the way, so I'm not coming, but know that I'm thinking of you. You're going to kill it!"

Denise felt a pang of remorse, but there was no time for regrets. She pulled Maggie over to introduce her to Alexander.

"Maggie, this is Alexander Aspen our new CEO," she said with a big smile, hoping she was doing a good job of hiding her nerves. "Alexander, this is Magdalena Petricova, our consultant and the owner of the gym where I train." Alexander shook Maggie's hand, smiled, and said, "Hi Maggie, good to see you again after all these years. We did a little project together when I was at Daimler. Remember?"

"Sure do, Alex, and it is great to be working with you again," Maggie replied, also with a big smile.

Denise was floored. *They know each other. How can that be? Why didn't she tell me? Maggie certainly is a woman of mystery ... I'll have to ask her more about her experience with Alexander....*

"Congratulations on the gym," said Alexander. "I hope we'll see each other more often now. We certainly could make good use of your skills at Goldberg. We have a lot of work ahead, a lot of change to implement at all levels. We need a cultural shift, a plan to update our processes, you name it."

"That's very kind of you to say," Maggie replied with a sly smile. "But I don't want to let down my team at the gym. So, I'm not sure I can commit to working on all of that. But I will be glad to help when I can. And you have an open invitation to the gym."

Denise could tell Alexander wanted to say more, but the break was over. It was time for the big presentation. After everyone else had taken their seats, Denise, Sarah, and Ray walked to the front of the room. Denise tried not to feel like she was walking to the gallows. *Be reasonable, you have a lot of good data to present.* The rest of the project team sat in extra chairs along the periphery of the room. *Besides, you're not here alone this time. You have teammates.*

It was then that Denise noticed that Dick wasn't in the room. *What's this?* she thought, *Another one of his tricks? Where is he?* But she had no time to consider his absence further. All eyes were on her, waiting for the presentation to begin. To Denise's surprise, the presentation was actually fun. Once they got going, she felt like her team was unstoppable. Ray did a magnificent job, his natural charisma showed. Sarah stunned the room with the quality improvements they had achieved, but even more so with what they had learned about how they could control process quality on a much higher level. And the numbers spoke for themselves.

After they finished their presentation, Alexander was the first to speak.

"You've all done an incredible job," he said. "Thank you for all your effort over the last three months and for setting an example of how much success we can have when we work together to achieve difficult goals. We'll discuss your proposal as a management team and let you know about our decision later today."

It felt like a win. But would they really win? After they left the room, the team stayed together as they walked back to the manufacturing building. They all congregated in their project room, where they would maybe spend the next three months saving motors ... or where they might never step foot as a team again. One thing was for certain: Nobody wanted to go back to work. It was all just too exciting ... and frightening.

THURSDAY, JUNE 8 – 4:30 PM, THE JURY IS BACK

About 45 minutes after they had presented, Denise saw David's number pop up on her phone. She pressed "answer" as quickly as she could.

"Yes, what is it, David?"

"Denise, are you still in the plant?" David asked.

"Of course."

"Can you come up to the boardroom quickly so we can inform you about the decision?"

He's not giving me any clues, Denise thought. *Is that good or bad?*

"The team is still here too," said Denise, looking around the room at a series of expectant faces. "Can they come along?"

"Of course," David replied.

That's a good sign, Denise thought.

After they had settled in the boardroom, Alexander Aspen addressed them again.

"As I said earlier, you've done a great job. You got results and maybe more importantly pioneered a new management approach for Goldberg through this Kata thing. Seeing the processes firsthand, and talking with our engineers, it is clear that keeping motor manufacturing inhouse can be a strategic asset for our company. Not only does it let us control a large part of our pumps' performance, but I have learned that controlling the motor might allow engineering and manufacturing to more quickly introduce performance features for our customers, that is if they can follow your lead and work together.

"Now that we've drastically reduced the cost and you've shown a clear strategy for achieving our target cost, the decision was easy. Motors will stay inhouse. Congratulations on a magnificent piece of work!"

The team burst out in cheers. They had done it! They had saved the plant from a huge loss. Denise felt completely exhausted and sank into her chair. All the strain from the past months fell off her body. She looked around at her team. All smiles.

"Let's throw a party," Ray said as they left the room.

"I'm in," Sarah replied.

Everyone else nodded in agreement. Denise felt very tired but she went along. *I'll try to escape soon*, she thought. *I desperately need some sleep.*

Then she thought of Jason. He should have been part of the team today too. He had been the first to join her in practicing Toyota Kata outside the assembly team. Denise felt empty thinking of him. *I miss him*, she realized. *Maybe I was too harsh. We were both idiots.*

Still, the team's victory wasn't the only good news they celebrated at the party that night. David showed up at the bar, but said he could only stay for a half hour, slowly nursing a single beer. At a certain point, he took Denise aside.

"Denise, I realized I forgot to tell you, Sandra had the biopsy, and she's all clear. We're out of the woods."

Denise was so relieved to hear the good news that she spontaneously hugged him. But Denise knew she could count on her teammates not to make any assumptions about her relationship with David or take any photos. They knew she was a professional. It felt good to trust them, to be a part of something like what they had all built together.

33

New Beginnings

FIRST THING FRIDAY morning, Denise held an all hands with the first motor manufacturing shift to inform them of the good news. Of course, by now they all knew. Nonetheless there were lots of cheers and even some tears when Denise described the outcome of yesterday's management meeting. After the meeting, even Jack Van de Berg, the union president, came over to shake her hand and thank her for her leadership.

After Denise held the same meeting for the second shift, her phone rang. It was David.

"Denise, can you come by the C-level offices? Alexander and I would like to discuss something with you."

"Sure. I just need a few minutes to settle some things. I'm on vacation next week, remember? So, I'll get done here and then come over. Afterward, I need to rush home."

The thought of her vacation the following week was a little painful. She had originally taken the week off to allow for Jason to move in. At least, that's what they had initially planned. But plans change. *Ah, so stupid*, she thought.

When Denise stepped into Alexander's office, David was already there.

They all sat down at a beautiful, round mahogany table, sinking into big, overstuffed chairs. *This is a fabulous office*, Denise thought, looking out of Alexander's large windows and thinking of how uncomfortable her regulation desk chair was.

"I have to get rid of these stupid chairs," Alexander said, as though he could read her thoughts. "Everyone just wants to take a nap in them instead of getting work done."

DOI: 10.4324/9780429347023-37

They all laughed.

What he said next, though, was even more of a shock. He explained that Dick had been released from his position yesterday and security had escorted him out the door. An announcement would go out right after their meeting. *That's why he wasn't in the management meeting yesterday,* Denise suddenly realized. *I wish I could have seen him with his box of belongings being ushered out.*

Then she heard Alexander say, "of course, we need a new Vice President of Operations now. I asked David to fill the role. Luckily for us all, he's agreed. Now, of course he can't head global operations *and* fill the plant manager role. David and I have been talking and we both agree you've done a fabulous job on the motor manufacturing project."

No, they're not going to ask me to become the plant manager. I'm too young. This is too early.

"We would like to offer you the role of production manager Denise," Alexander continued. "It's a new role we want to create just for you. You would have responsibility for all the manufacturing teams as well as maintenance and logistics. David would continue as plant manager in name, but you would cover all of manufacturing."

Alexander looked sideways at David and gave him a clap on the shoulder.

Then he continued, "this may seem like a big ask, but in addition to being production manager, we would also like you to act as a project manager for one of our R&D projects. From what I've seen in the past weeks, and also from my experience as an advisory board member, I know R&D and production do not work well together here at Goldberg.

If we get them to work as partners we can create fabulous products and at much lower cost. Besides, you seem to thrive on impossible challenges," he added, with a big smile.

"If you do both well I don't see any reason why we wouldn't make you our next plant manager in 18 to 24 months."

Denise was stunned. It was hard to get her head around everything Alexander had just said. All this new responsibility, while still running the motors special project? Even though they had just celebrated a huge milestone, they still weren't finished. They had more hard work to do over the next three months to bring the cost reduction home.

"I guess you'll give me some time to think about that, right?" she asked.

Alexander and David looked at each other. Then Alexander said, "Well, we have a bit of time pressure. The announcement about the changes with

Dick leaving needs to go out today. You know Goldberg. The rumor mill is already running. We need to get out ahead of it as much as we can. So, I'm sorry to pressure you like this, but it would be great if you could give us an answer as soon as possible so our crew doesn't need to worry about what will happen to plant management."

Denise took a deep breath. She felt overwhelmed. But at the same time she was excited by the idea of becoming the production manager, a new position they had created just for her. A new challenge.

I'll be able to spread Kata throughout the whole manufacturing plant and even bring it to engineering. And I can introduce the 3-1-1 pacemaker deployment process as a model for the company, she thought. *This is an opportunity too good to pass up.*

Denise looked at Alexander, then at David, and then back at Alexander.

"OK," she said, "I guess it's a logical next step. Count me in. And I like the idea of working for straight shooters like you two."

"Thank you," Alexander said, his voice sincere, and Denise realized he really meant it. "I'm looking forward to a great working relationship, and learning from you. You can go now, Denise. I know you've got a vacation coming up."

With that, Denise got up and left David and Alexander to continue their discussion of the next steps.

FRIDAY, JUNE 9 – 5:00 PM, THE SURPRISES KEEP COMING

As Denise pulled out of her parking spot, she couldn't help but wonder what she had gotten herself into. *So much new responsibility, so much change*, she thought as she approached the exit. The red and white bar raised, and the security guard gave her a big smile and waved her on.

She drove home feeling both elated and empty. *Now onto my solo vacation.* She parked her car and then took the elevator to her apartment. When she stepped inside her apartment, she was surprised to see it was completely dark, even though the sun was still shining. *I guess I forgot to open the shutters this morning.* She went into the living room, walked to the windows and pulled up the blinds. Staring back at her was a shocking sight. She nearly fell over backward. Across the street, stretching across the two huge black walnut trees, was a big banner that read: "I love you, Denise!"

Jason, the thought rushed through Denise's mind. She grabbed her phone and called him. Jason answered on the first ring, as if he was waiting for her call.

"Are you crazy?" Denise exclaimed, but she couldn't hide it, she was also delighted. "How did you get that up there?"

"Don't you know I'm an expert climber?" Jason replied, laughing. But then he paused, his voice turning serious. "Denise, I've been so stupid. Can we please talk it over?"

Denise felt warmth flow through her body. She was so glad to hear his voice. "To be honest," she said, "I've been pretty stupid, too. I overreacted and have regretted it ever since. Why don't you come by for dinner and we can talk? I just want to get a quick run in first, and then I'll need to shower. This day's been crazy. You won't believe what you missed."

"That's fine, I'll bring some food. See you soon."

Jason arrived just minutes after Denise returned from her run. She was still in her running clothes and had her bottle of water in her hand when he buzzed. She let him in, but they both stood there awkwardly. They hadn't seen each other in a while. Neither of them seemed to know what to say or do.

"I guess I need a shower first," Denise said at last.

"Sure, I'll get dinner ready," Jason replied. He put two big grocery bags down on the counter. "Take your time."

And she did, partly because she wanted a good shower after her run and her crazy day and partly because she wanted to think about what she wanted to say to Jason.

When Denise stepped out of her room over a half hour later, the table was set, and the meal was about ready. It smelled amazing. Jason had cooked some of his Asian style favorites. *He's a good cook. That's handy to have around*, Denise thought fondly.

She walked over to the table. Then she saw an envelope on her plate. She reached for it.

"Wait," Jason called as he walked over from the stove. "Before you open it, I have to ask you something. Do you still have this next week off?"

"Yes," Denise replied slowly, a bit confused by his question. "We both took that week off for you to move in, right?"

"Ah, I just wondered," Jason said with a grin. "Now you can open it."

Denise opened the envelope. Inside were two airplane tickets for the following day … Fort Lauderdale. She looked at Jason.

"Fort Lauderdale, Florida?"

"My brother and family live there. His wife is the manager of the Marriott. I got a luxury suite, and we can take their boat for a spin if we like. I mean, that is if you want to come." He paused and looked at Denise, trying to read her expression. "Denise, I know I've been very stupid, but I love you. We both have the week off. Please come with me to Florida. The return flights are flexible. We could even make time for that move we had planned before all this craziness happened. Sorry if I am pushing things."

Denise took a long look at him. "Of course I'll go, Jason. Are you still thinking about moving in with me though? Is that what you mean?"

"Don't know. Would you still be up for that?"

Denise thought for a moment. "Yes," she said. "I would. But the way you ask sounds like you're not so sure."

"No, no," Jason replied, "I'm more than sure. I just wanted to check if our next target conditions are aligned."

"Oh, you moron," Denise said, laughing. "Shut up and kiss me."

THE END

Scan with your mobile to
go to Denise's
notebook.

QR CODE 33.1
Take a look at Denise's notebook.

Afterword

"People can outperform what is 'expected' – individually and in a group – via better coaching."

– Doug Lemov, Author, Teach Like a Champion

A NOTE FROM THE AUTHORS

We hope you enjoyed Denise's and Goldberg's journey. Our goal was to write a story that would captivate you, but, of course, there is a message here, too. We firmly believe that you and your team can also achieve what Denise and her colleagues at Goldberg set out to accomplish, whatever industry you work in and whatever your particular goals may be. By practicing scientific thinking and with the leadership of a good coach (hint: we hope it will be you), we believe that any challenge can be properly understood and thus can be overcome.

It took a few drafts for us to realize that the purpose of our book was not to teach better coaching by sharing as many practical tips as possible. In fact, we would never expect you to learn any of the skills we describe simply from reading this book. The real point of *Giving Wings to Her Team* is to appreciate the struggle, the highs and lows, that Denise goes through as she learns to be a better coach and develops her team – and then start your own learning journey as a coach too.

Denise was an especially fast learner and took each coaching session as an opportunity to reflect, identify one or two lessons, get feedback from Maggie, and then try out the new ideas at the next opportunity. Since she was initially coaching two people once or twice daily, she had lots of opportunities to learn. When David agreed to be her second coach, she got even more useful feedback to hone her coaching. The learning group with Jason and Mary was another excellent chance to practice as an improver, coach, and second coach, and thus learn even more. Then Denise upped her game and learned at an even higher level when she was forced to coach multiple teams in parallel to achieve a seemingly impossible cost reduction target and keep motors inhouse.

Unfortunately, we cannot read about Denise's journey and then start where she left off at the end of the book any more than we can watch a professional athlete and then just imitate what she or he is doing. We have to start by practicing Starter Kata and learn through struggle as Denise did – and it's best to do so with the help of an experienced coach.

We hope this book has inspired you to start a learning journey of your own, to find your own Maggie. Becoming a scientific thinker and a great coach is a lifelong process, and it can apply to any life or business goal, even to learning that complex skill you always wished you had mastered in your life – cooking, sewing, fitness, music, sports, or whatever.

One kata geek used the Improvement Kata to quit smoking. Another used it to guide his son who was born with half a heart through complex medical treatments, allowing him to live a relatively normal life after no physician they consulted thought that was possible.

Most of all, we hope you will evolve yourself learning and growing as a coach so you can help others grow too. Best wishes for your practice.

ACKNOWLEDGMENTS

When Tilo, a plant manager for a German power-tool manufacturer at the time, started his personal Toyota Kata learning journey as part of Mike Rother's groundbreaking research, there were no books, no recipes, and no best practice examples on the topic. Tilo and his management team experimented with the original coaching questions Mike had developed and called the Coaching Kata. To better learn and reflect Tilo wrote down what he and his team learned in a little notebook he carried around at the time. In a way, that notebook was the start of the book you now hold in hand.

This book is fiction, but in a way it is not. It is based on Tilo's experience as a plant manager. He was Denise and his Maggie was Mike Rother. Tilo can relate to the experiences of Denise. Tilo is grateful to his fantastic team and could not have written this book without all he learned from them, and to Mike as his coach.

Later Tilo developed the Kata Coaching Dojo as a way to help others develop and deepen their coaching skills, allowing them to move beyond the Starter Kata on Mike Rother's five-question coaching card. Working off a fictional case in the Dojo afforded coaches the opportunity to repeat the same scenario while trying different approaches and receiving immediate feedback, just as you would do drills in sports or music. It was intriguing to consider why such practices existed for improving skills in many high-performance areas such as pilots, musicians, and physicians but not for managers and coaches in a business context. Tilo's Dojo was meant to close this gap.

As Tilo developed the Dojo, he also came up with various micro-skills to deal with the common dilemmas coaches face which he published in several articles and blog posts. To make matters more engaging Tilo invented a character called Denise, whose experience in business was not so dissimilar from his own.

At the urging of colleagues, he turned those blog posts into the initial draft of this novel. An engineer and native German speaker, he soon found he wanted help making the novel readable and accessible. Luckily, Mike Rother paired him up with Jeff, and so Tilo enlisted Jeff to help him rewrite it.

Jeff did so, feeling very proud of himself, until he asked his daughter Em, a writer herself, to read a few chapters. Em appreciated that it was clearly written and a good story but advised him to read his favorite novel and think about how he could make it more like that. She suggested he rewrite it as best he could, and then hire a professional writer to rewrite it again.

Fortunately, Jeff found Sofia Groopman, and, as a result, you have just read a true business novel. Sofia brought it to life, enhancing character development, cutting out wasted words, and generally improving readability. We hope you found it engaging and enjoyed it, as much as we collectively enjoyed writing it.

ABOUT THE AUTHORS

Tilo Schwarz is a leadership coach, author, and founder. He supports organizations and managers in successfully leading change and empowering their teams for improvement, adaptiveness, and superior results. He was a plant manager at a renowned German power-tool manufacturer, where he and his management team started practicing Toyota Kata as part of Mike Rother's groundbreaking research in 2006. By doing so, Tilo and his team established continuous improvement as a daily working routine throughout all processes and areas of the plant. That led to winning the A. T. Kearny operational excellence competition "Factory of the Year" and a WHU/INSEAD Industrial Excellence Award. Tilo is co-founder of the Campus for Leaders at the University of Applied Science Ansbach and the author of several books on coaching and Toyota Kata.

Jeffrey K. Liker is Professor Emeritus, Industrial and Operations Engineering at The University of Michigan and President of Liker Lean Advisors, LLC. He is the author of the best-selling book, *The Toyota Way*, Second Edition, and has coauthored nine other books about Toyota including *The Toyota Way to Service Excellence* and *The Toyota Way to Lean Leadership*. His graphic novel with Eduardo Lander and Tom Root tells the story of lean transformation at a mail-order company: *Lean in a High-Variability Business*. A more compact graphic novel, *Engaging the Team at Zingerman's Mail Order*, illustrates how kata unleashed the creativity of their team. His articles and books have won 13 Shingo Prizes for Research Excellence. He was inducted into the Association of Manufacturing Excellence Hall of Fame and the Shingo Academy.

Index

Printed in the United States
by Baker & Taylor Publisher Services